The Fiscalization of Social Policy

The Fiscalization of Social Policy

How Taxpayers Trumped Children in the Fight Against Child Poverty

JOSHUA T. McCABE

OXFORD
UNIVERSITY PRESS

OXFORD
UNIVERSITY PRESS

Oxford University Press is a department of the University of Oxford. It furthers
the University's objective of excellence in research, scholarship, and education
by publishing worldwide. Oxford is a registered trade mark of Oxford University
Press in the UK and certain other countries.

Published in the United States of America by Oxford University Press
198 Madison Avenue, New York, NY 10016, United States of America.

Library of Congress Cataloging-in-Publication Data
Names: McCabe, Joshua T., author.
Title: The fiscalization of social policy : how taxpayers trumped children in
the fight against child poverty / Joshua T. McCabe.
Description: New York, NY : Oxford University Press, [2018] |
Includes bibliographical references.
Identifiers: LCCN 2017044632 (print) | LCCN 2017054722 (ebook) |
ISBN 9780190841317 (updf) | ISBN 9780190841324 (epub) |
ISBN 9780190841300 (hardcover)
Subjects: LCSH: Family allowances. | Child tax credits. |
Poor families—Government policy. | Economic assistance, Domestic. |
Public welfare. | Fiscal policy.
Classification: LCC HD4925 (ebook) | LCC HD4925 .M35 2018 (print) |
DDC 362.7/2561—dc23
LC record available at https://lccn.loc.gov/2017044632

9 8 7 6 5 4 3 2 1

Printed by Sheridan Books, Inc., United States of America

Contents

The Fiscalization of Social Policy

1

American Exceptionalism Revisited

THE YEAR 1972 was a gloomy one for advocates of the poor. That was the year that Congress put the final nail in the coffin of President Richard Nixon's proposed Family Assistance Plan. It was supposed to revolutionize income security in the US by guaranteeing a minimum standard of income to all American families. Despite coming so close to passage—the bill had the support of Nixon and passed the House but could not make it through the Senate—the failure of the proposed Family Assistance Plan in 1972, according to scholars, "foreshadowed the diminishing prospect of a system that provides basic economic security for the nation's citizens" (Steensland 2008: 2). It seemed as though this was the beginning of the end of the war on poverty.

In 1974, a single mother with two children working full-time at the federal minimum wage in the US received no direct cash benefits from the federal government to help her raise her children. Forty years later, after a period often characterized as one of austerity and welfare state retrenchment, that same mother would receive $7,460 in federal benefits. It is something that might be overlooked by those who lived through the Reagan cuts in the 1980s or Clinton welfare reforms of the 1990s. These benefits would not come from social assistance, family allowance, or other programs we traditionally see as part of the welfare state. Instead, she benefits from the Earned Income Tax Credit (EITC) and the Child Tax Credit (CTC)—two tax expenditures considered part of the US' "hidden" welfare state. Tax expenditures are "provisions of tax law, regulation or practices that reduce or postpone revenue for a comparatively narrow population of taxpayers relative to a benchmark tax" (OECD 2010). This includes exemptions, deductions, credits, and allowances that lower an individual's total tax burden and sometimes provide refunds above and beyond official tax liability.[1] In the past decade, scholars of American political development have paid increasing attention to the use of tax expenditures to pursue social policy goals (Faricy 2015; Hacker 2002; Howard 1997; Martin 2008; Mettler 2011; Prasad 2011). There is good reason for this. As one OECD (2010) report notes, the use of tax expenditures is "pervasive and growing" in the United States and across the globe.

The situation now stands in marked contrast to that of forty years ago. In 1974, when the US Congress first mandated the recording of tax expenditures in the federal budget, the US had no tax credits for low-income families. In 2014, the combined value of the CTC and EITC amounted to $126.2 billion (US Congress 2014), dwarfing traditional welfare programs aimed at low-income families and making them the fourth and third single largest tax expenditures, respectively. This trend, the expanding use of tax expenditures for social policy purposes, is part of a broader phenomenon that I call the *fiscalization of social policy*.

Other liberal welfare regimes have seen similar explosions in fiscalization. In 1970, neither the UK nor Canada had child or in-work tax credits. By 2013, the value of the CTC and the Working Tax Credit (WTC) in the UK amounted to £28.8 billion (HM Revenues and Customs 2014). In 2012, the value of Canada's two CTCs and the Working Income Tax Benefit (WITB) amounted to C$12.9 billion (Canada Department of Finance 2013). The vast majority of research on the politics of tax expenditures focuses exclusively on the US, but the OECD finds that the total value of tax expenditures relative to GDP is now greater in the UK and Canada than in the US (OECD 2010). Despite these international trends, there is still almost no cross-national research on the politics of these tax credits.

Recent surveys confirm the fiscalization trend across a number of welfare regimes and varieties of capitalism. In their survey of child benefits in eighteen OECD and Development countries, Ferrarini, Nelson, and Höög (2012) find that Denmark was the only country with a CTC in 1960. By 1980, ten countries had a CTC. In 2005, thirteen of the eighteen countries they examined had some sort of CTC. Banks et al. (2005) find parallel results for in-work tax credits across OECD countries. Not a single country examined had an in-work tax credit before 1970; swift proliferation followed in subsequent decades.

These trends should be of interest to both scholars of the welfare state concerned with changing political dynamics and policymakers or advocates concerned with poverty, for two reasons. The first is that they give us an interesting puzzle, in that the expansion of these tax credits occurred during a period characterized as an "era of austerity" (Pierson 2001) in which welfare states across the globe were subject to cost containment and retrenchment.

It is significant that these tax credits arose at a time when governments were cutting back on traditional social assistance programs aimed at what many perceived as the "undeserving poor" and implementing workfare requirements. Rather than being administered by a benefits agency, these tax credits are administered by the respective revenue authority in each country. Thus there has been some confusion over how to characterize them (see Prasad 2011). This, in part, has led some scholars to ignore their impact on low-income families. Though several scholars have noted this trend (Bashevkin 2002; Brodie 2010; Ferrarini, Nelson, and Höög 2012), they have little to say about its causes or potential consequences. This leaves us with an important question: How were policymakers able to expand these programs in an otherwise austere environment? Part of the answer, as I will explain in this book, is that tax credits have unique characteristics that enable policymakers to obfuscate their real cost in budgets. Unlike traditional social spending, tax credits are usually classified (or perceived to be classified) as "revenues not collected" and thus do not show up as spending in budgets. This distinguishing feature has given tax credits a political advantage relative to other programs since the 1970s.

The second puzzle concerns child poverty. One of the primary motivations for the growth of these tax credits during this period was that they were part of conscious strategies for tackling child poverty. Beginning in the late 1980s, leaders in all three countries turned their attention to the plight of poor children, promising to tackle the problem of child poverty head-on. Despite similar goals and broadly similar policy outcomes (welfare reform, in-work tax credits, and CTCs), the effects on child poverty rates were surprisingly different (see Figure 1.1). The US and Canada have similar child poverty rates before accounting for the role of taxes and transfers. The UK's rate is actually higher. When we take taxes and transfers into consideration, though, Canada's and the UK's child poverty rates both drop significantly. The US child poverty rate on the other hand barely budges, staying high above the rate for the other two countries.[2]

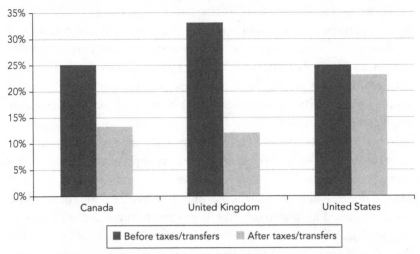

FIGURE 1.1 Child poverty in liberal welfare regimes, 2008.

Source: Jonathan Bradshaw, Yekaterina Chzhen, Gill Main, Bruno Martorano, Leonardo Menchini, and Chris de Neubourg, *Relative Income Poverty among Children in Rich Countries*, Innocenti Working Paper 2012–01. Florence: UNICEF Innocenti Research Centre, 2012.

This is not for a lack of trying by US policymakers. In a recent address to the Population Association of America, economist Robert Moffitt revealed the new research finding that US spending on poor families has actually gone up substantially since the 1980s (Moffitt 2015). The reason that this has not translated into reductions in child poverty is that these programs, including the EITC and CTC, are poorly targeted, excluding the poorest families from receiving any benefits at all. Why would policymakers exclude families most in need when constructing policies designed to tackle child poverty? The most popular answer, one that Moffitt himself puts forward, is that the legacy of the Poor Law tradition in the US leads policymakers to make cultural distinctions between the "undeserving" welfare poor and the "deserving" working poor (Handler and Hasenfeld 2007; Katz 1996; Steensland 2008). Most of the new benefits since the 1970s in the US have gone only to those who are working.

This explanation becomes problematic when we examine it in comparative perspective, though. The Poor Law tradition originated in the UK and is found in Canada as well. Yet this cultural legacy has not prevented policymakers from increasing benefits for families both in and out of work during the same period. Unlike families in the US, families in Canada and the UK have received CTCs regardless of whether either parent is working (see Figure 1.2). In fact, the poorest British and Canadian families receive larger CTC benefits relative to the working poor. This difference is key to explaining the diverging child poverty rates. But how is the divergence to be explained if it does not stem from the cultural legacy of the Poor Law tradition? The policy discourse used by advocates in each country points us toward the answer. Advocates had the same goal—tackling child poverty—in all three countries. However, they differed crucially in the logic by which they decided who was deserving of benefits and why.

In Canada and the UK, the logic that resonated the most was what I call "income supplementation." According to this logic, all children in low-income families were seen as the target population whether their families were perceived as part of the welfare poor or the working poor. They were deserving of benefits simply because having children is expensive and wages do not account for it. Advocates in the United States sometimes tried to use this logic but without the same success. Instead, the logic that resonated the most was what I call "tax relief." According to this logic, it was only children of low-income taxpaying families who were seen as the target population. They were not deserving of benefits simply because they were poor children but because they were part of taxpaying families pushed into poverty by an ever-growing tax burden. As a result

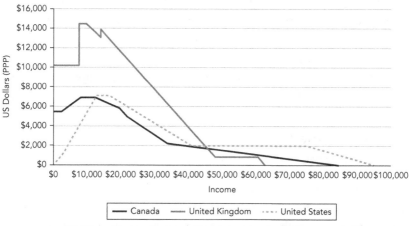

FIGURE 1.2 Child and in-work tax credits, 2011 (single parent, two children).

Source: Author's calculations. United States Internal Revenue Service, Revenue Procedure 2011-12, https://www.irs.gov/pub/irs-drop/rp-11-12.pdf; Canada Revenue Agency, General Income Tax and Benefit Package for 2011, https://www.canada.ca/en/revenue-agency/services/forms-publications/previous-year-forms-publications/archived-previous-year-tax-packages/archived-general-income-tax-benefit-package-2011.html; HM Revenue and Customs, http://www.hmrc.gov.uk/rates/taxcredits.htm

of the progressive nature of federal taxes, this meant the exclusion of the poorest families from the benefits of these tax credits.

The fiscalization of social policy is important because tax credits are unique, in that either logic could justify them. The public universally perceives both children (Cook and Barrett 1992; Gormley 2012; Iyengard 1991) and taxpayers (Michelmore 2012; Zelenak 2003) positively and as worthy of benefits. The question remains why one logic resonated more than the other in each country. It is unclear, when put into conflict, which group would be deemed more deserving (Meanwell and Swando 2013).

The answer is that scholars have been looking at the cultural legacy of the wrong public policy. Rather than to social assistance, we can trace these differences back to the adoption, or lack thereof, of family allowances in the 1940s. Prior to this period, policymakers envisioned children as beneficiaries of direct cash benefits in one of two ways: either as children of welfare recipients via social assistance or as children of taxpayers via tax exemptions. The introduction of family allowances in Canada and the UK institutionalized a third logic for children in those countries, which served as a springboard for the later growth of tax credits. The US on the other hand never introduced a family allowance, so children continued to be recognized only as part of either welfare or taxpayer families.

Building on theories about the institutionalization of cultural categories, I argue that policies also institutionalize distinct "logics of appropriateness" (March and Olsen 2008) that can constrain policymakers' efforts to expand benefits, even to seemingly deserving target populations such as children. For a policy to be implemented, it is not enough that recipients are seen as deserving. There must also be an appropriate match between the type of benefit and the category of beneficiary.

Explaining the Growth and Distribution of Tax Credits

This book will tackle two puzzles vital to understanding the causes and consequences of tax and social policy in the US and abroad. First, how do we explain the growth of tax credits for social policy purposes across liberal welfare regimes? Second, how do we explain the unique distribution of child and in-work tax credits in the US relative to other liberal welfare regimes?

Explaining the growth of these tax credits is important because they are considered part of the "hidden" or "submerged" welfare state (Hacker

2002; Howard 1997; Mettler 2011). Critics argue that the politics of tax expenditures are detrimental to democratic values of transparency and access in the policymaking process. Tax expenditures, some argue, are incomprehensible to the average citizen, who understands neither what they are or how they work. Powerful interest groups on the other hand have both the knowledge and resources to manipulate tax expenditures to their narrow benefit at the cost of the greater public good. As the process of fiscalization continues unabated both at home and abroad, it could harm democracies already under duress from increasing inequality (Bartels 2010; Hacker and Pierson 2010). I argue that tax credits are not "hidden" but are indeed obfuscated in important ways. This is one of the reasons these tax credits have thrived in recent years. Whereas democratic theorists might see this as a negative factor, proponents of a more expansive safety net for children should see this as a positive factor. Fiscalization, as I will explain, enables policymakers to expand family benefits by obfuscating their real costs in an environment otherwise hostile to new spending. While this sometimes results in unfair benefits for the rich and powerful, it has also been a critical avenue for benefits for working- and middle-class families.

Explaining the unique distribution of tax credits in the US relative to other countries is important because it will allow child poverty advocates to devise the best strategy for expanding child benefits, given historical obstacles. Advocates often complain that their expert advice goes un-heeded, but the academic literature on child poverty is clear: broad and generous child benefits, such as family allowances and refundable CTCs, have a dramatic effect on the reduction of child poverty (Brady 2009; Brady and Burroway 2012; Garfinkel, Rainwater, and Smeeding 2010; Immervoll, Sutherland, and Vos 2001; Smeeding 2006). Even with the more limited US CTC and EITC, researchers have found (relatively lim-ited) positive effects on a number of important life outcomes, including child poverty (Chetty, Friedman, and Rockoff 2011; Holt 2006). Armed with this knowledge, advocates go on to propose that the US emulate other countries (i.e., Waldfogel 2010; Kenworthy 2014) with little under-standing of the political and institutional obstacles that stand in the way.

To explain the US's unique historical trajectory is to explain the specific obstacles to reform. The single most important obstacle is not American individualism, antistatism, racial animosity, aversion to welfare, or right-wing resistance. Rather, it is the cultural legacy of institutions that were set up long ago and that have given a discursive springboard to taxpayers for making claims on the government but have left families more generally without an effective voice for making similar demands. The more advocates understand why the demands of taxpayers resonate more than those of families with policymakers and the public, the better equipped they will be to develop a strategy for overcoming this obstacle. Having made a case for the importance of understanding these two puzzles, I turn now to the theory behind my approach to explaining them.

Fiscalization as an Obfuscation Strategy

Obfuscation is usually seen as a primary strategy for retrenchment (Battle 1990; Pierson 1994), but the growth of tax expenditures is an example of an obfuscation strategy to *expand* the welfare state. Much in the same way that policymakers need to obfuscate the effects of retrenchment on policy beneficiaries in order to avoid blame and meet demands for austerity, the same strategy has an inverse effect for expansion. Policymakers wishing to expand the welfare state need to claim credit for increasing benefits while simultaneously meeting demands for spending restraints so as to claim credit for austerity. In the latter case, the targets of obfuscation are financial watchdogs—the International Monetary Fund, credit markets, and deficit hawks—rather than program beneficiaries.

Like traditional social security benefits, tax credits provide real income for their beneficiaries. The key difference is that tax credits appear in the budget as "revenues not collected" rather than as spending. The classification of tax expenditures as nonspending is their single most important attribute in explaining their proliferation since the 1970s. This facet allows policymakers to obfuscate their true effect on the budget and on deficits. We often take modern accounting for granted, assuming that it gives us an objective measure of reality, with debits and credits clearly differentiated on separate sides of the budget ledger. As important as this technical aspect is to the success of budget practices, it is not the only one. In addition to this technical dimension, Carruthers and Espeland (1991) argue that accounting also has a rhetorical dimension. Despite the simplicity and seeming objectivity of accounting, it must still be interpreted and still must convince its audience of the firm or state's legitimacy. The technical and rhetorical dimensions of government budgets are especially important to examine during times of "permanent austerity," when the politics of spending have become particularly contentious. It is tax credits' taken-for-granted classification that makes fiscalization so effective.

Government classification schemes have major consequences for politics (Bowker and Star 1999; Starr 1992; Steensland 2010), including budget politics. Government budgets themselves are a classification scheme that distinguishes revenues from outlays in accounting for state actions. As Carruthers and Espeland (1991: 57) point out, "double-entry bookkeeping edits and frames information. The complexity of economic reality is reduced, and decision makers are presented with a simple 'bottom line,' one that does not reflect all possible interpretations and judgments." The same applies to government budgets, where the complexity of political reality is reduced and reshaped by policymakers.

Rather than conceptualizing tax credits as hidden, Maryl and Quinn (2016) argue that such policies lead us to misrecognize the situation as actors "engage in classification struggles" over the meaning of policies. Under circumstances where the technical analysis of bureaucrats—in places like the US Congressional Budget Office, the UK's Office of National Statistics (ONS), and Canada's Auditor General—have an almost hegemonic quality, the right classification can lend legitimacy to efforts to classify tax credits as nonspending. Joyce (2011), for example, documents how Congressional Budget Office scoring and administration attempts to manipulate the process had major impacts on the failed and successful healthcare proposals of Presidents Bill Clinton and Barack Obama, respectively. Similar classification struggles took place in the case of CTCs and in-work tax credits, for two reasons.

First, the conversion of traditional social security benefits into tax credits served as a signal to financial watchdogs that governments were serious about pursuing austerity. Deficit reduction is a medium-run process that unfolds over multiple budgets, but financial watchdogs must make upfront decisions about whether to finance government deficits in the short run. As in most financial markets, there is a major information asymmetry that works in favor of borrowers (Carruthers 2010; Rona-Tas and Hiss 2010). As a result, lenders must rely on an imperfect combination of available standardized measures of risk and fuzzy signals from potential borrowers. Because austerity became synonymous with reducing spending, it made spending reductions advantageous as a credible signal (Clift and Tomlinson 2008; Gaillard 2012), but retrenchment was still highly unpopular with politically powerful program beneficiaries (Starke 2006). Fiscalization allowed policymakers to send two contradictory signals: one to program beneficiaries and antipoverty advocates, who were concerned only with the level of benefits rather than the form they took, and another to financial watchdogs, who were more concerned with total spending levels (often measured as a proportion of GDP) than the size of the deficit in the short run.

Second, tax credits equipped policymakers seeking to expand benefits with a rhetorical weapon they could use to defend budget changes in light of austerity. This included both left-party defense against conservative critics in opposition and giving cover to right-leaning parties against internal criticism that they were raising taxes or increasing deficits. The emphasis on aggregate measures (taxes and spending as a proportion of GDP) obfuscated changes within these measures. This made them less salient and their effect on the deficit harder to trace back to particular actions.

The classification of tax credits as revenues not collected played a crucial role in the decision to introduce and expand child and in-work tax credits across liberal welfare regimes. Policymakers had to make a credible claim to financial watchdogs and other relevant stakeholders that they were pursuing austerity. Relevant stakeholders would look to official budget accounts to determine whether spending was being contained or reduced. By classifying tax credits as revenues not collected, policymakers could accomplish this goal.

Austerity in Theory and Practice

As I will show, the stagflation that followed the 1973 oil crisis ushered in a new era of "permanent austerity" among rich democracies (Blyth 2013; Pierson 2001; Schäfer and Streeck 2013). Attempts to restore the value of inflation-eroded tax and social security benefits led to stagnating revenues and mounting spending commitments, the combination of which resulted in unsustainable budget deficits. In addition, welfare states were increasingly exposed to new economic pressures from several sources, including slower productivity growth, a shift from manufacturing to service employment, the maturation of welfare state responsibilities, and shifting employment expectations within families (Pierson 2001). As revenues faltered, spending commitments continued to grow, and interest rates climbed, persistent deficits became the new norm.

This shifted the landscape for policymakers. Keynesian emphasis on the advantages of deficit spending gave way to new pressures for austerity. In theory, the goal of austerity is debt and deficit reduction, which can take the form of tax increases, spending reductions, or some combination of each. In practice, however, policymakers since the 1970s have focused primarily on spending reductions as the best way to achieve this goal (Blyth 2013; Kato 2003; Pierson 2001). Part of the reason, especially in liberal welfare regimes, was popular opposition to raising taxes. Inflation-induced erosion of tax exemptions and bracket creep led to intense antitax backlashes in the 1970s. The lesson for policymakers was to avoid raising "painfully visible" income taxes lest voters punish them at the polls (Prasad 2006; Wilensky 2002).

At the same time, powerful financial organizations, fearful of arresting economic growth, increasingly shied away from reliance on increasing taxes to close budget gaps. Credit rating agencies, which began moving back into the business of rating sovereign debt in the 1970s, had a subtle bias in favor of spending reduction over tax increases (Gaillard 2012; Gill 2015). The International Monetary Fund shared a similar bias (Clift and Tomlinson 2008: 549), which eventually became de facto policy under the banner of "expansionary austerity" by the 1990s (Blyth 2013). In practice, policymakers looking to pursue austerity were reluctant to rely on revenue enhancements because voters and financial organizations discouraged it.

Instead, according to Pierson (2001: 423), the fight against spending is a "defining characteristic of the era of austerity." This intense focus on government spending opens the door for advocates to seek out policy alternatives, which may not show up on the budget as spending. In this new environment, the relative costs and benefits of using tax credits tipped to the point where they began to appear more politically attractive than traditional social security benefits.

The shift toward austerity explains why we begin to see a shift toward fiscalization during this period. Prior to the 1970s, policymakers had more incentive to provide benefits in the form of straightforward social spending. Revenues were abundant, so the costs were not salient, and there was no need to use the more complicated tax system. In addition, tax credits were the domain of treasury departments, making them less accessible to antipoverty advocates housed in social security departments. Austerity changed the costs and benefits of using the tax system for social policy purposes. New pressures for austerity, when they delegitimized tax increases and legitimized spending cuts, inadvertently made tax credits more attractive to policymakers who could pursue a strategy of obfuscation to expand benefits.

In the US, the EITC was first introduced in 1974 and has subsequently been expanded multiple times over the years. Historically, it has been successfully framed as an offset against income, payroll, and gasoline taxes, but it was the subject of classification struggles in 1995, when congressional Republicans attempted to portray it as an out-of-control spending program. In contrast, technical differences in the classification of the CTC, introduced in 1997, made it much less open to contestation from deficit hawks.

In Canada, the introduction of the first refundable CTC (RCTC) in 1978 was a direct response to pressures for austerity. Initially, government officials classified all of the RCTCs as revenues not collected, making it an attractive alternative to the popular and functionally similar family allowance program, which it completely displaced by 1992. Classification struggles came to the surface in the early 2000s as the auditor general of Canada called this classification scheme into question. Under pressure, the government reclassified the Child Tax Benefit (CTB) as spending. This changed the calculus for the Conservative government that took power in 2006. Instead of increasing the CTB, as previous governments had done, the spending-averse Conservatives introduced a new nonrefundable CTC and the WITB—both of which were classified as revenues not collected according to the new budget standards.

In the UK, fiscalization came much later with the introduction of the Working Families Tax Credit (WFTC) in 1999 and its later split into the CTC and WTC in 2003. Classification struggles became prominent in the government's ongoing dispute with the ONS over the classification of the tax credits as revenues not collected when the WFTC's very similar predecessor program has been classified as spending. The decision to split the WFTC into two credits was influenced by the ONS's decision to reclassify the portion of the credit greater than total income tax liability as spending, as is the standard in the US.

During the "golden age" of the welfare state, when governments were flush with revenue, the use of tax credits was not necessary. It was only with the onset of stagflation and the deficits that followed that these unique characteristics of tax credits became important. While this explains the broad convergence among these countries toward fiscalization, I now turn to explaining divergence in the distribution of these tax credits between Canada and the UK on one hand and the US on the other.

Children, Taxpayers, and the Cultural Legacies of Public Policies

The last decade has seen the relationship between cultural sociology and historical institutionalism flourish. In particular, there has been a new appreciation for the process through which policy legacies exert a cultural influence that shapes later actors attempting to make significant policy changes (Best 2012; Brown 2013; Pedrianna and Striker 1997; Schneider and Ingram 2005; Skrentny 2006; Steensland 2008). The dominant approach focuses on how particular target populations or cultural categories become institutionalized through policy and shape whom policymakers and the public sees as worthy of benefits. Steensland (2008), for example, documents the inability of US policymakers to introduce a guaranteed annual income program in a relatively favorable environment because of concerns over giving unrestricted cash benefits to the "undeserving poor." Similarly, Best (2012) notes that policy changes affecting how medical research was funded eventually led to less support for diseases perceived to be related to poor lifestyle choices (i.e., where the affected are "unworthy") relative to those perceived as unrelated to personal decisions.

While it is well established that moral distinctions between types of recipients affect policymakers' generosity, it is less clear why certain categorizations become salient at some moments but not others. In Canada and the UK, debates over in-work and CTCs focused on children and their needs; the distinction between taxpayers and welfare recipients never had much traction, even though it was central to other political conflicts in Canada and the UK at the time. In the US, by contrast, the taxpayer/welfare recipient distinction quickly came to dominate the conversation about both the EITC and the CTC, and the unifying category of "children" became less relevant.

To understand this divergence, we must look not only at which target populations are seen as deserving of benefits, but at *what it is* that they are deserving of exactly. As Skrentny (2006: 1803) notes in his study of how various groups were included or excluded in affirmative action policy, "worthy/unworthy are indeed important basic categories in all social policy making, but by themselves they do not explain which policies go to which groups. Elites may perceive two groups as both worthy of policy but not . . . the same policy." In order to understand why otherwise sympathetic groups may be excluded from the benefits of a given policy, we must examine the particular "logic of appropriateness" behind the policy in question.

March and Olsen (2008) argue that logics of appropriateness "define what are legitimate arguments and standards of justification and criticism in different situations." The legitimacy of a policy depends not only on *who* are receiving it and whether it is effective but also on *how* they are receiving it. There must be a match, so to speak, between particular categories of beneficiaries and particular types of benefits. Skrentny (2006) shows how this worked in the case of affirmative action: because the policy was first developed with African-Americans in mind, groups perceived as definitionally similar to African-Americans (American Indians, Asian Americans, Latinos) had the easiest time being incorporated into affirmative action policy, while women had more difficulty, and white ethnics had no success at all.

Others have shown that changing perceptions of target populations can lead to a shift in which logics are most prominent. When policymakers came to see disease victims, not doctors, as the primary beneficiary of medical research funding, they concomitantly shifted from a logic of science to a logic of mortality in deciding which diseases to fund (Best 2012). And in the aftermath of US welfare reform, Brown (2013) finds that states that perceived *Hispanic* immigrants as threatening followed a racial logic in determining the severity of punitive new rules, while policymakers who thought *illegal* immigrants threatened them used a legality logic instead.

The question then becomes why any particular logic dominates in a given situation. Building on the work of these scholars, I argue that in addition to institutionalizing cultural categories, policies also institutionalize distinct logics of appropriateness that are reinforced over time and constrain future policymakers. This occurs because actors in particular fields orient themselves to these policy legacies and internalize their logics, taking them for granted (Popp Berman 2012: 9–10). In addition, to a lesser degree, these legacies shape the perceptions of low-information publics who rely on policymakers for cues on how to interpret policies in light of existing policies. Once institutionalized, certain logics of appropriateness become dominant. Competing logics do not become unthinkable, because fields often overlap and actors may try to draw on the dominant logics in other fields, but they are put at a severe disadvantage (Popp Berman 2012; Schneiberg 2007).

Advocates of policies based on alternative logics find themselves unable to garner comparable resources in the political field because their rationale is less resonant for the field's actors relative to the dominant logic. It is not that policies adhering to nondominant logics lack merit. Rather, the problem is that their merits are overshadowed by the perception that they are simply inappropriate relative to policies that adhere to the dominant logic. This becomes clear in the case of children—a cultural category universally perceived as deserving in the abstract.

Three Logics of Social Policy

Families with children have been receiving direct cash benefits in liberal welfare regimes in one form or another for over a century. Three logics, though, and the policies in which they have become institutionalized have been crucial in determining whether families are seen as deserving of specific benefits.

The first is the *logic of income support* for destitute families. According to this logic, families are deserving of relatively generous benefits to keep them out of deep poverty if they find themselves unable to earn income because of unemployment beyond their control. Most famously institutionalized in the English Poor Law of 1834, but also through the creation of "mothers' pensions" in the US and Canada, this logic governs what later came to be called social assistance or welfare (Little 1998; Skocpol 1992).

The second is the *logic of tax relief* for taxpayers. According to this logic, families should be exempt from paying taxes until they have enough income to avoid poverty and support themselves. This logic was institutionalized in tax exemptions tied to the number of dependents during the rise of mass income taxation around the turn of the twentieth century (Carluccio 1993; Seltzer 1968). By the 1920s, both of these logics were firmly institutionalized in public policies across the industrialized world. In the US, they continue to be the dominant logics governing direct cash benefits to families with children.

In other liberal welfare regimes, including Canada and the UK but not the US, a third logic emerged in the 1940s: the *logic of income supplementation* for families with children. According to this logic, neither wages nor unemployment benefits take into consideration the fact that some people support dependent children while others do not. This necessitates providing small universal cash supplements to families with children, which prevents poverty among working families without removing work incentives for the unemployed (Blake 2009; Macnicol 1980). This logic was institutionalized in the family allowance policies that were introduced in every liberal welfare regime except the US in the 1940s, as part of a larger process of postwar reconstruction.

The first two logics make categorical distinctions between families in different situations: the truly destitute versus income earners of modest means. Providing tax relief to the welfare poor is seen as inappropriate because these families do not pay income taxes. Providing income support to working families is seen as inappropriate because they are not destitute and therefore lack the need for it (and likely wish to avoid the stigma attached to it). But the logic of supplementation transcends these boundaries. Policymakers may appropriately provide income supplements to all families, including both the welfare poor and taxpayers, because the logic is based on family size rather than ability to work or tax burden. Beginning in the 1970s, budget pressures made targeted income supplements more attractive, but the same logic still operates, as I will show in the case of the UK's Family Income Supplement in chapter 5.

It was this third logic that served as the springboard for refundable tax credits in Canada and the UK but was absent in the US. Beginning in the 1970s, all three countries increasingly channeled benefits through the tax system for the obfuscation reasons discussed earlier. In this environment, tax credits became a popular policy option for expanding family benefits. By the time child poverty became a major issue across the English-speaking world in the early 1990s, a consensus had formed that child and in-work tax credits were the best policy options for tackling poverty in families.

Child and in-work tax credits could be justified using either of two logics. Were they child benefits governed by the logic of income supplementation, in which case refundable credits were most appropriate, or tax credits governed by the logic of tax relief, in which case only partially refundable or nonrefundable credits were appropriate? The answer, rather than being contingent on the party in power or the country's general level of conservatism, hinged on whether the logic of income supplementation had been institutionalized through past policies. In all three countries, policymakers saw these tax credits as a way to ease the economic pressures families were experiencing. But they drew on different policy legacies in thinking about who were appropriate recipients of tax credits.

Social assistance ("welfare") was increasingly seen as problematic in all three cases. One of the keys advantages for Canadian and British policymakers was being able to frame tax credits as alternatives to social assistance rather than synonymous with it. In Canada, CTCs were seen as an off-budget way to restore the value of family allowances, which had been eroding due to inflation. Following the logic of income supplementation, it was only appropriate that such a benefit would go to all low-income families and thus that the tax credit would be refundable. Those families' status as workers or taxpayers was irrelevant. Indeed, Canadian policymakers explicitly argued that the RCTC would "take children off welfare." In the UK, the trend toward enriching the in-work benefits that would eventually become the WFTC grew out of the perception that welfare created a "poverty trap." Targeting benefits toward workers was a technical, not moral, decision to avoid this poverty trap. The subsequent conversion of part of the WFTC into a fully refundable CTC reveals that distinctions between the "welfare poor" and the "working poor" were not an issue outside the confines of social assistance, because policymakers could draw on the logic of income supplementation.

In the US, however, the EITC and CTC were quickly defined as forms of tax relief. Since only taxpayers were deserving of tax relief, making either fully refundable was perceived as inappropriate, and equivalent to "welfare." Those proponents who tried to argue for the legitimacy of income supplementation across a wide range of families were quickly shut down, as the US had no historical legacy of family allowances to institutionalize this logic. Instead, the US created a nonrefundable CTC, which avoided the problem of expanding "welfare" but did nothing for the poorest children, whom CTCs were originally intended to help. Even with the EITC, often touted as a success story, we find that the logic of tax relief has severely limited the size and scope of benefits after the 1990s.

The rest of the book traces these cultural legacies from their origins in the 1940s to their increasing salience in the 1970s and 1980s, and ends with the zenith of fiscalization in the 1990s.

Overview of the Book

Chapter 2 looks at what I call the "great divergence," when these logics of appropriateness were institutionalized into public policies. This chapter challenges the view that American exceptionalism is deeply rooted in some unique American culture or the country's shameful racial history by showing just how similar all three countries were in the interwar period. Prior to World War II, American, British, and Canadian policymakers held similar views on when it was appropriate to provide direct cash benefits to families with children. The first view, which was part of the old regime of local "mothers' pensions," was cast anew as social assistance and insurance programs were introduced and institutionalized on the state/provincial and national levels. The second view arose with the movement toward mass income taxation as policymakers introduced dependent exemptions for the purpose of tax equity between childless taxpayers and those supporting children. Children were recognized as dependents either of social assistance/insurance beneficiaries or of taxpayers.

Nascent projects for postwar reconstruction changed this in Canada and the UK as each country introduced family allowances in the mid-1940s. Children were recognized for the first time ever as deserving of direct cash benefits according to a new logic of income supplementation. The US on the other hand never introduced family allowances. I show that the reason for this was not a cultural tradition of individualism nor the result of racial animosity, two factors that might explain the later failure of fully refundable tax credits. Instead, it was contingent on the sequence of events during this critical juncture. Specifically, this chapter shows how the famous Beveridge Report in the UK served as a benchmark event at home and abroad, opening a new path for policymakers in North America by legitimizing family allowances for the first time. Canada, which had previously been on the same path as the US, switched paths by copying the Beveridge blueprint for a postwar welfare state that included family allowances. This might have happened in the US as well were it not for a fateful decision by President Franklin D. Roosevelt to choose as the US blueprint a report by the National Resource Planning Board that preceded the Beveridge Report, closing off the possibility for family allowances in the process. The unintended result was the noninstitutionalization of the logic of income supplementation for families. The policy legacies established during this period were crucial for shaping later responses to inflation and child poverty.

Chapter 3 looks at the transition from the "era of easy finance" to the "era of permanent austerity" when these logics, institutionalized in the 1940s, were reinforced in the 1970s. The onset of stagflation across the developed world led to new and intense economic pressures on families. Most of the scholars who have studied this period focus on the confusion policymakers faced as the Keynesian consensus broke down and they were forced to recalibrate monetary and fiscal policy to fight inflation and unemployment. Policymakers also faced uncertainty in how to deal with inflation as it increased economic pressures on families by eroding tax and social benefits. I demonstrate that in countries with family allowances, like Canada and the UK, policymakers and the public traced these pressures to the erosion of family allowances. In the US, which had no family allowance, policymakers and the public traced these pressures to the erosion of dependent exemptions and bracket creep in the tax system. In doing so, they reinforced the salience of dominant logics of appropriateness determining policy responses in each country.

Whereas US policymakers relied almost entirely on increases in the dependent exemption to help families, Canadian and British policymakers relied on increases in family allowances. Family allowances in Canada offered an alternative logic, which was neither "welfare" nor limited to taxpayers. This proved crucial as policymakers looked to relieve the pressure on families in the 1970s and 1980s under stagflation. The decision to triple the value of family allowances in 1974 was a direct response to inflationary pressures on families. British policymakers had the same response to inflation, tracing the economic pressures on family to the erosion of family benefits rather than the erosion of tax exemptions. The government, for example, explicitly framed the new Child Benefit introduced in 1977, which doubled the value of the family allowance, as a way to help families with children who were suffering from inflation. The antitax rhetoric of the government of Margaret Thatcher, I will show, was actually a distinct issue unrelated to the economic effects of inflation on families. Income supplementation, not tax relief, took center stage from the 1970s onward.

In addition to reinforcing dominant logics, the stagflation of the 1970s brought with it deficits in the 1980s, as a result of policymakers' attempts to shield families from its effects. These deficits ushered in an era of austerity as policymakers sought to constrain spending so as to curb deficits and inflation. In this new environment, cost containment became much more important as growth slowed and revenues became scarcer. Fiscalization, and income-testing in the case of the UK, became much more attractive to those trying to protect programs from retrenchment or even expand them. Tax credits were not technically nor popularly perceived as spending, which gave them an advantage from the 1970s onward.

In Canada, prior to the 1970s, there was little interest, in either the Department of National Health and Welfare (DNHW) or the Department of Finance, in using the tax system to distribute child benefits. This began to shift in the 1970s as countries around the world sought to constrain spending in the face of stagflation. In October 1975, Finance Minister Donald McDonald announced that "Canada [was] in the grip of serious inflation" that would require the containing of government spending. He pledged to hold spending growth to the rate of GNP and look for possible spending cuts (Savoie 1991: 149). With prospects for increased funding looking grim, the DNHW started to rethink the benefits of tax expenditures, which are not considered spending in the budget. Whereas traditional expenditures would be seen as new spending, tax expenditures were simply revenues not collected and thus did not contribute to the growth of government. In 1978, under intense pressure to cut spending, the federal government cut family allowances while simultaneously introducing the first refundable CTC. The change had a neutral effect on the deficit but was considered a spending reduction. As persistent deficits plagued Canada over the next two decades, policymakers looking to defend child benefits against retrenchment repeatedly used fiscalization as a means to protect the program from spending cuts by reframing benefits as revenues not collected.

In the US, it was the perception of tax exemptions as nonspending and tax credits as offsets that gave them an advantage. The Senate Finance Committee, for example, in drafting the legislation for the EITC, specified that the "credit is set at 10% in order to correspond roughly to the added burdens placed on workers by both employee and employer social security contributions" (US Senate 1975). As long as it was offsetting taxes, even if they were not technically counted against income taxes, it satisfied policymakers as nonspending. The dependent exemption and EITC thrived in this environment, becoming the glue that helped hold together the 1986 tax reforms.

Fiscalization came to the UK much later than the other countries. I trace this to the decision of the Thatcher government to shift to the value added tax (VAT) as a larger source of revenues. This helped shore up the government's finances and avoid the larger deficits found in the US and Canada. Instead, policymakers undertook a strategy of introducing income-tested benefits, starting with the Family Income Supplement (FIS) in 1970. Because it excludes middle- and upper-income families, FIS helped the government constrain spending relative to universal child benefits. The program is not only important because it was the predecessor to what later became the WFTC in the late 1990s. Because FIS was limited to the working poor, some might predict that it would institutionalize distinctions between the "undeserving" welfare poor and the "deserving" working poor, as some have argued about the EITC (Bertram 2015; Steensland 2008). So FIS serves as an important test case for this theory in other Poor Law legacy settings.

Chapters 4–6 move into the 1990s, looking at changes in each individual country. It was during this decade that child poverty became a major political issue leading to the culmination of fiscalization in liberal welfare regimes. Policymakers in all three countries placed efforts to tackle child poverty at the center of their agendas, but their responses were powerfully shaped by the cultural legacies of family benefits. Whereas children dominated in the UK and Canada, taxpayers trumped children in the fight against child poverty in the US.

Chapter 4 looks at how Canadian policymakers' renewed promise to tackle child poverty translated into the CTB, the nonrefundable CTC, and the WITB. Whereas the logic of tax relief served as the springboard for fiscalization in the US, the process was largely driven by the logic of income supplementation in Canada. These differences had important implications for the shape and scope of Canadian tax credits, enabling them to significantly affect rates of child poverty relative to much weaker outcomes in the US. The fiscalization of social policy was not the result of any antitax backlash or taxpayer identity. Children, not taxpayers, were the primary cultural category on which policymakers based their justification of relevant tax credits. Policymakers still had to be careful not to expand "welfare" in their pursuit to help children. Family allowances, which were the institutional predecessor to the CTB, offered policymakers an alternative to welfare as the primary method of delivering cash benefits to children. Expanding CTCs was seen as a way to "take children off welfare." Thus reformers were able to avoid the dual-clientele trap that hindered welfare reform. Policymakers could punish "undeserving" welfare parents while ensuring benefits for "deserving" children through the CTB. The initial change occurred under the right-leaning Progressive Conservative government in 1992 and was consolidated under the left-leaning Liberal government in 1997.

In addition, changes under Prime Minister Stephen Harper suggest that classification issues can also have effects on the advantage of using income supplementation or tax relief as the relevant logic for tax credits. A sudden change in the classification of the RCTC from revenues not collected to spending shifted the government's calculus and gave those who favored limiting tax relief to taxpayers the upper hand. Policymakers were still able to tap into antitax sentiments and frame tax credits as tax relief for taxpayers. As demonstrated by the introduction of the new nonrefundable CTC under Harper, tax expenditures remain flexible enough that policymakers can tailor their frames to fit changing circumstances.

Chapter 5 looks at the introduction of the WFTC and its subsequent split into the WTC and the CTC. The UK case follows the Canadian case in terms of tracing the dominant target population of children to the cultural legacy of family allowances and ends up with the same combination of refundable in-work tax credits and CTCs. As noted, the shift to fiscalization occurred much later in the UK. Policymakers first turned to income-testing, but this is only half the story. When the New Labour government reached the limits of this strategy in the late 1990s, the Treasury quietly turned to fiscalization as the solution to further expand the welfare state in the face of pressures for austerity. By introducing the WFTC, according to one observer, the Treasury "lopped some pounds 2.5bn off what is conventionally called 'welfare spending' yet was able to claim credit for more than doubling the amount of financial help the Government is offering families in low-paid work" (Walker 1998). The limits of fiscalization were soon tested as the ONS called the government's reclassification into question. The ensuing battle shows what can happen when the technical dimension of tax credits as revenues not collected comes into conflict with its rhetorical dimension.

It is worth highlighting here what makes the UK case study so important (in addition to reinforcing the findings from chapter 4). In terms of the sequence of policy innovations, the UK resembles the US more than Canada. This may matter for the institutionalization of cultural categories. Some scholars have argued that the introduction of the EITC in 1974 institutionalized the "working poor" as a distinct target population, further entrenching Poor Law distinctions between the "deserving" and "undeserving" poor (Bertram 2015; Steensland 2008). Because the UK also introduced a wage subsidy for the working poor in 1970, the FIS, we might expect it to similarly entrench categorical distinctions based on work. The subsequent split of the WFTC (the successor to the FIS) into the refundable WTC and CTC suggests that the cultural legacy of the Poor Law is not enough to explain the US situation but strengthens my case that the cultural legacy of family allowances was what really mattered.

Chapter 6 looks at the US experience with the EITC and the nonrefundable CTC in light of the previous two cases. Most crucially, the growth of these tax credits, tracing their legacy to the dependent exemption in the tax system, was premised on the logic of tax relief rather than the logic of income supplementation. These changes are reflected in the EITC expansions in the 1990 and 1993 budgets and the subsequent defense of the EITC against attempts by congressional Republicans to cut the program in 1995. Policymakers expanded the EITC several times without issue during the 1980s and early 1990s. As a smaller credit, they could credibly claim that it was a form of tax relief for taxpayers, in that it acted to offset income, payroll, and sometimes gasoline taxes. The 1993 expansion pushed beyond this boundary, calling into question the EITC as a pure tax relief mechanism for the first time. As a result, congressional Republicans subsequently targeted the EITC for cuts as a "welfare" program. Despite favorable conditions, they failed, because Democrats were able to respond to criticisms by arguing that EITC beneficiaries were indeed taxpayers deserving of tax relief. The fact that they were working families played, at best, a secondary role.

For the CTC, the logic of tax relief resulted in controversies over full refundability, "credit stacking," and eventual introduction as part of the Taxpayer Relief Act of 1997. In both cases, intense discursive battles were fought in order to define the cultural boundaries of who exactly constituted a taxpayer versus a welfare beneficiary and what that meant for policy goals. Child poverty became a major concern, as was evidenced by the creation of the National Commission on Children (NCC) in 1988. The NCC later released recommendations for a fully refundable CTC as the best way to tackle child poverty. This served as a successful springboard for the introduction of fully refundable CTCs in Canada and the UK. This was not the case in the US, where the logic of tax relief remained dominant. It was not that poor children were undeserving in general but that they were undeserving of tax credits because their parents were not technically taxpayers. Expending the benefits of the CTC to them by making it fully refundable would result in a form of symbolic pollution by giving tax relief to nontaxpayers. It would become "welfare," with the entire stigma that comes along with the label.

Although proposals for a fully refundable CTC were quickly defeated, Democrats were able to extend more of the CTC's benefits to the working poor—but not based on their status as workers. Controversy ensued over the issue of "stacking": whether families would be able to claim the refundable EITC before or after the nonrefundable CTC. Having learned their lesson after the defeat of the fully refundable CTC, Democrats strategically adopted the more resonant logic of tax relief rationale in order to extend benefits to the working poor based on their identity as taxpayers deserving of tax relief. The strategy proved highly effective, giving Democrats a victory in an otherwise unfavorable environment.

Chapter 7 reviews the evidence presented in the previous chapters. It summarizes the evidence for my theories of fiscalization and argues that traditional alternative arguments cannot explain the timing or the shape fiscalization took in the US, the UK, and Canada. I conclude with a discussion of the implications of my theories in regard to the study of culture and political institutions, as well as their practical implications for advocates who are interested in learning more about the politics of tax and child poverty policies in order to reform them.

2

The Great Divergence

IN ORDER TO understand why taxpayers trumped children in the debate over tax credits in the US—but not in Canada or the UK—we need to start at the beginning. As discussed in the previous chapter, policymakers were guided by what March and Olsen (2008) call logics of appropriateness institutionalized in certain policies. Social assistance/insurance, tax exemptions, and family allowances are all aimed at helping children, but each of these benefits is governed by a different logic as to why children are deserving of it.

Prior to the advent of World War II, public policies across these three countries institutionalized two distinct logics justifying benefits for children. First, the Poor Law tradition led to laws institutionalizing the logic of income support for the destitute. By the 1930s, most states and provinces had passed "mothers' pension" laws providing income support for very needy families with children; eventually, these programs became federal. Alongside social assistance, these governments all introduced unemployment insurance, adding a contributory principle to the logic of income support (Amenta 1998; Glennerster 2007; Guest 1999; Harris 1997; Little 1998; Skocpol 1992).

Second, the creation of tax exemptions for children established another way government could legitimately assist families. As tax expenditures, child exemptions have received less attention from historians than other welfare state measures. Nevertheless, they were a major social policy innovation during this period. As policymakers shifted to mass income taxation in order to fund wars and budding new welfare states, they awarded special recognition to taxpayers with children. Tax exemptions for dependents were added to all income tax systems as taxes were raised to generate revenue for World War I (Carluccio 1993: 82; Daunton 2002: 41; Seltzer 1968: 39–40).

Heading into World War II, the three countries had institutionalized two appropriate ways for governments to assist families: through income support, for the destitute; and by reducing the tax burden, for everyone else. By the end of the war, liberal welfare regimes—with the sole exception of the US—had introduced family allowances, institutionalizing a new logic of income supplementation for all families. This is the critical juncture during which the logic of tax relief came to dominate American politics.

Why was the US the only rich democracy not to adopt family allowances? The policy of providing universal direct cash benefits to families with children took root in every other rich democracy during the interwar and World War II periods (Macnicol 1992; Misra 2003; Wennemo 1992). Even among liberal welfare regimes, which provide few universal benefits otherwise, there was a rapid adoption of family allowances in the short period between 1941 and 1946.[1] Whereas other aspects of "American exceptionalism" have been the topic of countless studies, the literature on the absence of family allowances in the United States is virtually nonexistent.[2]

This chapter establishes, through a comparative analysis focusing primarily on the US and Canada between 1939 and 1945, that contingent events, rather than more durable differences in political culture or racial animosity, best explain American exceptionalism. It was during this critical juncture that these two similar countries diverged, with Canada introducing family allowances in 1944. Though there are subtle differences that make the UK case less useful in this instance, the UK too adopted family allowances in 1945.

Building off of Amenta's (1998) pioneering work on American "work and relief" policy during the Great Depression, I argue that Canada was on a similar "work and relief" trajectory as late as 1942. Both American and Canadian policymakers saw public works projects—not family allowances—as the best strategy for comprehensive postwar reconstruction. It was only with the publication of the Beveridge Report in the UK that year that this changed. The Beveridge Report acted as what I call a benchmark event, opening the possibility for the reorientation of policymakers and legitimation of family allowances in North America.

Contrary to Amenta (1998), the failure of family allowances in the US was not an inevitable consequence of path dependency. Nor was the success of family allowances in Canada a preordained outcome. The contingent sequence of policy crafting in each country explains the two countries' divergence. Although both countries released blueprints popularly described as the "American Beveridge plan" and the "Canadian Beveridge plan," respectively, only the latter was crafted after the benchmark of Beveridge. Whether policy crafting takes place before or after a benchmark event is important, for two reasons. First, benchmark events allow for the activation of strategically placed reformist actors. Family allowance advocates headed important committees prior to the publication of the Beveridge Report, but it was only afterward that it became possible to translate personal support into the institutional advocacy that was necessary for policy change (Weir and Skocpol 1985). Second, benchmark events enable the legitimation of previously unpopular policy innovations on new rationales. Early proposals for family allowances were justified on a number of grounds, including feminist, pronatal, and antipoverty grounds, all of which were deemed unconvincing by policymakers. The Beveridge Report offered a new rationale—family allowances as work incentives—that was acceptable to conservative policymakers.

These findings challenge a number of alternative historical explanations positing that the US's distinct welfare state trajectory was the result of differences in political culture, racial animosity, fiscal capacities, macroeconomic environments, or conservative forces (Amenta 1998; Hacker 2002; Lieberman 1995; Katz 1996; Prasad 2012a). Instead, the US-Canada comparison shows that the divergence was contingent on specific choices made by liberal state builders in the 1940s. Because it was the decision to introduce family allowances that institutionalized the logic of income supplementation, these choices had unintended consequences that went on to shape the policy preferences and institutional constraints of political actors from the 1970s onward.

Explaining Divergence in Postwar Possibilities

In order to understand the failure of family allowances to take hold in the US, we must go back to the critical juncture where the US diverged from other liberal welfare regimes. Canada introduced its family allowance in 1944, but the great divergence took place earlier, between 1941 and 1943. It was during this period that elites in governments were creating the blueprints for postwar reconstruction that would fundamentally shape social policy after the war ended.

The best known of these is Sir William Beveridge's *Social Insurance and Allied Services* (1942), popularly known as the Beveridge Report, in the UK. The US and Canada released similar reports. In the US, the report of the National Resource Planning Board (NRPB), *Work, Security, and Relief Policies* (1941), was known popularly as the "American Beveridge plan." In Canada, Leonard Marsh's *Report on Social Security for Canada* (1943) was known popularly as the "Canadian Beveridge plan." All three were discussed at length by contemporaries as analogous documents laying out national strategies for postwar reconstruction via Keynesian economic management and comprehensive social security measures (Beveridge 1943; Burns 1943; Cassidy 1943; Witte 1945).

Most analyses of critical junctures focus on how the material interests of stakeholders are shaped and reshaped during specific windows in time that are then reinforced by the new institutional arrangements in subsequent periods (Hacker 2002; Prasad 2012a). Historical institutionalists have spent far less time exploring cognitive or cultural factors, with a few significant exceptions (Lieberman 2003; Skrentny 2006; Zollars and Skocpol 1994).

Lieberman (2003), for example, looking at key moments in constitutional negotiation in South Africa and Brazil, argues that the resulting constitutions helped define "national political communities" in ways that put the two otherwise similar countries on different trajectories in regard to tax compliance.[3] Lieberman's study of constitutions in particular brings our attention to the possible importance of major documents in shaping the cognitive schemas (Sewell 1992) actors see as relevant as they begin to craft policies. In much the same way, the US, UK, and Canadian reports on postwar reconstruction acted as blueprints, guiding policymakers as they set out to strengthen and consolidate their welfare states after the war. These reports were not simply a reflection of broader national cultures. Though there was budding support for family allowances in the UK, it was completely absent in North America. Instead, support came from autonomous elites within governments. "Strategically placed actors," according to Capoccia (2015), "may use their position of influence to diffuse ideas that legitimize particular institutional innovations and through this process prevail over others affected by the institutional change at stake, including social groups that may be substantially larger."

In creating these blueprints, government elites were filling up empty political space provided by the uncertainty of the immediate postwar period. A severe recession with high unemployment followed World War

I. Policymakers sought to prevent a similar recession at the conclusion of World War II. To do so, they created committees to look into possible policy options. The results were "unofficial" reports about postwar reconstruction that filled this previous open political space. As Pierson (2004: 71) notes, "actors arriving later may find that resources in the environment (e.g., potential supporters) are already committed to other patterns of mobilization." These reports quickly morphed into plans or blueprints setting the boundaries of postwar possibilities. The crucial determinant of whether these countries adopted family allowances was whether any such proposals were included in postwar blueprints.

Supporters of family allowances were strategically placed in all three countries for this. Beveridge, a member of the Family Endowment Society, was tasked with creating the blueprint for British postwar reconstruction. As Rodgers (1998) has documented, a vibrant transatlantic network of social reformers flourished across the first half of the twentieth century. The authors of both the American and Canadian blueprints were part of this network. In fact, both hailed from Britain. Leonard Marsh, author of the "Marsh Report," was a student of Beveridge at the London School of Economics before joining the faculty of McGill University in Montreal. Eveline Burns, author of the NRPB report, had served on the faculty of the London School of Economics alongside Beveridge before joining the faculty of Columbia University in New York City. Both favored the introduction of family allowances.

Despite these commonalities, the three reports diverged in their treatment of family allowances. Both the Beveridge and Marsh reports included proposals for family allowances as part and parcel of a larger set of social security reforms. The NRPB report on the other hand was totally silent on the issue, containing no mention of family allowances. A program for family allowances was subsequently introduced in Canada; discussion of such a program was totally absent hitherto in North America, and none was ever even proposed in the US. We might expect that the presence of strategically placed advocates would have at least ensured the placement of family allowances on the political agenda (Weir and Skocpol 1985), but the US case defies this prediction. Conversely, we might expect that the lack of any historical legacy would have hindered the development of family allowances (Amenta 1998), but Canada defies this prediction.

In order to explain the great divergence between the US and Canada, we need to look closer at the sequence of events as they unfolded. The importance of sequence to historical institutionalists is well established

(Pierson 2004). Most often, their accounts look at the sequence of events before or after critical junctures in time,[4] but sequences often matter during critical junctures. Pearson (2014), for example, argues that the 1960s and 1970s was a critical juncture in the growth of state fiscal capacities as US states searched for new sources of revenue to support growing spending commitments. She finds that the sequences of popular ballot initiatives, whether they were launched before or after the implementation of new taxes, played a pivotal role in whether the public approved or repealed them.[5]

Sequence mattered during this critical juncture, in that blueprints may be created before or after what I am calling *benchmark events*. These are major events that orient government elites to new standards for evaluation of future policies. Skrentny (2006), for example, argues that the early institutionalization of African Americans in the development of affirmative action policy acted as a "legitimate benchmark" for the inclusion or exclusion of later social groups. Similarly, Martin (2008) argues that Proposition 13 in California reoriented policymakers' views on tax limitation. In this case, the Beveridge Report served as a benchmark event, legitimizing family allowances at home and abroad. According to Beveridge's biographer, "the benchmark of 'Beveridge' continued to exercise a powerful constraint over the boundaries of social policy for many years after the war" (Harris 1997: 471). This was true in North America as well, where family allowances had no prior political support.

The Beveridge Report influenced the development of social policy in two ways. The first was through the activation of strategically placed reformist actors. Key actors may have the right ideas and be in the right place but may not act on them if the timing is not right. Bureaucratic inertia favors conservative, tried-and-true policy ideas over new and untested reformist ideas (Amenta 1998; Weir and Skocpol 1985). Both Burns and Marsh favored family allowances yet never made this explicit in interim reports for the government prior to the release of the Beveridge Report. Instead, both wrote in favor of a renewed emphasis on public works projects as the best way to deal with expected postwar unemployment. I call these recommendations conservative-oriented because they looked to the past—the Depression—for policy solutions. It was only after the publication of the Beveridge Report that longtime advocates officially proposed policies, such as family allowances, that were reform-oriented, in that they looked to the postwar future.

The second influence of the Beveridge Report was its legitimizing of previously discounted policy innovations based on new rationales. Family allowances can be justified on a number of different grounds. They can be seen as feminist measures recognizing the contributions of mothers, as pronatalist policies for increasing the birth rate, or as antipoverty tools to help provide a living wage to workers and their families. Each of these rationales had failed to resonate with policymakers at various times in the past. The Beveridge Report legitimized family allowances not based on any of these rationales but as vital to the proper functioning of a comprehensive social insurance system. Without universal family allowances, unemployment benefits for larger families might be worth more than full-time employment. In order to avoid work disincentives, Beveridge argued that family allowances were a necessary component of any social insurance system. Using this new rationale—ensuring work incentives—subsequent proposals for family allowances became much more politically acceptable to key policymakers.

Sequence was crucial to the success or failure of family allowances. Prior to 1942, the US and Canada were on the same conservative path for postwar reconstruction, what Amenta (1998) calls a "work and relief" policy. They only diverged after the release of the Beveridge Report. Although released in 1943 and dubbed the "American Beveridge plan," the NRPB report authored by Burns was actually written and published in 1941—one year before the Beveridge Report. President Roosevelt held off on releasing it until pressure from the popularity of the Beveridge Report provided him the opportunity to do something to show his concern with social security. The blueprint for American postwar reconstruction had already been written before this benchmark event. The Marsh Report, however, was written and published months after the Beveridge Report and was based directly on it. The result, stemming from Roosevelt's fateful decision, was the proposal and eventual introduction of family allowances in Canada and their complete absence in the US.

Comparison of the US and Canada during this critical juncture provides us with an excellent set of cases for a most similar system research design. The fact that the US has a deviant outcome on family allowances that is not immediately explicable makes it a useful negative case (Emigh 1997). This strategy follows a number of recent comparative studies looking at US-Canada divergence during this time period in areas such as healthcare (Maioni 1998), financial regulation (Prasad 2012a), and industrial relations (Eidlin 2015). During the period in question, the two countries were remarkably similar in terms of a number of factors scholars see as important to the development of welfare states, including liberal political culture (O'Connor, Orloff, and Shaver 1999), working-class strength (Eidlin 2015), federalism and regional cleavages (Maioni 1998), fiscal capacity (Smith 1995), involvement in World War II (Higgs 1987), and child-related social policy legacies (Guest 1999). In addition, I demonstrate that the US and Canada were similar in terms of several relevant factors that are believed to have stunted the development of family allowances in particular, including preference for public works projects (Amenta 1998), the historical failure of family allowances to take hold (Pederson 1993), and a lack of strategic placement of policy advocates (Weir and Skocpol 1985).

Family Allowances in North America before 1939

While there was a major (if unsuccessful) movement for family allowances in the UK prior to World War II (Macnicol 1980), the situation in North America was in stark contrast. Writing in 1926, the official publication of Canadian social workers saw family allowances as "entirely foreign to present Canadian and United States practice" (Guest 1999: 80). Brief flurries of interest arose in Canada and the US but quickly fizzled out. Years later, one observer remarked that "virtually no study has been given to the subject on this continent and it is totally new to the general public" (Cassidy 1943).

During the 1980s battles over the future of family allowances, the Canadian public saw them as part of a "sacred trust" at the heart of the Canadian welfare state, but early proponents of family allowances had failed to overcome fears that providing unrestricted cash benefits to families would lead to dependency and illegitimacy. The proposal first gained public attention in a series of parliamentary hearings before the Select Standing Committee on Industrial and International Relations in 1929. Primary support came from the province of Quebec, which was home to the country's largest Catholic population. At the hearing, support for family allowances was expressed by Father Léon Label, a Catholic priest from Quebec, who argued that such allowances were needed to keep larger families from falling into poverty. The problem, according to Label, was that employers did not adjust wages based on the number of children a breadwinner was supporting. Given the importance of the family as a basic unit of society and the inability of the industrial system to support families, Label argued that it was necessary for the government to provide some sort of family allowance based on the number of children.

Opposition was strong and widespread. Ironically, this opposition was strongest among social workers worried about giving cash benefits to the poorest families (Blake 2009: 23–29; Guest 1999: 122–123). Instead, they argued for a more active role for social workers to ensure that families were not wasting their benefits. Charlotte Whitton, head of the Canadian Council on Social Welfare, advocated in-kind transfers to untrustworthy poor families. Other social workers worried that cash benefits would lead to higher birthrates among "less desirable" kinds of people, with the cost being picked up by taxpayers. According to one social worker from Montreal, "since it is not desirable to encourage the increase of families from such stock, whose children inherit poor physical health and mental defect, with the certainty that a large proportion of such children will be weaklings, becoming consumers and dependents, rather than producers, because of their unfitness, physically and mentally, it would seem undesirable and dangerous to encourage larger families among such a class of people" (Canada. House of Commons 1929:69).

The idea of family allowances prompted familiar fears about "undeserving" populations receiving cash benefits. Others worried about the religious and racial implications of introducing such a program, given the already higher birth rates of Catholic Ukrainians in the west and French Canadians in Quebec (Vadakin 1958: 52). Father Label's proposal gained no traction, and proposals for a family allowance program were not seriously considered again for over a decade. According to Guest (1999: 81), "the subject was a dead issue in Canada until the Second World War era."

In the US, there were "scattered discussions" of family allowances in the 1920s (Schorr 1966: 149). The most prominent proposal came from University of Chicago economist (and later US senator) Paul Douglas, who made the case for family allowances in *Wages and the Family* (1925). The "living wage" principle was strong in the US as well. Douglas argued: "it would not be practicable to pay each adult male worker enough to maintain a family of five under the present structure of society" (Douglas 1925: 25). Employers could not afford it, and it would be wasteful to pay higher wages to account for 48 million "fictitious dependents" of single workers. Family allowances could remedy this problem. It should be noted that Douglas also anticipated objections from opponents on a number of grounds, including the fear that it would encourage an increase in the birthrate among the "least desirable class," but wrote nothing about racial animosity (Douglas 1925: 253–257).

A number of New Deal allies supported family allowances in principle as well. Also basing his argument on living wage principles, Social Security architect Abraham Epstein argued that family allowances would "distribute among all employers the burden of relief which a few humane corporations now carry on account of the larger family needs of some of their workers" (Epstein 1938: 637–651). Beyond these isolated islands of support, proposals for family allowances did not catch on in the interwar period.

Work and Relief in North America before 1939

In terms of tax and social security policies in place by 1939, the US and Canada were broadly similar. Each provided benefits for children in the form of social assistance and tax exemptions for dependents but lacked universal programs. Importantly—though largely unnoticed by political sociologists—the two countries took similar approaches to providing employment through public works projects.

Amenta (1998) argues that the US was exceptional in pursuing what he calls a "work and relief" policy during this period. It is often taken for granted that the welfare state as we traditionally see it today was preordained to become the model set of social policies in rich democracies.[6] In this view, US social policy in the 1930s was only partially developed. Amenta convincingly challenges this view, arguing that US policymakers were actually building a different kind of welfare state that was based on work and relief programs that provided public employment to displaced workers.

Early in his administration President Roosevelt called for a "definite program of putting people to work" (Amenta 1998: 3). Soon after, the US introduced the familiar alphabet of programs such as the Federal Emergency Relief Administration (FERA), Works Progress Administration (WPA), Civilian Conservation Corps (CCC), and National Youth Administration (NYA). These programs were designed to provide economic stimulus and employment during economic downturns, especially to men with families.

By 1939, these programs provided employment to over 30% of the total unemployed population (Amenta 1998: 145). As such, they constituted a major social policy innovation.

Amenta characterizes this as a distinctly American approach, but an examination of Canada during this same period reveals that it is really a distinctly North American approach. Scholars have documented how the Conservative government of R. B. Bennett, following Roosevelt, introduced his own "New Deal" in Canada, which included the Unemployment and Social Assistance Act of 1935 (Guest 1999). Less often discussed is Bennett's importation of work relief policies as part of the same New Deal. Writing in 1975, Leonard Marsh recollected that "many Canadians in those years advocated study and suitable emulation" of the American work relief programs (Marsh 1975: xv). Following Roosevelt, the Conservative government passed the Public Works Construction Act in 1934 as a work relief measure (Bryce 1985: 24).

This strategy was first employed as a "temporary" response to the onset of the Depression. As was the case in the US, the federal government was initially reluctant to get involved. Between 1929 and 1932, provincial and municipal work relief was the primary response to mass unemployment. It soon became clear that the provinces were ill-equipped for dealing with the problem, leading the federal government to step in. The 1934 Act promised $40 million for a series of public works projects throughout Canada (Keck 1995: 50). Smaller than the US effort, the various projects still employed around 20% of unemployed workers in 1934 (Bryce 1985: 10).

The defeat of the Conservative government by Mackenzie King and the Liberals in 1935 resulted in a scaling back of work relief programs over the next three years. Another recession in 1938 forced King to re-think his stance on work relief. That spring, the government appropriated $40 million for federal work relief projects. In addition, the government passed the Municipal Improvements Assistance Act, which provided $30 million in low-interest loans to municipalities for public works projects, and later the Civic Improvement Act, which provided federal grants worth 50% of the labor costs on municipal projects (Pal 1987: 42–43; Strikwerda 2013: 212–214). Although a much smaller effort than the one under the Conservatives, the new programs still employed about 13.5% of unemployed workers in 1939 (Bryce 1985: 10). Work and relief was the dominant policy in Canada as well. This was the policy trajectory in North America as World War II got under way, shaping early proposals for postwar reconstruction.

Planning for Postwar Reconstruction, 1939–1942

In late 1939, the NRPB appointed the Committee on Long-Range Work and Relief Policies to draft the US report on postwar reconstruction. In Canada, the government created the Committee on Demobilization and Re-establishment, which had the power to appoint advisory committees and did so in 1941, creating the Advisory Committee on Reconstruction. The early work of these committees prior to the publication of the Beveridge Report in 1942 reflected a preference for work and relief policies and completely lacked any discussion of family allowances.

The National Resource Planning Board

The NRPB began work on what would eventually become *Work, Security, and Relief Policies* in June 1940. Eveline Burns was appointed director of research for the project. The British-born Burns was an expert on social security policy. She had been educated at the London School of Economics, where she had earned her PhD in 1926. While there, she had taught alongside Beveridge, and she was very familiar with his work (Kasper 2012). Burns followed the work of Eleanor Rathbone's Family Endowment Society and looked approvingly on the movement for family allowances across Europe (Burns 1924). She moved to the US in 1928 to take a position at Columbia University and first became involved in social security policy in 1934 as a junior staff member on the Committee on Economic Security (Kasper 2012). As director of research, she worked alongside representatives from the Works Progress Administration, the Federal Security Administration, the Children's Bureau, and the Farm Security Administration, but she was ultimately in charge of planning the research and writing the final report.

The committee's primary concern was postwar unemployment. The experience of the recession that had followed World War I had taught policymakers that the country would slide into a recession after World War II if the government did not step in to boost demand as the conventional Keynesian thinking of the time dictated. Rather than focusing on countercyclical spending through social security, the committee very much viewed possible responses through the lens of work and relief policy. They saw public employment through public works projects as the best way to deal with the impending economic downturn (Amenta 1998: 193–194).

Burns and the committee worked on the report for almost two years, completing it in December 1941. What would later be dubbed "America's Beveridge plan" was completed a year before the actual Beveridge Report. The NRPB report argued, first and foremost, for the need to "provide work for all who are able and willing to work" (National Resources Planning Board 1941: 1). This was to be achieved through full employment policies and a new federal work agency to be tasked with working with state and local agencies to create and run public works projects. Social insurance was to play a secondary role, while social assistance was tertiary (National Resources Planning Board 1941: 545–549). Family allowances were not mentioned at all.

The NRPB report was a conservative document from beginning to end, in that it was the product of Depression-era thinking. As Amenta has documented, the committee looked backward to the tried-and-true programs based on work and relief policies. No new policy innovations, such as family allowances, were put forward, despite the strategic placement of Burns as director of research. Several years passed before any kind of political reaction to the report occurred. Three days after it was submitted to President Roosevelt, the attack on Pearl Harbor pulled the US into World War II. The war effort took up the bulk of Roosevelt's attention for a year, before the NRPB report was given fresh attention after the publication of the Beveridge Report in 1942.

The Advisory Committee on Reconstruction

While the NRPB was working on their report, Canada's earlier entrance into World War II meant that interest in social policy was taking a backseat to mobilization among most policymakers in government. The almost lone exception was Ian Mackenzie, who had recently been appointed minister of pensions and national health. Mackenzie was keen on pushing social security reforms but found the war had left little power with his department (Owram 1986: 279). The situation began to shift when the government set up a number of special parliamentary committees, including the Committee on Demobilization and Re-establishment, tasked with preparing Canada for postwar reconstruction. Mackenzie was to chair that committee.

As was the case in the US, policymakers saw the problem of postwar reconstruction in light of their experience after War World I. The expectation was a period of recession and high unemployment unless the government stepped in to boost demand and ensure full employment (Granatstein 1975: 256). In September 1941, the government formed the Advisory Committee on Reconstruction at the behest of Mackenzie. Looking outside government, it was made up of researchers from McGill University. Cyril James headed the committee; Leonard Marsh served as research advisor.

Like Eveline Burns, Marsh was a British-born expert on social security. He had studied as one of Beveridge's protégés at the London School of Economics, where he had earned his PhD in 1928. He had moved to Canada in 1930 to take a position at McGill University (Owram 1986: 281). He had been active with the League for Social Reconstruction through the 1930s, helping write *Social Planning for Canada* (1935), an early outline for Keynesian economic management that included proposals for family allowances. He eventually went on to write the *Report on Social Security for Canada,* but social security policy was far from his agenda in 1941–1942.

In fact, social security was far from any agenda. The last government report on social security, in 1939, the Rowell-Sirois Report, had made no mention of the possibility of family allowances. Serious proposals were not mentioned even once in Parliament between 1939 and 1942 (Bruel 1953: 271). Mackenzie complained bitterly throughout 1941 that there was little interest "in government circles on problems of social security" (Christie 2000: 273). Much to his chagrin, the Advisory Committee on Reconstruction focused almost exclusively on employment policy. "The central problem of postwar reconstruction," James said in 1941, "is the finding of adequate employment opportunities for returning soldiers and the men who are no longer required in munitions factories" (Granatstein 1975: 256). Even Marsh later admitted that employment policy preoccupied the committee's time at this early stage (Blake 2009: 38). Marsh himself had written extensively in the 1930s on the need for government-created jobs (Christie 2000: 281).

In April 1942, Mackenzie appeared before the Special Committee on Reconstruction and Re-establishment to update them on the work of James's committee. Mackenzie told the special committee that James and his committee had established four subcommittees: on agriculture, postwar employment, conservation and development of natural resources, and construction projects. Descriptions of the latter two subcommittees mention employment as part of their goals, indicating that work and relief policies were still on the agenda. Mackenzie also told the special committee that social security reforms should be deferred until after the war (Canada. House of Commons 1942).

James's committee released an interim report in the fall of 1942. It was modest, with few sweeping reforms. The only major proposal was for a "Construction Reserve Commission" that would assist in undertaking public works projects. It would assemble a "shelf" of public works projects "ready for quick implementation, as needed, to counteract the expected postwar depression" (Owram 1986; Young 1981: 603). This early proposal was very similar to those of the NRPB in many ways. Rather than calling for new social security programs, the Advisory Committee on Reconstruction proposed creating a federal agency to work with provincial and local agencies on public works projects. Family allowance proposals were nowhere to be found. As late as January 1943, Marsh continued to argue that "employment measures for the transition period" were an essential part of any reconstruction plan (Christie 2000: 280).

The Beveridge Benchmark, 1943–1945

No pressure for family allowances existed in North America in 1942. Across the Atlantic in the UK, though, the movement was finally culminating in something concrete. The report that put family allowances on the government's agenda, according to Glennerster (2007: 23), was "something of an accident, and certainly not what the wartime Coalition government originally had in mind." The soon-to-be-formed committee, as the cabinet envisioned it, was to be practical and limited in scope. Its narrow goal was "to undertake, with special reference to the inter-relation of schemes, a survey of the existing national schemes of social insurance and allied services, including workmen's compensation and to make recommendations" (Glennerster 2007: 25–26).

The report produced was a blueprint for a comprehensive social insurance system unlike anything the government had imagined when it commissioned the committee. In addition to the consolidation and rationalization of existing social insurance programs, the report proposed universal family allowances as the first of three "assumptions" underlying the rest of the system (Beveridge 1942: 154). Whereas previous proponents advocated for family allowances based on feminist, pronatal, or child poverty rationales, Beveridge differed in framing them as integral to the larger system of social security. He outlined three problems that family allowances solved.

The first was the need for uninterrupted income in case of lost earning power. Universal family allowances would ensure that families would still receive benefits in the gaps between immediately losing and gaining a job. Second, Beveridge recognized the traditional "living wage" argument that wages do not account for family size. Family allowances would help prevent poverty among larger families, but this principle was connected to the third problem. This was the problem that unemployment benefits, in accounting for the number of children, could end up becoming larger than total income from work. This problem would be more severe for larger families. If not remedied, the social security system would create disincentives to move from benefits into work. By providing for children via universal family allowances, policymakers could ensure that work was always more remunerative than the dole without pushing benefits well below poverty levels (Beveridge 1942: 154). This new rationale played a crucial role in winning over opponents in the Treasury.

The "benchmark of Beveridge" reoriented policymakers around new standards of evaluation, becoming the new standard by which all social security reforms would be measured. The cabinet and the Treasury, which had successfully fought off pressures for family allowances for decades, quickly shifted from opposition to support. The key to their changing stances, according to Macnicol (1980: 196–202), was Beveridge's argument about work disincentives. Family allowances became part and parcel of employment policy, helping to ensure full employment after the war. Within three years, family allowances would become public policy.

The "benchmark of Beveridge" soon extended itself across the Atlantic Ocean. As late as the end of 1942, the odds that the US or Canada would introduce family allowances continued to look grim. The publication of the Beveridge Report in December 1942 fundamentally changed the terrain of social policy, opening up new possibilities for reform in North America. The report made its way through a powerful transatlantic network of policy reformers to the US and Canada. Historian Daniel Rodgers (1998: 488–489) called it a "social-political blueprint of instant, transnational importance" and a "foundational document of welfare state politics." Beveridge himself went on a tour of North America to extol the virtues of the report that same year. The US and Canada soon published analogous reports of their own, described among policymakers and the public in reference to the UK's report as the "Canadian Beveridge plan" and the "American Beveridge plan" (Beveridge 1943; Burns 1943; Cassidy

1943; Witte 1945). Only one of these reports would lead to the adoption of family allowances, though, determined by the timing of its writing.

The Canadian Beveridge Plan

It was no secret that Ian Mackenzie wanted the Advisory Committee on Construction to make social security reform the primary objective of their work. He had told James as much on several occasions (Blake 2009: 41). Despite Mackenzie's prodding, the committee continued to place employment policy, not social security, at the center of their agenda throughout 1942 (Christie 2000:272–273; Struthers 1987: 6). The publication of the Beveridge Report in December had a transformative effect on the environment in Canada. Within three months, social security would eclipse employment policy and set Canada on a new trajectory.

Within days of Beveridge Report's release, Prime Minister King and President Roosevelt were discussing it at a White House dinner (Blake 2009: 41). Looking back, Marsh (1975: xvii) reflected: "in 1943, social security was in the air as never before." The Beveridge Report was the benchmark event Mackenzie needed to finally bring his agenda for social security reform front and center. He jumped on the chance to reorient policymakers in the new environment created by the buzz over the Beveridge Report (Christie 2000: 275; Granatstein 1975: 257–258; Owram 1986: 288–290). With the prime minister expressing support for social security reform in his January 1943 Speech from the Throne, Mackenzie set his plan in motion. He relayed to James that he would like the Advisory Committee on Reconstruction to come up with a report on social security. James, in turn, tasked Marsh with writing what would become the *Report on Social Security for Canada* (Blake 2009: 52).

James indicated that he would like to have a completed report similar to the one Beveridge had produced as soon as possible. Marsh began work almost immediately and finished in six weeks. Under these circumstances, it is not surprising that Beveridge's protégé Marsh produced a report strikingly similar to the Beveridge Report. Marsh followed the same rationale as one of Beveridge's "assumptions," arguing that family allowances were the "key to consistency," providing "administrative simplicity and efficiency" to the entire system of social security. This rationale so permeated the report that by the time he came to discussing family allowances specifically, he remarked that this point "requires no further emphasis" (Marsh

1943: 200). Beveridge's rationale became the new standard for family allowances. This aspect was noted by contemporaries and has been well documented by historians (Blake 2009). Less noted has been the inclusion of work relief and employment policies.

Marsh proposed a national employment program for undertaking needed public works projects and combating postwar employment slump, arguing that such a program had a "special place" in postwar reconstruction. In contrast with the more revolutionary social security proposals in the report, Marsh wrote that there was "nothing new in the idea of a works programme" in Canada. He was simply improving on previous programs so as to avoid the earlier mistakes of some inefficient "make work" schemes (Marsh 1943: 76–86). Work and relief policy was still very much present in the report. It was not that Marsh had abandoned his earlier policy preferences for employment policy. Rather, he simply elevated alongside them his preferences for social security, by including them in an Advisory Committee on Reconstruction report for the first time. Some contemporaries even believed that this was part of Marsh's ambition the whole time (Christie 2000: 277). This was not an unreasonable inference.

The reason Marsh's work relief proposals are overlooked is that they were almost instantly overshadowed by the new social security proposals. Marsh's report was supposed to be included as a subsection of a larger and much anticipated full report of the Advisory Committee on Reconstruction. By February, James was already worried that the Beveridge Report and Marsh's work were diverting attention away from employment policy. He was right. Prime Minister King, hoping to ride the wave of excitement over the Beveridge Report, soon intervened personally to have Marsh's research published early as a separate report (Christie 2000: 274–277). In releasing the report in March, before the publication of the committee's full report, the government ensured that the Marsh Report became the "Canadian Beveridge plan."

The Marsh Report was discussed far and wide. Public reaction to its proposal for a universal family allowance was mixed. The Canadian Institute of Public Opinion conducted a poll in October 1943. They found that 49% of respondents thought a $9 per month allowance was a "good idea," whereas 42% said it was a bad idea, and 9% were undecided (Blake 2009: 59–71). King's Liberal government was on the fence as well. Cabinet discussions of family allowance proposals revolved around what were perceived as two major political issues: one ethnic, the other class-based.

Political cleavages in Canada often run along regional lines, often overlapping with ethnic lines. It was no coincidence that earlier proposals for a family allowance had come out of French Catholic Quebec, and this latest proposal generated the same sorts of worries about regional and ethnic favoritism. Internal memorandums circulated in the Finance Department showed that some officials were worried that family allowances might exacerbate regional and ethnic animosities because they would be seen as favoring groups who had more children—Catholics in Quebec and Ukrainians in the west (Blake 2009: 64–65). One public opinion poll conducted in 1944 asked respondents whether they thought the proposal was a "necessary law" or a "political bribe." Nationally, it appeared that Canadians were split (34% v. 29%), but this appearance hid regional differences. In Quebec, 49% of respondents saw it as a necessary law, while only 13% saw it as a political bribe. Responses in Ontario were similarly inversed—only 26% saw it as a necessary law, while 39% saw it as a political bribe (Blake 2009: 117). Some opposition MPs in the Progressive Conservative Party hammered the proposed family allowance as an election year tactic to buy votes in Quebec, alleging that it meant taxing eight provinces for the benefit of one. The premiers of Ontario and Manitoba both opposed the introduction of a federally administered family allowance, seeing it as a provincial prerogative (Blake 2009: 106–116).

In King's cabinet, C. D. Howe was the most vocal opponent, telling King that the proposal meant "taxing people of medium incomes to support others who were in many cases not deserving of support" (Blake 2009: 85). Outside the cabinet, the same Progressive Conservative MPs who criticized family allowances as political bribes to Quebec also criticized them on the grounds that they would require taxing hardworking Canadians to subsidize those with questionable work habits (Blake 2009: 106). Worries about ethnic minorities and the work habits of the poor, often seen as impenetrable barriers to the introduction of universal policies in the US, were present in Canada as well but were not insurmountable.

Political support for family allowances came from two sources. The first, coming directly out of the Beveridge Report, was the idea that family allowances guaranteed the proper functioning of the larger social security system by ensuring that work was more remunerative than life on the dole, especially for larger families. The second, based on the work of American Keynesian Alvin Hansen and novel to North America, was the idea that family allowances could be a tool of Keynesian demand management on a par with public works projects (Christie 2000: 280).

Marsh testified as much before the Special Committee on Reconstruction and Re-establishment. "Children's allowances," he told the committee, "should be considered on that score alone" (Canada. House of Commons 1943). Looking back, Marsh (1975: xxv) saw the "purchasing-power floor" argument as vital in winning political support. These twin arguments were what won over King and his cabinet in their discussions of the proposal. After legislation was introduced in June 1944, King repeatedly made these arguments in the House of Commons debates that summer (Blake 2009: 88, 93–94).

By 1944, the Liberals, Progressive Conservatives, and Co-operative Commonwealth Federation parties all supported some sort of proposal for family allowances. With no official opposition from rival parties, King's Liberal government passed the Family Allowance Act in 1944 (Blake 2009: 94–95).

At the beginning of the 1940s, any regular observer of Canadian politics would have told you that public works projects—not family allowances—would be the policy program of choice for postwar reconstruction. By the end of the 1940s, public works as an employment strategy, which began to fall out of favor after 1943, was dead (Keck 1995: 65–72; Pal 1987: 44–46). Family allowances, which were not even on the radar prior to 1943, were now considered part of the logical and inevitable evolution of the Canadian welfare state. How do we explain this seismic shift? The Beveridge Report clearly served as a key benchmark event, reorienting Canadian policymakers toward a new path for social policy via the Marsh Report. More important, as an examination of the American response to the Beveridge Report makes clear, the sequence of these events was crucial to the outcome. Marsh was able to incorporate the idea for family allowances into his "Canadian Beveridge plan" only because he wrote in the wake of the original Beveridge Report. Eveline Burns did not have this same advantage when she wrote the "American Beveridge plan."

The "American Beveridge Plan"

The Beveridge Report made a big splash in the US as well. Over 50,000 copies of an American edition of the report were sold within the first six months of its release. Beveridge himself sailed to the US and toured the country talking about his report to crowds of eager Americans in early 1943 (Harris 1997: 426–427). Days after the report's release, President Roosevelt discussed it favorably with King, suggesting to his Canadian counterpart that they should undertake a similar program of social security reforms, along the lines of what was proposed in the Beveridge Report (Blake 2009: 41).

Roosevelt and his cabinet saw this as an opportunity to ride the wave of the Beveridge Report's popularity. He discussed releasing "a kind of Beveridge plan" among colleagues, and word soon leaked to the press that he would soon release his own "American Beveridge plan" to Congress. Whereas Canadian policymakers scrambled to put together a report, however, Roosevelt instead dusted off an already existing one on his shelf. In March 1943, Roosevelt released the NRPB's long-dormant *Security, Work, and Relief Policies* to Congress and the public. Roosevelt was pleased that the press instantly billed it as an American Beveridge plan (*New York Times* 1942; Rodgers 1998: 496–497). This was the decision that fundamentally shifted the trajectory of American social policy.

Eveline Burns and her working group had begun work on the NRPB report at the request of Roosevelt back in 1939 and had completed their work two years later. On December 5, 1941, the NRPB had submitted their report to the president with a draft transmittal letter to Congress with a date of December 15. The December 7 attack on Pearl Harbor intervened, though (Reagan 2000: 220). The effect on Roosevelt's social security agenda was profound. As he would later tell the public, it transformed "old Dr. New Deal" into "Dr. Win-the-War." American military mobilization moved to front and center on the president's agenda, and nonmilitary concerns like the NRPB report abruptly fell by the wayside. The NRPB continued their work with the tacit support of Roosevelt, but he did not directly involve himself from that point onward (Jeffries 1990: 410). Although Roosevelt quickly forgot about *Security, Work, and Relief Policies*, the NRPB continued to pressure him to release it as part of a broader social security agenda. They were rebuffed until the popular response to release of the Beveridge Report and concern for the 1944 election worked in conjunction to force him to take plans for postwar reconstruction seriously again.

While Prime Minister King used the renewed attention to social security as a reason to commission a fresh report from Marsh, Roosevelt never asked Burns for a new report. The exact reasons for this are unclear, but the available historical record suggests that several factors explain the divergent reactions of King and Roosevelt. First, unlike the King government in Canada, Roosevelt already had a suitable plan ready in Burns's unreleased *Work, Security, and Relief Policies*. It made little sense to shunt aside the six-hundred-plus-page report and ask the NRPB to write a new one from scratch. Second, unlike King, Roosevelt had never shown any personal interest in the details of social security policy. Whereas King himself had authored books on social security in the past and continued to take an active interest in it, Roosevelt always relied on the expertise of those around him, especially while fighting the war. It is unsurprising that King would be more open to emulating the specific details of the Beveridge Report rather than the broad ideals. Third, senior members of the NRPB had spent a great deal of political capital pushing for the release of *Work, Security, and Relief Policies* for several years. They could hardly get a meeting with Roosevelt about it, so they likely perceived pushing him to scrap the existing report in favor of a brand new one as a risky strategy (Clawson 1981: 140; Jeffries 1990: 411–412; Reagan 2000: 229; Warken 1979: 224–226).[7] As a result, a report that was finished long before Beveridge even began his work was selected to become the "American Beveridge plan."

Despite being inspired by the release of the Beveridge Report and being labeled as the "America Beveridge plan" for postwar reconstruction, the NRPB report was entirely a relic of pre–Beveridge Report thinking among government elites. Amenta aptly summarizes the differences between the British and American blueprints: "The American plan dealt mainly with work and relief; new social programs and the nationalization of Unemployment Compensation were secondary. By contrast, the British plans concentrated on the rationalization and extension of existing social insurance. The new British proposals for family allowances and the national health service had nothing to do with unemployment and Depression, and the reform of relief programs was an afterthought. Moreover, the British plans for preventing postwar unemployment were conspicuously underdeveloped compared to the elaborate American proposals for public works and public employment" (1998: 236). In contrast to the progressive Beveridge Report, which looked forward to building a social security system for the postwar era, the NRPB report was a conservative blueprint looking backward to the Depression era. Amenta argues that these two reports diverged for several reasons. The first was that the US had already built a legacy of "work and relief" policy on which it drew in creating its blueprint for postwar reconstruction. Reformers wanted to "build on what had already been constructed" (242).

While this argument makes sense within the narrow scope of Amenta's US–UK comparison, it is unsatisfactory in light of the Canadian experience during this same period. Canada's Advisory Committee on Reconstruction was similarly staffed with bureaucrats wedded to the Depression-era idea of work and relief policy, yet the Marsh Report included a proposal for family allowances. At the same time, Weir and Skocpol's (1985) argument affirming that the strategic placement of actors was more important than the publication of the Keynes's *General Theory* for the adoption of Keynesian policies would likewise affirm that the strategic placement of family allowance supporter Eveline Burns would be more important than the publication of the Beveridge Report. Why did Marsh's support for family allowances find its way into postwar reconstruction blueprints while Burns's support had no effect?

The strategic placement of reform-friendly actors was important, but it was the sequence of events within this critical juncture that was decisive for the outcome. By using the pre–Beveridge Report NRPB report, written in 1941, as the American blueprint for postwar reconstruction, Roosevelt inadvertently denied his administration the advantages that would have come with crafting a blueprint after the "benchmark of Beveridge"—the activation of strategically placed reformist actors and the legitimation of new policy innovations.

Burns was strategically placed as research director for the NRPB, but she was not able to activate her support for family allowances in a post-Beveridge report as Marsh had in Canada. Marsh was able to write his report in six weeks. There is little reason to think that Burns could not have done the same if Roosevelt had asked her. The demise of the NRPB through defunding by Congress in June 1943, often seen as putting the lights out on Roosevelt's agenda, was of secondary importance. The Advisory Committee on Reconstruction was similarly disbanded several months after the release of the Marsh Report, to no effect. Burns spoke favorably of family allowances in the Beveridge Report and subsequently became a strong public advocate (Burns 1943, 1944; Freeman 1948), but none of this was done through her official capacity with the Roosevelt administration. Although activated, she was no longer strategically placed.

Nor could the NRPB report take advantage of recent legitimations of family allowances as a new policy innovation. The program could be justified on a number of grounds, but some were more conducive to concrete policy formation than others. As Macnicol (1992: 246) argues in his survey of family allowances development, "arguments about child poverty, pronatalism, and the role of women were usually secondary to the prime causal factors." The Beveridge Report had the effect of elevating the work incentive rationale and putting it front and center. In framing family allowances as vital to the proper functioning of a comprehensive social insurance system by reinforcing the popular principle of "less eligibility," the Beveridge and Marsh reports made them politically acceptable to conservative policymakers. This rationale—encouraging work over welfare dependency—surely would have been convincing to otherwise intransigent conservative members of Congress had it been made to them.

Instead, what had been otherwise open political space ripe for new proposals was quickly filled with familiar work and relief policies, institutionalized as the blueprint for postwar reconstruction. Family allowances were never introduced in the US because they were never proposed during this critical juncture. With no family allowance proposals to entertain, Congress turned to the most tried and true method of providing benefits to children—the dependent exemption. The Revenue Act of 1944 raised it from $350 to $500; the Revenue Act of 1948 raised it again to $600. The $600 exemption amounted to 42% of per capita personal income at the time. It effectively closed the window on family allowances by providing significant child-related benefits for the majority of working families. The closing of that window locked in support for the status quo, making family allowances proposals seem less necessary and much less politically attractive in the prosperous postwar economy. In the process, the expansion of the dependent exemption ensured that the logic of tax relief would dominate discussions of family policy for the next seven decades.

Discussion

Of course, having a blueprint does not necessarily guarantee translation into concrete policies. However, the consequent failure of the NRPB report's proposals in the 1940s should not be interpreted, as many political scientists and historians have done, as signifying the inevitable failure of any new spending program that might have been proposed at the hands of a new conservative Congress. Nor does the report's political failure offer any evidence that racial animosity played any role in Congress' decisions during this period. In order to establish the counterfactual that family allowances would have been introduced had they been included in an "American Beveridge plan," it must be shown that what some scholars see as obstacles to new spending would not have applied to any proposal for family allowances.

Much has been made of two episodes in the immediate postwar period to argue that congressional conservatives were anti–New Deal or antispending in general. Comparisons to Canada show that neither episode warrants such a conclusion. The first argument is that the failure of Congress to include government-guaranteed employment in the watered-down Employment Act of 1946 was a repudiation of Roosevelt's work relief policies. As Amenta (1998: 219–225) shows, though, this was a result of distrust of executive discretion over public works programs. Moreover, the Marsh Report included proposals for similar employment strategies that likewise went nowhere after the war. Work relief, not spending per se, had fallen out of favor in both countries.

The second argument concerns the failure of the Wagner-Murray-Dingell bill, which proposed comprehensive reforms for social security and health insurance. It is important to note that it was the health insurance components in particular that brought down the entire bill (Hacker 2002: 222–228). When brought before Congress separately, the Social Security Amendments of 1950 and 1954 expanded coverage and benefits without issue. Again, a comparison with Canada is very telling. Family allowances were passed there as a stand-alone bill with the support of Conservatives in 1944. As in the US, expansion of the rest of Canada's social security system did not occur until the 1950s (Guest 1999: 137–139). Given these factors, one may counterfactually predict that a stand-alone bill for family allowances would have similarly passed in the US if it had ever been proposed.

What about racial animosity among southern members of Congress and the public at large? It is possible that family allowances would have upset the racial status quo by distributing benefits to black families. Some scholars argue that racism undermined early support for the US welfare state (Alesina and Glaeser 2005; Katznelson 2005; Lieberman 1995; Quadagno 1994). While there is no doubt that many social assistance programs became racialized in the 1960s, the evidence that race was key to the decisions of Congress or the Roosevelt administration in the 1930s and 1940s has been strongly challenged by others who view the US case in comparative perspective. Proponents of the racial animosity thesis point almost exclusively to the decision to exclude farm workers and domestic servants, which disproportionately excluded black workers, from coverage under the Social Security Act as evidence that the Roosevelt administration caved to pressure from southern members of Congress enforcing a rigid racial hierarchy (Quadagno 1994; Lieberman 1995). Prima facie, this seems like good evidence, but the case for the racial animosity thesis fails when we view these actions in light of similar countries at the time.

Davies and Derthick (1997) challenge this thesis (also see DeWitt 2010; Rodems and Shaefer 2016). They argue that it was the Roosevelt administration—not Congress—that pushed for the exclusion, for fiscal rather than racial reasons. Importantly, both Canada and the UK initially excluded farm workers and domestic servants as well, for the simple reason that it was harder to collect payroll taxes from them. It was the British experience that American Treasury officials had in mind when they made the decision to push for the exclusion of these workers (Rodems and Shafer 2016). What seems like a response to uniquely US race relations was actually part of a broader trend among all early liberal welfare regimes. Despite my best efforts, I could find absolutely no evidence that the absence of family allowance proposals by Roosevelt or Congress during this period had anything to do with racial animosity.

One might argue that racial animosity would have acted as an obstacle to family allowances had they been proposed, though. Canada offers a compelling analog here. As noted, initial proposals for family allowances in Canada ran into opposition partly because they were seen as favoring one particularly salient ethnic group: French Catholics in Quebec. The premier of Ontario continued to attack family allowances as favoritism for French Canadians well into 1944 (Blake 2009: 116). Despite this backlash, all three federal parties went on to support the government's family allowance proposal. Rather than mounting a wholesale opposition, Canadian policymakers designed the system in such a way that it favored the Anglo-Protestant population over ethnic minorities. First, the value of the benefit for each additional child declined, as a way to explicitly prevent larger Catholic families from receiving a disproportionate share of the benefits (Whitton 1944: 416). Second, the government set up a separate registration and administration process for Aboriginal families, whom they believed could not be trusted with the money (Blake 1999: 140). There is little reason to think that the US could not have done something similar—as was the case with the racialized administration of Aid to Dependent Children during this period.

Instead, the evidence points to contingency and differences in the sequence of events as the best explanation for the divergence between the US and Canada on the adoption of family allowances. Prior to the publication of the Beveridge Report, both countries were on the same "work and relief" trajectory of welfare state development. The introduction of family allowances was highly unlikely in either country. The Beveridge Report was a benchmark event that had the effect of opening up radical new possibilities by reorienting policymakers in North America around a new set of policies previously deemed unacceptable.

In Canada, the crafting of the Marsh Report following the publication of the Beveridge Report allowed a longtime advocate of family allowances to activate his dormant support for the policy in his official capacity as the author of the country's blueprint for postwar reconstruction. In addition, the Beveridge Report provided a new rationale for family allowances—as a necessary policy for avoiding work disincentives in the new social security system. This new rationale made the family allowance politically acceptable even to conservative policymakers. The Marsh Report set Canada on a new trajectory in line with other liberal welfare regimes, including the adoption of family allowances in 1944.

In the US, the publication of the Beveridge Report similarly opened the possibility of setting the country on a new path. The fateful decision by President Roosevelt to reach for the pre-Beveridge NRPB plan instead of tasking longtime family allowance advocate Eveline Burns with crafting a new blueprint for postwar reconstruction essentially put an end to this possibility. The administration stuck with its familiar work and relief proposals without ever considering family allowances. The transatlantic network that brought the ideas of Beveridge across the Atlantic soon dissolved (Rodgers 1998), and an enlarged dependent exemption satisfied demand that might have been met by a family allowance. As a result, the US ended up being the only liberal welfare regime without universal child benefits in the postwar era.

Traditionally, scholars working in a historical institutional framework have argued that the nonintroduction of family allowances in the US was significant because it robbed the US of an important universal program. Universality, according to these scholars, builds powerful cross-class coalitions in defense of social spending—an important line of defense against retrenchment in other countries (Korpi and Palme 1998; Prasad 2006; Skocpol 1991). Research by Brown (1999) suggests that much of the racialization of the US welfare state stems from its reliance on means-tested welfare programs, stereotyped as handouts to poor black families, and contributory programs, premised on regular employment, from which black workers were excluded. Family allowances had the potential to create cross-racial coalitions otherwise unheard-of in the US. This suggests that the salience of race in American social policy is, in part, a result of the failure to introduce family allowances.

Although important, these material approaches miss the crucial cultural effect that the early introduction of family allowances—or lack thereof—had on countries. The three countries had already similarly institutionalized logics of income support via social assistance programs and logics of tax relief via tax exemptions for dependents. Family allowances institutionalized a third logic of appropriateness in the UK and Canada: the logic of income supplementation. Family allowances made it legitimate for government to provide cash supplements to families, without stigma, solely on the basis of their containing children.

This was the critical juncture where the US and the other two countries—previously on very similar welfare state paths—diverged. The US, which pursued postwar reconstruction without seriously considering family allowances, never institutionalized a logic of income supplementation; Canada and the UK did. This divergence would have lasting ramifications; the most important of these would not become evident until the 1970s. It is to this decade that I turn in the next chapter.

3

From the Era of Easy Finance to Permanent Austerity

THE GREAT DIVERGENCE of the 1940s set the US on a unique path relative to Canada and the UK. These paths remained stable as each country navigated similar circumstances in the conservative 1950s and launched its own version of a "war on poverty" in the 1960s. Existing social programs were expanded, and some new healthcare programs were created, but direct cash benefits for families saw little significant change in terms of structure or administration. At this point, the consequences of the earlier divergence were masked by the sustained economic growth that marked the postwar period. Poverty rates dropped as a result of a historic boom in well-paying employment opportunities. For those left out of the labor market, the growing economy provided governments with ample revenues to fund enlarged social safety nets. Historians have dubbed this period the "era of easy finance" for policymakers who used buoyant tax revenues to fund popular social programs (Brownlee 1996). It seemed as if the Atlantic world had entered a new golden age of prosperity, the fruits of which would be shared by all.

The era of easy finance was short-lived though. The fragility of its foundations was first exposed in 1973. In October of that year, the OPEC declared an oil embargo that hit the US, UK, and Canada especially hard. The price of oil nearly quadrupled, with severe repercussions for the economies that depended on it. The oil shock "ended the world that the rich democracies of the West had taken for granted and brought inflation, unemployment, and recession into everyday life" (Prasad 2006: 1). The public even coined a new word to describe the unprecedented combination of economic stagnation and rampant inflation—stagflation.

Scholars recognize the 1973 oil crisis as a turning point in the politics of tax and social policy. The event acted as an exogenous shock, opening up the possibility for institutional change in rich democracies. In many scholars' accounts, the oil crisis served to overturn dominant models and policy paradigms such as social democracy and Keynesianism. In their search for explanations of and responses to the crisis, policymakers turned to new models and paradigms, such as neoliberalism and monetarism (Blyth 2002; Prasad 2006; Streeck and Thelen 2005). This chapter argues that 1973 was indeed an important turning point but that the shift was much more subtle and we need not depend on transformative ideational changes to explain it. Instead, mundane "pocketbook politics" best explains the reactions of policymakers working in a period of chronically high inflation. As the annual rate of inflation reached upward of 10% in the 1970s and 1980s, it had two primary effects that led to institutional continuity on the one hand and change on the other.

First, inflation helped reinforce the salience of dominant logics of appropriateness through its interaction with existing policies. One consequence of inflation was to put economic pressures on families through the erosion of tax and social security benefits. Depending on how policymakers traced the sources of these economic pressures, they concluded that the proper response was either to provide tax relief for taxpayers or expand income supplements for families. In Canada, the early decision by policymakers to index the value of tax exemptions for children in 1973 protected these exemptions against erosion by inflation and prevented the popular backlash against taxes that occurred in the US and UK. Instead, the public traced growing economic pressures on families to the erosion of family allowances. Policymakers responded by emphasizing the plight of all families with children. In the UK, policymakers delayed indexation of tax allowances until 1977 (and then only reluctantly accepted it) but had already begun the process of completely phasing out the child tax allowance and folding it into family allowances. As a result, the antitax backlash that culminated in the Thatcher government's famous 1979 budget was unconnected to concern for growing economic pressures on families. As in Canada, the British public traced economic pressures to the erosion of family allowances and income supplements, and policymakers responded accordingly. In the US, the decision to delay indexation until 1984 and the unique absence of family allowances led the public to trace the economic pressures on families to the erosion of the dependent exemption and rising payroll taxes. As a result, US policymakers differed from the

Canadian and British counterparts in that they sought provide relief to the more limited target population of taxpayers rather than families with children more generally.

Second, attempts to restore the value of inflation-eroded tax and social security benefits led to stagnating revenues and mounting spending, a combination that resulted in unsustainable budget deficits. The era of easy finance gave way to what Paul Pierson (2001) calls the "era of permanent austerity," as policymakers looked for ways to trim deficits while avoiding political unpopular tax increases and benefit reductions. In this new environment, the relative costs and benefits of using tax credits tipped to the point where they began to appear more politically attractive than traditional social security benefits. The US was the first country to make the shift toward fiscalization with the introduction of the EITC in 1974. In Canada, historical aversion to the use of tax credits for social policy purposes gave way with the introduction of a refundable CTC in 1978. The UK on the other hand saw no movement toward fiscalization during this period, as early attempts were thwarted by gender politics. Policymakers there instead relied on a combination of tax increases and a shift toward selective benefits, which allowed them to delay the process of fiscalization much longer than their North American counterparts.

The divergence that began in the 1940s became fully entrenched by the 1980s. The end result was a whole new environment for policymakers working in the 1990s. This chapter shows how the onset of chronically high inflation and the persistent deficits that followed changed the calculus for policymakers, leading to an accelerated shift toward fiscalization at the end of the century.

What Hath Inflation Wrought?

Price stability is an underappreciated factor that contributed to postwar prosperity. While it is important to investors and businesses trying to make long-term plans, it is essential for families trying to live from paycheck to paycheck. Periods of chronically high inflation can disrupt the stability necessary for planning one's life. The 1960s was a period of low inflation in the US, UK, and Canada, with the decade average ranging from 2.4% to 3.3%. This is the range we have come to expect today. When inflation is this low, people can make plans with the expectation that the cost of living will not radically change each month or year. Families living in the 1970s and 1980s were not so lucky. In contrast with the relatively stable 1960s, the ten-year period between 1973 and 1982 saw the average rate of inflation nearly quadruple (see Figure 3.1).

The combination of high inflation and economic stagnation upended the Keynesian consensus and sent policymakers in search of new strategies for monetary and macroeconomic stability. It also had a profound impact on what historian Meg Jacobs calls "pocketbook politics" (Jacobs 2005), as the public searched for strategies for dealing with the escalating cost of living. Inflation put an economic squeeze or pressure on families as general price levels quickly outpaced family income growth. Pocketbook politics manifested itself most notably in intense labor conflicts as unions sought to keep wages in step with the cost of living. Less noticed but more critical was the way pocketbook politics manifested itself in conflicts over the indexation of tax and social security benefits.

Prior to the 1970s, the values of most tax and social benefits were set in nominal terms. The government, for example, would establish the value of family allowances or tax exemptions in terms of so many dollars per year. In periods of low inflation, the real value of these benefits declined only slightly each year. From time to time, the government might legislate increases to make up for this decline. Minimal pressure was exerted on

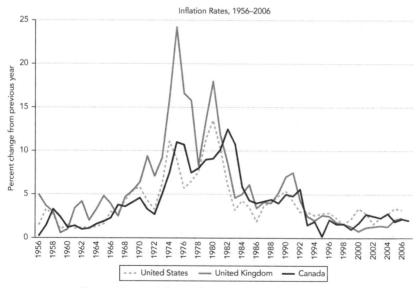

FIGURE 3.1 Inflation rates, 1956–2006.

Source: Organization for Economic Cooperation and Development, Consumer Prices (MEI), stats.oecd.org/Index.aspx?querytype=view&queryname=221, Data extracted on 29 May 2015.

families, especially when family incomes were growing at a reasonable rate. In high inflation periods on the other hand the real value of these benefits erodes quickly and substantially. Even annual ad hoc adjustments may not be enough to prevent their erosion when high inflation is chronic.

In these scenarios, families suffer losses in real annual income despite no legislative changes taking place, because inflation erodes their benefits or increases their tax burden. This is an example of the phenomenon of policy drift (Streeck and Thelen 2005). This occurs when policies themselves do not change but their effects change as a result of shifting factors external to the policies. In other words, the more policies stay the same, the more they change. In this case, the nominal value of benefits stays the same, but the effects of inflation on the wider economy alter their real value and coverage. The question of what to do about this problem vexed policymakers on both sides of the Atlantic throughout the 1970s and 1980s. One simple answer was to do nothing and hope nobody noticed. Another was to make policy changes on an ad hoc basis. Both of these were politically risky if voters got wind of the fact that their benefits were eroding or that any given "tax cut" or "benefit increase" did not actually make them any better off than they were in the previous year. The last answer was to introduce some sort of automatic indexation mechanism into the system. By linking the value of benefits to an external metric that accounted for inflation, such as the consumer price index (CPI), the real value of benefits would remain stable even in time of high inflation.

As a technical solution, indexation had widespread support among experts (Tanzi 1980). As a political solution, its support depended on the power of the particular policy's constituency (Weaver 1988). Policymakers often preferred having discretion in these matters. Indexation took this power away from them. In some cases, such as old age pensions, influential interest groups mobilized quickly to force policymakers to index benefits. In other cases, policymakers put off making any adjustments for inflation as long as possible. There was a built-in incentive for this. Policymakers seek to avoid blame for politically unpopular benefit cuts or tax increases, even if done for sound reasons. Policy drift through inflation-induced erosion allows policymakers to do both in a less salient manner. They do not need to pass legislation that might be flagged by advocacy groups or blocked by opponents. They simply do nothing and lay the blame on external economic forces. While a viable short-term strategy, this runs into trouble as the effects of inflation become significant and take their toll year after year.

By the mid-1970s, the growing economic pressures on families became the subject of extensive public debate and discussion (Deacon and Bradshaw 1983: 151–153; Michelmore 2012; Wilensky 2002: 379–380). By any objective measure, inflation was hurting families. As political pressures to do something about it mounted, governments responded by raising benefits, lowering taxes, introducing indexation, or instituting some combination thereof. Distinct policy legacies in each country influenced the choices they made and were in turn reinforced by these choices. The threat of inflation was obvious. Not so obvious was the best strategy for protecting families from it.

Policymakers had to first locate the source of economic pressures on families in order to craft ameliorative policies. This process is subject to diagnostic framing, in which actors seek to identify problems and attribute causation to a particular source (Benford and Snow 2000). This is where the policy legacy of family allowances was critical. Similar economic experiences interacted with unique policy legacies in each country to produce distinct diagnostic frames. These diagnoses entailed different prognoses for different target populations.

In countries with family allowances, the source of economic pressures on families was traced to the erosion of family allowances. This affected all families with children. The solution was to increase the value of child benefits for the families with children who were most in need. This included children from all but the highest-income families. The situation was remarkably different in the US, where the absence of family allowances led policymakers to trace these same economic pressures on families to the erosion of tax exemptions. Instead of diagnosing the problem as one of declining benefit levels, policymakers on both the left and the right saw the problem as one of growing tax burdens on the working and middle classes. The solution was to provide tax relief, which by its nature was limited to those families who were paying taxes. Children whose parents were not considered taxpayers were excluded from the benefit of subsequent policy changes.

As inflation served to open all sorts of new contingencies in other policy areas, it ended up reinforcing the logic behind the policies (income supplementation or tax relief) and the cultural categories (children or taxpayers) that were inherent in the policy legacies of family allowances and tax exemptions. Ultimately, inflation made these dormant logics and cultural categories more salient to policymakers and the public at large, setting the stage for a showdown between the two in the 1990s.

From Easy Finance
to Permanent Austerity

The second effect of stagflation was that it ushered in a new era of "permanent austerity" among rich democracies (Pierson 2001; Schäfer and Streeck 2013). Up until the 1970s, policymakers had been able to safely assume that the tax revenues needed to fund relatively generous welfare states would appear like manna from heaven. As the world rebounded from depression and global war, productivity and economic growth had boomed at astounding rates. The result was an ample flow of tax revenues and a population less reliant on state benefits as their primary source of income. This changed in the 1970s as welfare states were increasingly exposed to economic pressures from several sources, including slower productivity growth, a shift from manufacturing to service employment, the maturation of welfare state responsibilities, and shifting employment expectations in families (Pierson 2001). Together with inflation, these changes had the effect of increasing spending commitments while decreasing government revenues (see Schäfer and Streeck 2013). The so-called golden age of the welfare state was simply never sustainable in the long run.

The aforementioned battles over tax and benefit indexation were a symptom of the inevitable fiscal reckoning. Indexation of social benefits in times of high inflation was very expensive. For a short time, policymakers could rely on the erosion of tax allowances and bracket creep to raise taxes by stealth. The public soon caught on to the scheme, and antitax backlashes eventually forced policymakers to include indexation provisions in their tax codes. This satisfied taxpayers but also laid bare the reality of the situation. As revenues faltered, spending commitments continued to grow, and interest rates climbed, persistent deficits became the new norm (see Figure 3.2).

Demands for welfare state expansion soon gave way to demands for deficit reduction. Technically, austerity can take the form of tax increases, spending reductions, or some combination thereof. Since the 1970s, however, policymakers have focused primarily on spending reductions as the best way to achieve this goal (Blyth 2013; Kato 2003; Pierson 2001). Priorities on both the left and the right have shifted to cost containment as the best method of deficit reduction. Pierson (2001: 423) goes so far as to argue that the fight against spending is a "defining characteristic of the era of austerity." The rise of chronic deficits in the 1970s and the subsequent

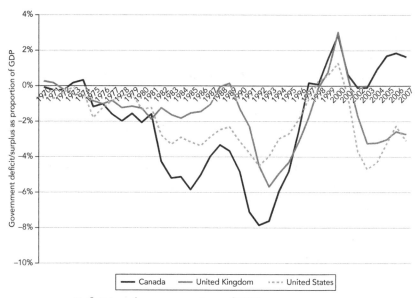

FIGURE 3.2 Deficit/surplus as percentage of GDP, 1970–2007.
Source: Organization for Economic Cooperation and Development, Economic Outlook No. 90. Paris: OECD.

turn against spending explain why a shift toward fiscalization began during this period across the US and Canada and was delayed in the UK.

Among liberal welfare regimes, where cost containment was a major priority, fiscalization became an attractive alternative to retrenchment. In an environment where spending cuts are seen as an economic necessity, policymakers have three choices for achieving this goal. The first is broad welfare state retrenchment. Policymakers can reduce various state benefits in order to contain the total costs of the welfare state. Though highly effective at reducing spending, as a rich literature has documented, this strategy is problematic from a political standpoint (Starke 2006). Program beneficiaries who would be adversely affected by the cuts are likely to mobilize in opposition to stop them. Cuts to universal programs, which provide the most bang for the buck, are more likely to garner a backlash than cuts to targeted programs, which provide relatively little savings (Korpe and Palme 1998; Pierson 1994; Prasad 2006). As even hardcore conservative policymakers quickly discovered, broad-based retrenchment was, at best, a mediocre strategy for reducing spending.

The second strategy is to pursue "income-testing at the top" by reducing spending on universal benefits through the exclusion of high-income beneficiaries (Levy 1999; Myles 1998). This is exemplified by the growing attractiveness of "negative income tax"–style programs that provide relatively generous benefits to the poor, less to the middle class, and none to the rich. Policymakers are able to take credit for cutting spending while making antipoverty programs more cost-effective by concentrating the cuts affecting those who have little or no material need. This may also involve shifting spending from more expensive universal programs to less expensive selective programs. Policymakers pursued this strategy with some success in Canada and the UK, shifting spending from the universal family allowances to income-tested programs. As a deficit reduction strategy, it is relative effective but quickly reaches its limits when cuts begin to hit the middle class, creating pushback from the public similar to those that occur with broader retrenchment strategies.

These first two strategies assume that the new impetus for policymakers is avoiding blame rather than claiming credit for policy changes (Pierson 2001; Weaver 1986). Together they can explain many of the changes in regard to austerity that have taken place in rich democracies since the 1970s. At the same time, the politics of blame avoidance tell us little about the shift to fiscalization. Fortunately, one does not need an entirely new framework to understand it. The politics of fiscalization are the politics of welfare state expansion, modified for times of austerity. As such, the politics of fiscalization can be analyzed as the same politics of credit claiming that marked the earlier postwar period.

Tax credits, as I have argued, are functionally equivalent to traditional social spending. Prior to the 1970s, policymakers had more incentive to provide benefits in the form of straightforward social spending. Revenues were abundant, so the costs were not salient. In addition, tax credits were the domain of treasury departments, making them less accessible as a policy lever to antipoverty advocates housed in social security departments. Austerity changed the costs and benefits of using the tax system for social policy purposes. The legitimization of spending cuts as the primary way to reduce the deficit inadvertently made tax credits more attractive to policymakers looking to claim credit for both deficit reduction and providing benefits to their constituencies. Families clearly see that they benefit from tax credits but their budget classification obfuscates their nature to budget watchdogs.

As a result of the taken-for-granted nature of accounting discussed in chapter 1, fiscalization began to become attractive to policymakers in the 1970s and 1980s. It allowed them to obfuscate the true costs of welfare state expansions by classifying such expansions as tax cuts or nonspending in the budget during times of intense pressures for spending restraint.

Policymakers were able to do this because of what Carruthers and Espeland call the technical and rhetorical dimensions of accounting. The technical dimension of tax expenditures is their classification as revenues not collected in official government budgets. The rhetorical dimension of tax expenditures is their popular perception as reductions in spending and/or taxes. The manner in which policies are framed influences whether they resonate with wider cultural schemas (Ferree 2003; Steensland 2008). There is some evidence that the public does care about restraining and reducing spending, especially if there is a large deficit (Gallup 1999). The issue is that while this support is often strong in the abstract, it wanes considerably when specific programs are put on the chopping block.

In order to claim credit for spending reductions, policymakers must also be able to credibly claim that they will not affect benefits for programs that help deserving populations, such as children. Beneficiaries see an increase (or at least no reduction) in their benefits, but the introduction of tax credits is not perceived as an increase in spending. The conversion of traditional programs into tax credits is actually perceived as both a spending and a tax reduction. This comes in handy for policymakers, whether they face popular demands to shrink "big government" and provide tax cuts or pressure from stakeholders to curb inflation through spending restraints.

Together, these dimensions of tax credits allowed policymakers to gain the legitimacy of two different audiences, each focused on a different aspect of the budget. On the one hand those who were concerned with cost containment, such as the International Monetary Fund and the elusive yet powerful financial markets, cared only about one goal: the reduction of spending, signaling concrete efforts to do something about deficits (Blyth 2013). On the other hand those concerned with benefits levels, such as beneficiaries and antipoverty advocates, cared only about a different goal: increasing benefits for families. Fiscalization focuses the attention of the former on the total level of government spending narrowly defined and the attention of the latter on the distribution of benefits broadly defined. Fiscalization allowed policymakers to have their cake and eat it too.

The remainder of this chapter traces these developments as they affected child and in-work tax credits as well as their predecessor policies. All three countries followed the same broad pattern in which these changes began under left-leaning governments in the 1970s and were simply continued under right-leaning ones in the 1980s. Given the popular and scholarly perception that the 1980s marked a conservative break from an earlier period (usually focused narrowly on social assistance or top income tax rates), it is necessary to stress the continuity between liberal and conservative approaches to social policy aimed at families. Policy legacies and macroeconomic changes—not resurgent conservative movements—are responsible for the shape and timing of major policy changes during this period.

Canada: Swift Response to Inflation

Inflation had barely surpassed normal rates when it crept onto Canadian policymakers' radar in 1972. The concept of indexation was a radically new idea when Progressive Conservative opposition leader Robert Stanfield first proposed it in May 1972. In parliamentary debates, Stanfield argued that the government had a "vested interest in inflation" because it enabled the government to raise taxes without having to vote to do so. He went on to propose indexing tax allowances and brackets as a way to "protect citizens from tax increases imposed upon them by inflation rather than imposed upon them as the result of an increase in their real income" (Canada. House of Commons Debates, 15 May 1972: 2267–2268). The Progressive Conservatives saw indexation as a way to constrain spending by limiting automatic revenue increases resulting from inflation. The issue was so important to Stanfield that it made it onto the party's 1972 election platform.

When Stanfield first proposed indexation, there was little reason to believe it would receive much political support. The Carter Commission on tax reform had recently recommended continued nonindexation of income taxes. Inflation was still relatively low. Taxpayers were unlikely to notice the small loss in real income stemming from exemption erosion and bracket creep, but ministers of various spending departments did notice the aggregate sum of revenues that they could use for their favored purposes. The Liberal government retained only a minority government after the election, but an uptick in inflation beginning in 1973, moving above 5% for the first time since 1951, led finance minister John Turner to co-opt the issue from the Conservatives. The government had provided broad-based tax relief in 1971, removing a substantial number of families from the income tax rolls altogether. Turner worried that the government might face a backlash from taxpayers who soon found themselves paying income taxes again. In his 1973 budget speech, Turner proposed a small increase in tax exemptions in order to protect low-income taxpayers. He then went on to echo Stanfield's earlier concern about the effects of inflation on taxpayers before proposing full indexation of exemptions and brackets in the personal income tax system (Canada. House of Commons Debates, 19 February 1973: 1433–1435; Gillespie 1991).

The budget passed, and indexation took effect in 1974. Unbeknownst to the government, Canada had just enacted a radical policy change that would become the blueprint for other countries facing similar problems with the effects of inflation. The oil crisis struck in October 1973, and inflation skyrocketed. The economic pressures from erosion of exemptions and bracket creep faced by families in other countries never affected Canadian families. The value of the dependent exemption had steadily increased since 1958, so that by 1977 the poverty threshold was still approximate to the level at which families hit the tax threshold (Carluccio 1993: 85; Kesselman 1979: 658). According to Hale (2002: 151), "these policies were immensely popular, and arguably helped the federal government avoid the middle-class anti-government backlash embodied in the tax revolts of California's Proposition 13 and its imitators in the United States in the late 1970s." Canadians were never "taxed into poverty" as US (and to some extent British) families were. Although the Progressive Conservatives would sweep into power in the 1980s, there would be no Canadian Thatcher or Reagan coming to the rescue of aggrieved taxpayers.

Income tax indexation ensured that the Progressive Conservatives would not outflank the minority Liberal government on the right. There was also the issue of the New Democratic Party on the left. Prior to the 1972 election, the government had been looking into income-testing family allowances and redistributing the savings to lower-income families. After the election, the government not only abandoned this plan but pulled a complete U-turn, tabling legislation to increase the value of family allowances while making them taxable for the first time ever. There was good reason for this. The nominal value of family allowances had only been increased once since their introduction in 1944. Even in a period marked by low levels of annual inflation, this resulted in a substantial erosion of the real value of family allowances. The uptick in inflation at the end of 1973 drove this point home. The government passed an amendment to the Family Allowance Act at the end of 1973 that tripled their value, beginning in 1974 (Blake 2009: 231–242; Haddow 1993: 100–101).

The decision to index the income tax system and family allowances proved wise, as the inflation rate shot up the following year, and the government adjusted each accordingly. As politically wise as it was, it was also very expensive. The growing cost of family allowances helped usher in a new era of austerity that would soon lead to a fundamental shift in child benefits. Fiscalization would begin before the Liberals left office.

Child tax credits had been proposed twice before in previous years. The first proposal was in reaction to the proposed Family Income Security Plan in 1972. This plan was a proposal to income-test family allowances, along with several other programs aimed at families with children. Federal officials encountered opposition from the provinces, though. Ontario's minister of social and family service, John Yaremko, put forth the alternative idea that family allowance payments should be linked to the income tax system so families could receive them by filing their taxes rather than applying though the welfare office. This would eliminate any fears that making the program more selective would result in stigma for the families (Blake 2009: 196). At the time, officials at the DNHW opposed integration of the tax and welfare system (217). On a practical level, Family Income Security Plan benefits were to be assessed on the basis of total family income, while income taxes were assessed on an individual level. This would make family assessment administratively difficult. Politically, it had the unattractive effect of transferring control over social policy from the DNHW to the Department of Finance. Incoming DNHW minister Marc Lalonde dropped both the Family Income Security Plan proposal and its tax credit alternative after the 1972 election.

The second proposal was made during the Social Security Review of 1973–1976, an effort to come up with proposals for a comprehensive overhaul of the entire social security system (Torjman 1995), which sought to explore the possibility of introducing a guaranteed annual income program. One issue discussed was how to best deliver benefits. Once again, Ontario pushed for a refundable tax credit approach, based on a 1972 green paper from the UK (discussed later in this chapter) and its own experience with provincial tax credits. The tax credit approach now had the support of officials in the DNHW who worried that any new spending proposals would not stand a chance in the increasingly austere environment. The tax credit approach still ran into opposition from officials in the Department of Finance, who objected to the delivery of benefits through the tax system (Carluccio 1993: 21–22; Canada Federal-Provincial Social Security Review 1975: 61; Haddow 1993: 109–110). By 1976, the entire review collapsed due to the provincial resistance and the Finance Department's reluctance to undertake any new spending initiatives. The tax credit proposal lost out once again.

Within two years, the Liberal government would introduce what, according to one observer, was the "most revolutionary step in the use of the federal income tax system since its inception in 1917" (Kitchen 1979: 44). The Refundable Child Tax Credit (RCTC) marked the beginning of a shift toward fiscalization. How do we explain the political success of tax credits in 1978 after their failure only a few years earlier? Chronically high inflation worked in conjunction with the earlier decision to index the income tax system and most social benefits to create persistent and unsustainable budget deficits almost immediately. By 1978, the estimated cumulative revenues losses stemming from income tax indexation reached C$4 billion (Tanzi 1980: 157). As revenue growth slowed to a halt, indexation of social benefits led to an unprecedented growth in spending. It was the latter change that gained the attention of policymakers concerned with the growing budget deficit.

In October 1975, new finance minister, Donald McDonald, announced: "Canada is in the grip of serious inflation"; he traced it back to the growth of government spending and the deficit. The consensus was that any successful response would need to target spending. He pledged to hold spending growth to the rate of GNP and look for possible spending cuts (Savoie 1991: 149). The government subsequently cut C$2 billion in spending, spread out over the least politically popular programs, but quickly ran out of "fat" to cut. In 1976, the government made the decision to forgo automatic adjustment of family allowances. With the inflation rate averaging 10% that year, it saved the government (and cost families) C$220 million. A backlash led by the New Democratic Party forced the government to reinstate indexation as usual the following year (Blake 2009: 243–245). Despite the temporary deindexation, the cost of the family allowance rose by almost half a billion dollars in four years. It was clear that even popular social programs might be targeted for spending cuts if the situation worsened. Spending increases were out of the question.

This is part of the reason the DNHW became increasingly interested in the use of tax credits during the social security review. Prior to this, few government departments took interest in tax expenditures because they were under the control of the Department of Finance. This changed as the government sought to bring the budget under control by containing spending more strictly. Tax expenditures were not counted in the total expenditure budget, which made them much more attractive to department officials looking to increase funding for their constituencies (Savoie 1991: 92–94). The turning point came in 1975 with leadership changes in the Department of Finance. Both Finance Minister Turner and Deputy Finance Minister Simon Reisman were adamantly opposed to the use of the tax system for the delivery of social benefits. It was Reisman who sank tax credit proposals during the social security review. Following the reelection of the Liberal government with a stronger majority in 1974, Turner and Reisman both resigned and were replaced by ministers who were more open to the idea of integrating Canada's tax and transfer systems (Blake 2009: 244).

The new leaders in the Department of Finance, in conjunction with the DNHW, agreed to form the Interdepartmental Task Force on Tax-Transfer Integration in the summer of 1976 to study the issue. The task force began meeting immediately and reported their initial findings to the cabinet the following summer. Buoyed by the positive reaction from the prime minister's office, task force members began crafting internal proposals for a refundable child tax credit (RCTC). By 1978, the task force published its official report, which found that tax-transfer integration was feasible; but Finance Department officials remained skeptical of tax credit proposals in the face of pressures to cut spending (Canada Department of Finance 1978). Although the Liberal government passed a small, $50 nonrefundable CTC in 1977, there was no indication that it would pass a much larger refundable credit in the near future.

Changes in the Department of Finance facilitated the introduction of the RCTC, but they were not the proximate cause of its passage in 1978. Instead, it's introduction was an austerity measure. The proposal reached the cabinet in the summer of 1977, but they sat on it without acting for over a year (Leman 1980: 131). The DNHW still preferred to keep family benefits under their auspices, the Department of Finance still preferred not to take on responsibility for administering social programs, and cuts elsewhere in the budget dampened pressures for austerity. This respite holding back fiscalization was short-lived.

In the summer of 1978, Prime Minister Pierre Trudeau attended an international economic summit in Bonn, Germany, where world leaders came to the conclusion that the runaway inflation faced by most Western countries was the result of continued government spending. Trudeau returned to Canada ready to take swift action. In August Trudeau announced, after little consultation with cabinet ministers, that the government needed to cut $2 billion in spending from the federal budget over the next several years. Monique Bégin, the DNHW minister, and Jean Chrétien, the finance minister, feared that family allowances, as one of the largest programs, would be a target and that cuts would be very politically unpopular. The proposal for an RCTC came out of cabinet discussions on how to divert attention away from child benefits by obfuscating their true cost in the budget (Blake 2009: 248).

Within weeks, Bégin and Chrétien, both of whom had had little appetite for the proposal prior to Trudeau's announcement, crafted legislation to simultaneously cut family allowances and introduce a new RCTC. The bill they tabled reduced the universal family allowance from $25.68 to $20 per month and deindexed its value from inflation. It also amended the Income Tax Act to create a $200 RCTC. The credit was income-tested, such that its value was reduced 5% for each dollar over $18,000 that a family earned. It was estimated that 2 million families stood to gain from the changes, while 1.7 million would see an overall reduction in child benefits—very similar to the expected changes under the failed Family Income Security Plan. The poorest families saw the combined value of their family allowance and RCTC increase by about 34% (Carluccio 1993: 60–61; Haddow 1993: 152).

Most important, the use of tax credits enabled policymakers to redistribute benefits to poorer families without being perceived as increasing spending, which Finance Department officials feared might put too much pressure on capital markets (Canada. Commons Debates 1977: 4533–4539). Rather than show up on the spending side of the ledger, the RCTC, like previous tax expenditures, was counted as revenues not collected. On one level, the change had a relatively small effect on the deficit, in that family allowance reductions were shifted to the RCTC for a net savings of only C$35 million. On another level, the family reduction allowance was perceived as a C$690 million spending decrease. The RCTC was not classified as a spending increase. It was classified as a C$655 million revenue loss. This was crucial because Trudeau's political promise was based on the idea that runaway *spending* was the source of inflation. Furthermore, this classification scheme was politically, not technically, determined. The 1978 report on tax-transfer integration suggested that the RCTC could be classified as "reduction of (or offset to) revenue; as an explicit expenditure; or as part revenue reduction and part expenditure" (Canada Department of Finance 1978: 9). The government chose to count it wholly as a reduction of revenue.

In choosing the first option, Chrétien promised that this was "not the beginning of a round of social welfare measures disguised as tax reduction" (Canada. House of Commons Debates, 31 October 1978: 653).

Of course, that was exactly what the government was doing. Progressive Conservative MP Sinclair Stevens accused the government of "cooking the books" and using "cute accounting tricks" to mislead the public about the government's ability to constrain spending (Canada. Commons Debates 1978: 1235). This criticism fell on deaf ears in 1978. By 1984, the Progressive Conservative government of Brian Mulroney was using the same accounting practice to provide cover for tax increases elsewhere in the budget, citing similar concerns about avoiding "undue demands on Canadian capital markets" (Canada. House of Commons Debates, 8 November 1984: 98) through increasing taxes. This ensured that this favored classification lasted for another two decades.

This attribute of the RCTC proved to be the most important in the coming years. In this case, the advantage was not so much that the RCTC was perceived as a tax reduction (as was the case in the US) but that the RCTC was perceived as a spending reduction vis-à-vis the family allowance. In fact, the RCTC was decidedly not perceived as tax relief because of its connection to family allowances. There was little rhetoric about the RCTC being a tax cut for taxpayers. Instead, policymakers actively advertised it as a way to increase child benefits for the poorest families whether or not they paid taxes. Bégin was clear: "this reform is directed towards Canadian children" (Canada. House of Commons Debates, 31 October 1978: 670). With little opposition from rival parties, the reform passed soon after. Canada's RCTC followed a logic of income supplementation—not tax relief—from the very beginning.

The combination of increasing the RCTC while decreasing family allowances became the primary strategy by which the Liberal government sought to control spending in the face of increasing budget deficits. In 1982, the Liberal government partially deindexed family allowances, allowing inflation to further erode their value over the next two years, while increasing the value of the RCTC by another $50 per child in order to compensate lower-income families (Blake 2009: 252; Phillips 1999: 29). By 1984, low-income families were receiving more from the RCTC than from family allowances. The DNHW begin to undertake an official reevaluation of family allowances in 1984 when they lost a federal election to the Progressive Conservatives under the leadership of Mulroney. Rather than changing directions, the Mulroney government intensified the Liberal government's shift toward fiscalization and reforms aimed at injecting more selectivity into the program as ways to deal with still-persistent deficits.

The continued growth of federal deficits despite early federal attempts to control spending pushed the new Department of Finance under finance minister Michael Wilson to make deficit reduction their number one priority. The Department of Finance report *A New Direction for Canada* (1984) signaled a number of changes to come. First, it drove home the idea, initially brought up by the previous Liberal government, that Canada's deficits were the primary obstacle to renewed economic growth. Second, the report recommended spending cuts rather than tax increases as the best method for reducing the deficit.

The Progressive Conservatives' landslide victory in 1984 was, in part, based on their campaign promise to cut the deficit without making the same sorts of perceived draconian cuts to social spending that Canadians were witnessing in the United States. Prime Minister Mulroney said that universal programs in particular were part of Canada's "sacred trust," implying that they would be insulated from spending cuts (Bashevkin 2002: 28). Immediately on entering office, Mulroney announced a task force to review federal spending. The task force set out to look for duplicate, complex, and unnecessary federal programs that could be targeted for simplification, consolidation, or elimination. Unlike previous reviews, this one was led by the Department of Finance rather than the DNHW. In fact, the DNHW was kept in the dark until the report was released in 1985. The shift of the center of power from the DNHW to the Department of Finance that had started with the 1978 decision to cut family allowances and introduce the RCTC was consolidated under the Progressive Conservative government in the 1980s (Phillips 1999: 223–224).

Following the previous Liberal government's accounting classifications, the report referred to the "costs" of family allowances, while the child tax exemption and the RCTC were both said to "reduce federal tax revenues" (Canada Department of Finance 1984: 71–72). All three programs were perceived as benefits for children, but only family allowances were perceived as spending. Canada was able to reap the benefits of fiscalization without shifting to a logic of tax relief, even under a right-leaning government.

In 1985, the DNHW released a report titled *Child and Elderly Benefits, Consultation Paper*, proposing a number of options for slowing the growth of spending in Old Age Security and family allowances. The same year, as part of the budget, Finance Minister Wilson proposed partially deindexing both programs so that their value fell behind the rate of inflation. A negative reaction from seniors caused the government to backtrack on Old Age Security, but they held the course on family allowances. Just as the Liberal government had done in 1978, the Progressive Conservative government simultaneously increased the value of the RCTC (from $384 to $524) over three years while making it more selective (reducing the threshold for income-testing from $26,330 to $23,500). The value of the dependent exemption was also reduced over four years (from $710 to $384). The changes allowed the government to increase benefits for low-income families while putting savings into deficit reduction. The government followed up with several more policy changes redistributing child benefits from the rich to the poor, including the decision to convert the dependent exemption into a nonrefundable CTC in 1987 (Guest 1999: 217–226).

By the decade's end, Canada had made significant progress toward fiscalization with the introduction of both refundable and nonrefundable CTCs. Such tax credits were nonexistent prior to 1978. In 1988, they accounted for close to 60% of child benefits received by poor families. The shift was a result of choices made in 1973. Swift indexation helped Canada avoid an antitax backlash that might have put taxpayers at the center of policymakers' agenda. Instead, Canadians continued to think of families with children as the primary victims of chronic inflation. This focus on children continued even as policymakers began to use the tax system to deliver benefits to families as a way to obfuscate their actions. The ensuing budget deficits changed the calculus for policymakers who had previously been averse to using the tax system for such purposes. By classifying tax credits as revenues not collected, Canadian policymakers ensured their popularity even under Progressive Conservative rule.

The United Kingdom: Taking a Middle Path

Although the antitax ideology of Thatcher is usually thought to best characterize this period, there is clear evidence that the logic of income supplementation—not tax relief—dominated from the 1970s onward in the UK. The war on poverty that began in the 1960s continued in the UK under the Conservative government of Edward Heath, who was elected in 1970. The new government favored what was then termed the "supplementary family allowance," for which only working families were eligible (Lenkowsky 1986: 78–79).

The reasons were practical rather than ideological. Department of Health and Social Security officials discovered that the tax threshold had eroded so far over the years that there would be too little savings from eliminating tax allowances in order to supplement family allowances. Moreover, because families received no family allowance for the first child, many single-parent families would receive nothing from the benefit increase (CAB 129.152.20; Deacon and Bradshaw 1983: 79–80). The effect on child poverty would be underwhelming as a result. Instead, the government turned to a strategy of income supplementation in what would become the FIS (Family Income Supplement). The proposed FIS provided in-work benefits to families where at least one parent worked a minimum number of hours per week. In this case, those who worked at least thirty hours would receive a benefit large enough to bring them above the poverty line. This benefit was phased out by 50% for each new dollar earned above a given threshold.

The proposal was not new. Treasury officials under the Labour government had proposed something similar, but it had encountered opposition from Labour Party members, antipoverty groups, and trade unions, who preferred universal programs. These groups still opposed targeted benefits in 1970, but the Conservatives, who had been advocating for more selectivity in social policy as a way to contain costs since the 1950s, were much more open to the idea (Deacon and Bradshaw 1983: 80–81). The new policy was meant to be temporary, but it was never repealed and was only reformed—to serve as the predecessor to the WFTC decades later. The early introduction of the FIS gives us a remarkable test case for examining the institutionalization of cultural categories of worth. Much like the EITC, which passed only a few years later in the United States, one might theorize that the FIS would have institutionalized and strengthened categorical distinctions between the "undeserving" welfare poor and the "deserving" working poor in the UK (Bertram 2015; Moffitt 2015; Steensland 2008: 18). The evidence suggests that the introduction of the FIS did not constrain future policymakers as such theories might predict. I will return to this issue in later chapters.

No sooner had the new temporary FIS gone into effect than policymakers began to look for replacements. One opportunity came when the government undertook efforts to simplify the tax code. Arthur Cockfield, special advisor to the chancellor of the exchequer, was interested in ways to make the UK's pay-as-you-earn system more efficient. One way to smooth out fluctuations was to have a single tax rate and replace the personal and children's exemptions with refundable tax credits payable throughout the year. Cockfield soon realized that he could also fold the family allowance and the FIS into the same system to create one single tax credit (Lenkowsky 1986: 125–134).

The result was the green paper *Proposals for a Tax-Credit System* (1972). The paper identified complexity and poverty traps as major issues with the current tax and welfare system. The proposed tax credit would serve multiple goals, including reducing means-testing, simplifying the tax code, and eliminating 10,000–15,000 bureaucrats by integrating the tax and welfare systems (CAB 129.163.11). In his 1972 budget speech, the chancellor of the exchequer spoke of integrating "a taxation system which embodies a set of reliefs and allowances based on one set of principles, and a social security system which embodies a different set of benefits and allowances based on a different set of principles" (Rein 1973: 81). The proposal had the support of both the Trades Union Congress and the Confederation of British Industry. The government formed an all-party Select Committee to further study the proposal. The committee officially endorsed the plan in 1973, and then it began to run into trouble.

As they were preparing the proposal for approval, the Select Committee and the government received an avalanche of letters from angry mothers who resented the redistribution of their family allowances to fathers. Under the current system, mothers received family allowances while fathers received the benefits of tax exemptions. The new tax credit proposal threatened to transfer all payments to breadwinning fathers in their paychecks. In order to blunt criticism, the government announced that the new tax credit would be paid to the mother in March 1973 as a separate CTC.

While this appeased mothers, it had the effect of undermining the rationale for the reform in the first place. Instead of the tax-transfer system becoming simplified, it was becoming more complex. What had initially been framed as tax reform was increasingly seen as social security reform, leaving it open to new criticisms, especially from Conservatives themselves (Lenkowsky 1986: 134–138). Conservative Party members could support the £1.3 billion price tag for tax relief but balked at £1.3 billion in new public spending. Many Conservatives saw the proposal as just "another expensive welfare program" (138). The loss of support slowed the bill in Parliament. At this point, fiscalization was not worth the political price of angering voting mothers or the party's conservative base. The pace proved too slow, as the Conservative government called for an election in response to worsening economic conditions and labor unrest in the wake of the oil crisis. The Conservatives were ousted in February 1974, and the new Labour government did not take up the tax credit proposal.

Inflation soon took center stage as the top issue. Unlike the Liberals in Canada, the Labour government actively resisted calls for indexation of the tax and social security systems. As early at 1974, opposition MPs were accusing the government of redistribution "by stealth" and calling on the Treasury to index the tax system to protect the public from inflation. The government readily admitted that they were using inflation to increase tax revenues, calculating that the windfall in 1973 alone was £740 million, but argued that this was needed to help avoid larger deficits (HC Deb 10 June 1974, vol. 874, cols. 1230–1332). Conservative and Liberal opposition leaders intensified calls for indexation, making special reference to low-income taxpayers with families and citing Canada's experience as evidence that it would not hurt the economy (HC Deb 8 May 1975, vol. 891, cols. 1628–1757; HC Deb 20 May 1975, vol. 892, cols. 1341–1367; HC Deb 22 March 1976, vol. 908, cols. 46–105; HC Deb 11 May 1976, vol. 911, cols. 300–407). The government ignored the criticisms of the Conservatives and Liberals, prioritizing revenue growth over tax relief.

The inflation that crept up in the early 1970s exploded after the oil crisis, reaching double digits by the end of 1973 and staying there through 1977. This took a heavy toll on the value of the unindexed tax and social security benefits. Despite periodic ad hoc adjustments, the real value of tax exemptions declined by almost 20%. With nine different tax brackets, rate bands set in nominal terms shrank in real terms. Bracket creep meant that taxpayers found themselves paying higher rates without any real gains in income (Cropper 1978; Morgan 1977; *Economist* 1977). Family allowances' real value declined by one-third between 1968, when they were last increased, and 1974. Inflation was putting heavy economic pressures on families as their tax burden increased, their social security benefits shrank, and their incomes stagnated.

In this situation, the policy legacy of family allowances proved crucial in enabling the Labour government to shift the focus to income supplementation rather than tax relief. The situation the government faced was similar to that faced by the Democrats in the US, with the key difference that UK policymakers had the opportunity to eschew tax exemptions in favor of family allowances. Whereas both countries faced popular antitax backlashes as a result, this backlash did not spill over into family policy in the UK. Changes to the family allowances preempted the chance to trace economic pressures on families to the tax system.

Learning from the Conservative government's mistake, the Labour government took the opposite course of action, proposing to expand family allowances by eliminating the child tax exemption altogether. Once in power, the Labour government quickly moved to introduce a concrete proposal. Barbara Castle, the secretary of state for social services, was tasked with guiding a bill to replace the family allowance and child tax exemption with a new program called the Child Benefit (Lenkowsky 1986: 163–164). This improved on the old programs by increasing the value of benefits, especially for poor families, and extending them to the previously excluded first child. The government was motivated by and explicitly framed the new Child Benefit as a way to help families with children who were suffering under inflation (CAB 129.189.2; HC Deb 29 January 1974, vol. 868, cols. 252–378). Castle focused on poor children in general, with no reference to taxpayers, during the parliamentary debate: "what will the child benefit scheme achieve? First and most important the poorer families who have not been able to take advantage of child tax allowance in full, if at all, because of their low incomes, will in future do so, as the new benefit extends the cash advantage of the allowance to all these families. Those who are dependent on means-tested benefits will receive a larger part of their income from benefits as of right" (quoted in Greener and Cracknell 1998: 9). In folding the child tax exemption into the family allowance, the government effectively mooted discussion of the tax exemption's erosion and the necessity of indexation. According to one Labour MP, "the child's tax allowances have a limited life. We shall be seeing the passage of the Child Benefit Bill. Both the child tax allowances and the family allowances are to be replaced by the new child benefit scheme" (HC Deb 10 June 1975, vol. 893, cols. 244–317). Despite increasing economic pressures on families stemming from the erosion of tax exemptions, the Child Benefit Act successfully prevented the public from tracing economic pressures to that erosion by phasing out child tax exemptions altogether.

The Conservatives in opposition attempted to amend the bill to include indexation of the new Child Benefit. The Labour government rejected the amendment on the grounds that they would uprate it each year as needed but wanted to retain discretion in the face of growing economic problems. Still, Conservatives supported the bill in principle. Though they obviously preferred their own tax credit proposal, they were not opposed to tax-transfer integration even if it took the form of increased family allowances (HC Deb 28 March 1974, vol. 871, cols. 639–761). The Child Benefit Act of 1975 passed in April with all-party support. It provided an immediate boost to the value of family allowances. The full shift from child tax allowances to the Child Benefit for the first child was delayed until April 1977 so that the government could work out the full costs of what they could afford.

In the meantime, the inflation rate reached an all-time high of close to 25% in 1975 and 16% in 1976, quickly eroding the value of the Child

Benefit to a new low and sparking an economic crisis. To make matters worse, Prime Minister Harold Wilson abruptly resigned in early 1976. His replacement, James Callaghan, quickly moved to undermine the new Child Benefit, which he had previously opposed as a cabinet member. He immediately sacked Castle, who had championed the Child Benefit, and internal memos circulated ordering that full conversion would be delayed indefinitely in response to the new economic situation (Glennerster 2007: 119–120). The new secretary of state for social services still pushed for the Child Benefit, but its fate was now clearly in the hands of Treasury officials, who had their own reasons to delay it (CAB 129.189.2; CAB 129.189.5). A run on the pound in early 1976 precipitated a fiscal crisis so severe that the UK government was forced to turn to the International Monetary Fund for loans in order to remain solvent. One of the conditions attached to the loan was that the government reduce its deficit through spending cuts (Burk and Cairncross 1992). Austerity was imposed on the UK by external factors.

Although neutral in terms of its effect on budget deficits, the shift from tax allowances to the Child Benefit had the effect of increasing the total level of government spending in the budget. The Treasury had previously noted this while the Child Benefit was in the process of being passed, but it had meant little at the time (CAB 129.185.16). The IMF's conditions suddenly made the issue into a political problem. Part of the reason the Callaghan government wished to delay implementation of the Child Benefit was because of this technical dimension of accounting. This rationale was outlined in a confidential memo from the chancellor of the exchequer to the secretary of state for social security: "postponement would also have a presentational advantage. Whenever the CB scheme is introduced, it will look like a large addition to public expenditure on the social services. The fact that the greater part of it is offset by a reduction in tax reliefs will make little impression on the outside observer. By deferring the scheme the Government would look as if they were doing something about the level of public expenditure and this is a point on which there has been substantial home and overseas criticism" (CAB 129.189.18). This led to the decision to let inflation erode the value of both the child tax allowance and the Child Benefit in 1976 and again in 1977, saving the government billions. Members of the government who were unhappy with broken promises about child poverty soon leaked news of this strategy. Pressure from the Child Poverty Action Group and the embarrassment of the government backtracking on its own policy eventually forced the

Labour government to go through with the introduction of the Child Benefit between 1977 and 1980. When it was fully phased in, it more than doubled the value of family allowances relative to where they had been in 1974, bringing their real value even higher than its prestagflation peak in 1968. The shift from the child tax allowance to coverage for the first child increased the value of the benefit for the poorest families and decreased it for rich families.

In the end, the Labour government received less popular credit for the reform than expected. The episode did, however, teach the Labour government a very important lesson that would influence their decision to turn to the use of tax credits in the 1990s and early 2000s. The logic of income supplementation was not a blank check for policy expansion. In the new era of austerity, benefit expansion also needed to be antispending to help contain costs. The difference in classification would weigh heavily on future chancellor Gordon Brown's decision to convert existing programs into tax credits.

The decision to phase out child tax allowances in favor of the larger Child Benefit in 1975 made the broader category of children rather than the narrow category of taxpayers with children the focus of policymakers concerned with economic pressures on families. The continued nonindexation of the tax system still made taxpayers in general a salient target population for policy action. The problem was seen as a general increase in the tax burden on workers rather than on families in particular. The Labour government did not attend to the issue until the 1977 budget. In his budget speech, the chancellor argued that the "effect of inflation has been to put too high a proportion of the tax burden on to the income tax; to impose tax on too low a level of income; and to bring too many people into the higher rates of tax at each successive level, starting at a level not very far above average earnings" (HC Deb 29 March 1977, vol. 929, cols. 279–280). The budget originally proposed to increase the real value of tax exemptions and widen tax brackets to make up for previous erosion from inflation. There were no plans for indexation, despite continued expectations of high inflation.

The Conservative shadow chancellor of the exchequer Geoffrey Howe estimated that of the £6.6 billion in new revenues collected since 1973, £4.1 billion had been "imposed by stealth" from erosion of tax exemptions and bracket creep. The Labour budget would only provide tax relief worth £2.2 billion (HC Deb 25 July 1977, vol. 936, cols. 57–159). The continued intransigence on indexation spurred a rebellion from backbenchers in the

Labour caucus. Whereas prior amendments to require indexation were rebuffed by the Labour majority, two Labour members of the Parliamentary Standing Committee tasked with examining the budget bill defected on an amendment to index tax exemptions and sided with Conservative and Liberal committee members to attach it to the bill. Parliamentary rules prevented the government from undoing the amendment, and the government had no choice but to pass it, along with the budget (Barnett 1982; Cropper 1978). This marked the beginning of an antitax backlash that culminated in the election of Thatcher the following year.

By the time Conservatives returned to power in 1979, tax exemptions had been indexed, and the child tax allowance no longer existed. Some Conservatives wanted to reintroduce it in order to relieve pressures on working-class families, but the Treasury objected that it would lead to unacceptable revenue losses (Deacon and Bradshaw 1983: 163). Instead, the Conservative government introduced popular broad-based tax cuts and elimination of tax brackets to make up for the bracket creep long ignored by the previous government. Moreover, the government shifted much of the tax burden onto less salient consumption taxes. The VAT was almost doubled, from 8% to 15%, during the Conservatives' tenure (Daunton 2002: 335–338). Taxes might have risen on the poorest families, but in a much less salient way that garnered little backlash relative to the erosion of tax exemptions (Prasad 2006; Wilensky 2002).

Unable to make family tax relief a viable issue and unwilling to further expand expensive universal programs like the Child Benefit, the Thatcher government devised a strategy of shifting resources to more selective, less expensive income supplementation programs. The Conservative government avoided any direct attack on the Child Benefit, for fear of upsetting middle-class mothers and the Child Poverty Action Group, but allowed the benefit's value to erode 14% between 1979 and 1989 by deindexing it from inflation (Pierson 1994: 108–109). The FIS was substantially expanded during this period. This had less to do with the deservingness of the working poor and more to do with the FIS's structure. Children were deemed more deserving than the working poor, yet the Child Benefit eroded. They key difference was that the FIS, by targeting benefits narrowly, was less expensive and more cost-effective in terms of child poverty reduction. The growth of the FIS was part of a broader strategy for cost containment that consisted of income-testing universal programs or shifting funding from universal to targeted programs (Myles 1998; Levy 1999). Although superficially limited to the working poor, policymakers still saw the FIS, as its name indicates, as a form of income supplementation for families.

The Department of Health and Social Security attempted to tackle the issue with a comprehensive review of the social security system. The resulting investigation was published as a green paper, *The Reform of Social Security* (UK Department of Health and Social Security 1985a). It argued that the social security system had become too complicated over the years as programs had been added and altered in an ad hoc manner. This was connected to the issue of tax/benefit integration, as officials concluded that "overlap between social security and income tax means that significant numbers of people are paying income tax and receiving means-tested benefits at the same time" (1). The report's authors were especially concerned with child poverty, noting that families with children accounted for 48.5% of all individuals with low incomes in 1971 and had risen to 57.1% of them by 1982 (13).

The report traced this rise in child poverty to the decline in family benefits due to inflation, as well as the increase in social assistance and unemployment insurance benefits, which had led to an unemployment trap in which "low-income working families could be worse off than if they were out of work" (UK Department of Health and Social Security 1985a: 28). The report admitted that doubling the Child Benefit could alleviate child poverty and would also largely eliminate the unemployment and poverty traps for families with children but asserted that the cost (£4 billion) would be too high and ill-targeted. Cost containment took precedent over all competing goals.

Instead, the government proposed to further expand and entrench the "temporary" FIS in a white paper released later that year (UK Department of Health and Social Security 1985b). The proposal would replace the FIS with a similar program called Family Credit. The proposed Family Credit had several advantages over an increase in the Child Benefit. First, it was more selective and therefore less expensive and better targeted to the alleviation of child poverty than the Child Benefit. Beyond cost, the Family Credit, as it was first proposed, had important classification advantages. Unlike the FIS, which was paid directly to mothers, it was proposed that the Family Credit would be a tax credit, which, "paid through the wage packet offsetting national insurance and tax, would make much clearer the net family income in work" (31). This would have the effect of making the tax and benefit system less complicated by integrating them. It would also have the valuable effect of appearing as a spending reduction. It was duly noted that the Family Credit would appear as pure tax offset for about 60% of claimants (33).

Efforts to introduce the Family Credit as a tax credit ran into opposition, once again, from women's groups and employers. The former resented the redistribution "from purse to wallet"; the latter resented the costs associated with having to administer it. This opposition helped lead to the defeat of the bill in the House of Lords (Strickland 1998). The provisions that stipulated payment through the pay packet were stripped, and the bill eventually passed, but this meant that the Family Credit would be introduced as a traditional social security benefit rather than as a tax credit. The government continued on with their strategy of increasing selectivity, but fiscalization was again derailed by concerns expressed by women's and business groups.

The United States: The Perils of Policy Drift

One of the most enduring myths of American exceptionalism is that the US public has always been, to put it mildly, strongly skeptical of taxes. From the original Boston Tea Party to the modern-day Tea Party movement, it is often assumed that antitax sentiments are part of an American culture of antistatism or rugged individualism. A rich fiscal sociology literature suggests, however, that opposition to taxes is a relatively recent phenomenon. The early postwar period was marked by surprisingly little popular interest in taxes (Zelizer 1998). It was during the 1970s that taxes began to become, as Howard (2009) puts it, the "life of the party" in American politics. This section builds on more recent work in fiscal sociology (Martin 2008; Prasad 2012b) in order to show why taxpayers—not children—took center stage beginning in the 1970s. Unlike Canada and the UK, the US had no institutionalized logic of income supplementation on which it could build support for children in general. Combined with US policymakers' decision to delay indexation of the tax system well into the 1980s, this ensured that the logic of tax relief became more dominant than ever.

Though garnering the most attention, President Ronald Reagan's 1981 tax cuts were not the first movement for tax relief, nor were they the most consequential. Throughout this period, the antitax movement was largely concerned with lowering taxes on working- and middle-class families. What had begun in the early 1970s as a desire to relieve workers of increasing payroll taxes expanded into a wider antitax movement, as policymakers allowed exemption erosion and bracket creep to push the tax burden onto more and more lower- and middle-income families. All of these events can be traced back to the growing problem of chronic inflation beginning in 1973.

Fiscalization arrived in the US much sooner than elsewhere with the introduction of the EITC in 1974. The most popular explanation of this is that it was a reaction to the failure of President Nixon's guaranteed annual income proposal, the Family Assistance Plan (Bertram 2015; Steensland 2008). The EITC, it is argued, allowed congressional conservatives to undermine the Nixon proposal by substituting a program for it that, unlike Nixon's proposal, encouraged work and limited benefits to the "deserving" working poor. These accounts put the legacy of the Poor Law at the center of their story. In doing so, they ignore the aspect of the EITC that makes it so distinct. As a work subsidy, the EITC was neither new nor uniquely American. The UK had already introduced the FIS in 1970. What made the EITC unique was its introduction as a tax credit. On this issue, work-centered accounts have little to contribute. The evidence on the other hand demonstrates the explanatory power of my inflation-centered approach.

Rather than tracing the EITC to Nixon's failed Family Assistance Plan, I trace it to Nixon's proposal to index old age, survivors, and disability insurance (OASDI) benefits in 1969. In doing so, Nixon wanted to make the program "inflation proof" and remove benefit levels from politics altogether by making adjustments automatic (Zelizer 1998: 317–319). After some political wrangling, the Social Security Amendments of 1972 introduced indexation of benefits, to begin in 1975. The amendments also increased benefits by 20% on top of a 10% benefit increase enacted in 1971. Benefits were significantly higher than when Nixon had first proposed indexation three years earlier. Moreover, Congress enacted additional ad hoc benefit increases in the interim period before indexation took effect, as inflation began to erode previous increases (Weaver 1988: 74–89; Zelizer 1998: 340–343). Indexation and the political power of elderly beneficiaries ensured that increased benefits were here to stay. Chronic inflation pushed the costs of the program higher than anyone expected.

Structured as a trust fund, increased spending required increased revenues to keep the program financially solvent. This meant payroll tax hikes. The combined employee/employer payroll tax rate climbed from 6% in 1960 to 8.4% in 1970. Subsequent benefit increases forced it up to 9.9% by 1974. Payroll taxes nearly doubled as a proportion of personal income in a very short period (Bakija and Steuerle 1991). Policymakers on both the left and the right who were concerned with the rising burden on low- and middle-income families began to look for ways to ease payroll tax burdens (Campbell and Morgan 2005; Ventry 2000).

Representative Martha Griffiths, a liberal Democrat and member of the Ways and Means Committee, was one of the first policymakers to bring the problem of high taxes on the poor into the public discussion through her work as part of the Subcommittee on Fiscal Policy, where she pushed for a series of "Studies in Public Welfare." The studies examined the tax-transfer system as a whole in order to shed light on the effects of marginal tax rates on poverty and work incentives. Griffiths found that "Americans are becoming increasingly resistant to high taxes. Nearly two-thirds of all Americans feel that taxes have reached the breaking point. A rapidly growing number are expressing sympathy for a taxpayer's revolt, in which people refuse to pay their taxes" (US Congress 1972: v–iv). Griffiths, along with Senator Russell Long (D-LA), saw rising payroll taxes as the primary source of the increasing tax burden on the poor. By 1973, more than half of the country's taxpayers were paying more in payroll taxes than in federal income taxes. At the same time, Griffiths recognized that lowering this tax burden on low-wage workers was politically problematic, given the perception of Social Security as a contributory program. The injection of general revenues might help ease the burden but also threatened to undermine the program's cherished contributory principle, making this option unlikely to gain traction (US Congress 1974).

The second option was to relieve low-income workers of some portion of their payroll tax burden, as was the case with income taxes. Various personal exemptions guaranteed that workers making less than poverty-level wages were exempt from paying federal income taxes. The payroll tax had no such exemptions. Workers paid taxes starting with the first dollar they made. Senator Lawton Chiles (D-FL) raised this issue during a hearing on Social Security in 1972, asking: "why should we take a man's social security when we don't take his income tax; why should we take dollar one of the working man?" He subsequently filed a bill that would have allowed low-income workers to "qualify for a refund of the credit toward any unpaid income tax if his Social Security taxes exceeded the amount paid in income tax" (US Senate 1972a: 2053–2057). Then-governor Reagan testified at the same hearing, suggesting in his written statement that the government similarly solve the issue by exempting "low-income families from federal and state income tax (including withholding) and provide them with a rebate for their social security taxes. Including the employer's contribution thereto" (US Senate 1972a: 1926). The outlines of what would become the EITC were slowly gaining traction among policymakers.

It was in this environment that the powerful chair of the Senate Finance Committee, Russell Long (D-LA), first proposed what he called a "work bonus" program, attached to the same bill that eventually became the Social Security Amendments of 1972. Long's proposal would solve two problems. First, it would provide payroll tax relief to low-income workers with children by providing them with a tax refund equal to 10% of their income up to $4,000, at which point it would gradually be phased out through an income-test. Long made the connection to the payroll tax burden explicit by limiting the credit exclusively to those who paid payroll taxes. Low-income workers who were not subject to payroll taxes were not eligible for the credit. The rationale was based purely on a logic of tax relief from the very beginning. Second, the proposal stipulated that employers would continue to collect payroll taxes for deposit into the trust fund and that workers would still receive credit toward their pensions for these earnings. However, the tax refund would come out of general revenues (US Senate 1972b: 426). This would prevent the work bonus from undermining contributory principles and the solvency of the trust fund. Technically, much of the bonus would be scored as an outlay, but rhetorically it was perceived as tax relief from payroll taxes.

After the bill's legislative introduction in 1972, Long repeatedly made distinctions between his tax cut for working people and welfare benefits. He told colleagues: "we conceived this proposal initially as, in effect, relieving low-income working persons from the social security tax" (US Congress 1974: 67). Long characterized it as a "dignified way" to "prevent the taxing of people onto the welfare rolls." Setting the rate at 10% was not arbitrary. It was tied explicitly to payroll taxes, in that its purpose was to "prevent the social security tax from taking away from the poor and low-income earners the money they need for the support of their families." This was important after Congress passed payroll tax increases in 1972 and 1973; "it is just not fair that these poor people should be taxed so heavily," he told colleagues after the 1973 payroll tax increase, "especially when you recognize the fact that in many instances we are actually taxing these people into poverty" (quoted in Howard 1997:68–69). It was not just conservative and moderate senators who supported the bill. Walter Mondale (D-MN), among other liberals, championed it. Mondale gave the work bonus further publicity in his capacity as chair of the Subcommittee on Children and Youth during a hearing on economic pressures on families (US Senate 1973). In each and every case, the work bonus was discussed as a tax relief measure for alleviating payroll tax burdens on low-income families.

Although popular in the Senate, the bill did not have the support of Ways and Means Committee chair Wilber Mill (D-AR), who was able to block it in the House for several years (Ventry 2000: 995). In 1974, Al Ullman (D-OR) replaced Mills as chair of the committee. Ullman was much more open to a proposal like Long's work bonus. Also serving on the committee was James Burke (D-MA), a liberal representing the working-class district of South Boston. Burke had long worried about the rising payroll tax burden on low-income families. He had proposed several bills over the years to lower the burden but found his colleagues unwilling to tamper with the Social Security system. Burke discovered that Long's proposal could achieve the same result while avoiding prickly political issues about Social Security. He pushed Ullman to include a proposal for an "earned income credit" modeled on Long's work bonus as part of the Tax Reduction Act of 1975 (Shanahan 1975).

The Burke/Ullman proposal was more expansive than the Long proposal. Whereas Long limited his work bonus to workers with children, the earned income credit included all low-income workers subject to payroll taxes. In order to keep costs down, the House version reduced the credit to 5%. Despite cutting the size of the tax benefit in half, the increased eligibility still doubled the cost of the proposal relative to the Senate version (Bertram 2007: 227). For reasons that are unclear—perhaps because of the institutional power of Long relative to Ullman—the Senate version won out over the House version (Howard 1997). The Senate Finance Committee, in drafting the final legislation, specified that the "credit is set at 10% in order to correspond roughly to the added burdens placed on workers by both employee and employer social security contributions" (US Senate 1975). The Tax Reduction Act of 1975 was passed by Congress and signed by President Gerald Ford, introducing a "temporary" earned income credit that same year.

Like the FIS in the UK, this temporary program was not going anywhere. The earned income credit was extended over the next two years before it was renamed the Earned Income Tax Credit and made permanent in the Revenue Act of 1978. It had the protection of Long in Congress, while Jimmy Carter's administration put their support behind it because it was seen as a tax measure rather than a welfare measure and only part of the cost showed up on the budget as spending (Ventry 2000: 999–1001). Working-class tax relief was popular among Democratic constituencies, but the EITC was not enough to quell discontent among the wider public.

At the same time that payroll taxes were rising as a result of explicit legislative actions, income taxes were rising as a result of policy drift. The inflation-fueled rising cost of living polled as the most important issue facing the country between 1973 and 1981 (Michelmore 2012: 126). It was in this context that congressional Democrats and the Carter administration made "tax fairness" a central aspect of their political agenda. This was evident in their push for the EITC, such that tax fairness became synonymous with popular working-class tax relief. The meaning of tax fairness shifted when it came to the income tax, though. Democrats instead used the idea of tax fairness as a way to build support for tax reform focused almost exclusively on closing tax loopholes benefiting the rich. This was part of the traditional Democratic focus on making the tax code more progressive and raising more revenues (Michelmore 2012: 106–119; Zelizer 1998: 312–346). Broader tax relief dropped off the agenda.

Congress initially responded to inflation by enacting ad hoc tax cuts and adjustments in 1975, 1976, 1977, and 1978, but chronically high inflation ate them up faster than Congress could pass them. Despite the series of cuts, both marginal and average tax rates rose on families ranging from one-half to twice median income (Weaver 1988: 192). One Joint Economic Committee study found that "personal income and payroll taxes rose twice as fast as prices for food, housing, and transportation." Inflation had an especially severe effect on low- and middle-income families, as their total tax burdens increased by 31% and 26.5%, respectively (Michelmore 2012: 107). In 1974, Senator Mondale testified: "the average American family is being tortured by inflation and by higher taxes. Hearings before the Subcommittee on Children and Youth, which I chair, have brought home to me dramatically the economic pressures, which confront American families. These pressures are seriously threatening the stability of a growing number of families and are undermining the most important institution in our society" (US Senate 1974: 32). Mondale's Democratic colleagues did not share the same concern. They were more fearful that substantial tax cuts might lead to large deficits and more inflation. Inflation allowed them to increase revenues through the erosion of tax exemptions and bracket creep. Through a strategy of policy drift, Democrats "enacted" substantial tax increases throughout the 1970s. Inflation helped increase federal revenues by $25 billion in 1973 alone (American Enterprise Institute 1974). Federal personal income tax revenues as a proportion of GDP climbed from 8.3% in 1976 to a postwar high of 10.4% in 1982.

There was a broad consensus that low-income families disproportionately bore the brunt of inflation-induced tax increases. The Advisory Commission on Intergovernmental Relations produced reports in 1976 and in 1980 demonstrating that "inflation is especially hard on low-income families and all families with many dependents" (Advisory Commission on Intergovernmental Relations 1976: 6). A study by the Congressional Budget Office (1980) came to similar conclusions. As family incomes stagnated, bracket creep pushed taxpayers into higher tax brackets while the value of tax exemptions eroded (Aaron 1976; Smith 2007; Witte 1985: 236–238). Similarly, the property tax became problematic because assessed values were rising rapidly, despite no real gains for property owners (Martin 2008). It was no coincidence that poll respondents named income and property taxes as the two taxes most in need of reduction in 1978 (Campbell and Morgan 2005). The result was that both the public and policymakers traced the source of growing economic pressures to the tax system.

It was congressional Republicans who took up the call for tax relief. Beginning in 1974, they began to push for indexation of the tax system, but without a majority, there was little they could do in the face of Democratic intransigence (Advisory Commission on Intergovernmental Relations 1980). Events in California in 1978 helped turn the tide in favor of indexation. Most people are familiar with the effects of Proposition 13, facilitating a property tax revolt that eventually spurred a general tax revolt (Martin 2008), but California was a bellwether for indexation as well, becoming the first state to introduce income tax indexation in 1978. Congress and future presidential candidate Reagan closely watched these events and reacted accordingly. Support for indexation quickly grew among congressional Democrats, while Reagan endorsed the Roth-Kemp proposal for tax cuts, which included provisions for indexation (Brownlee 2004: 135–136; Brownlee and Steuerle 2004: 156; Weaver 1988: 195–197). By 1980, indexation had the endorsement of the *New York Times*, and the Advisory Commission on Intergovernmental Relations (1980: 35) called it a "reasoned and effective response to the political pressures of the taxpayers' revolt and the economic burdens imposed by inflation."

The tax revolt, stemming from Democrats' conscious strategy of policy drift, culminated in the election of President Reagan in 1980. Utilizing newly released documents from the Reagan administration archives, Prasad (2012a) affirms the arguments of former Reagan administration officials, such as Eliot Brownlee and Eugene Steuerle, that support for the 1981 tax cuts stemmed from popular opposition to inflation-induced tax increases throughout the 1970s (see also Witte 1985: 236–238). Prasad argues: "opinion polls also showed consistent, unwavering, and strong support for fighting inflation, and without the tax cut Reagan had nothing to offer that would take on that concern" (Prasad 2012a: 363–364). Unlike their counterparts in Canada and the UK, neither Reagan nor Carter before him could relieve growing economic pressures on families through any mechanism but the tax code. The absence of a family allowance left policymakers unable to channel public discontent toward policy changes outside the tax system. Consequently, American families could only think of how inflation affected them as *taxpayers*.

The 1981 tax cuts had one fatal flaw that ensured that tax relief remained on the political agenda for the foreseeable future. While the legislation included a provision for indexation, it would not take effect until 1984. Persistent high rates of inflation undercut even the mighty Reagan tax cuts almost as swiftly as they were phased in. This was not an oversight. The decision to delay indexation was an intentional strategy that Congress used to reduce the size of the deficit (Brownlee and Steuerle 2004: 161). The further erosion of tax exemptions continued to put economic pressure on families, despite broad rate cuts. Moreover, continued fiscal pressures on the Social Security trust fund led policymakers to accelerate a payroll tax increase that had been scheduled for 1990 in the Social Security amendments of 1983, once again disproportionately raising taxes on low-income families (Steuerle 1991: 63). Meanwhile, the real value of the EITC declined 35% between 1975 and 1984 (Ventry 2000: 1001).

The crucial turning point in the focus on family tax relief came in 1982. That year, the American Enterprise Institute asked Treasury economist Eugene Steuerle to write a book chapter on the taxation of families. When he began writing it, Steuerle himself was surprised by how much tax exemptions for families had declined since the 1940s. His research showed that the value of the dependent exemption had plummeted by over 50% since 1948, meaning that the effects of inflation hit families with children hardest relative to other taxpayers (Steuerle 1983). The popular press, Congress, and the Reagan administration picked up his research (Pear 1983). One Reagan administration official wrote Steuerle: "had I not read your paper . . . I would have missed what became the core argument of the family initiative I urged on the president, and which he adopted—and there never would have been a presidential decision to double the personal exemption" (Steuerle 1991: 123–124). The significance of Steuerle's report cannot be underestimated. Much as the Beveridge Report had done for the issue of family allowances, the Steuerle report acted as a benchmark event in the US. Not only did it reinforce the salience of tax relief as a political issue (so much so, as I will show in chapter 6, that Steuerle would later find himself constrained by his own earlier report), it reoriented two major coalitions that would play central roles in the politics of fiscalization in the 1990s. Liberal child poverty advocates and conservative profamily groups all converged around Steuerle's finding, citing it approvingly again and again before Congress and the public.

Prior to the publication of Steuerle's report, those concerned with child poverty had paid little or no attention to tax policy. If they did, they were pushing for higher taxes on upper-income earners to pay for social programs for the poor. When it was clear that new spending proposals would go nowhere under Reagan, fiscalization became more attractive. Led primarily by Robert Greenstein of the Center on Budget and Policy Priorities and Representative Charlie Rangel (D-NY), chair of the House Ways and Means Committee, a number of groups began to bring attention to the role of tax policy in poverty relief (Primus 1989). Beginning in 1984, Congress held an unprecedented number of hearings highlighting the growing tax burden on families below and near poverty (US House 1984; US House 1985a; US House 1985b; House 1985c; House 1985d; House 1987; House 1989; US Senate 1985). In each and every one of these hearings, advocates pointed to inflation-induced erosion of the dependent exemption and the EITC and to rising payroll taxes as the source of the problem. The issue gave liberal policymakers a new voice in tax debates, allowing them to become just as fervently pro–tax relief as their opponents.

The burgeoning profamily movement picked up on it as well. In a series of hearings leading up to the 1986 tax reforms, Family Research Council president Gerald Regier began connecting declining exemptions with a number of family issues, telling the Committee on Ways and Means: "greater economic pressure caused by this increased tax burden may very well be the cause of many national problems—including divorce, crime, drug abuse, child abuse and runaway children" (US House 1985c: 106; US House 1985d). Later that year, the White House Working Group on the Family (1986) released a report citing Steuerle's research as justification for further tax relief in order to restore the full value of the dependent exemption to its 1948 level. The report, dubbed the Bauer Report, was named for Gary Bauer, who eventually went on to lead the Family Research Council in the 1990s. Bauer, along with representatives of the Christian Coalition, would continue to cite Steuerle's research in their CTC advocacy.

President Reagan, who was ideologically opposed to taxes in general, put Steuerle in charge of the Treasury group tasked with coming up with a proposal for what would become the 1986 tax reforms. A strategic alliance between profamily conservatives and antipoverty liberals pushed Congress and the Reagan administration to include a doubling of the dependent exemption in the 1986 tax reform legislation (Brownlee and Steuerle 2004: 169–170). The Treasury report, which served as the template for the Tax Reform Act of 1986, reflected the policy changes advocated by both liberal and conservative groups. The broad consensus was that tax relief for lower-income families could be achieved through a combination of increasing the dependent exemption and expanding the EITC. Policymakers liked the EITC, in particular, because it concentrated benefits narrowly at the lower end of the income distribution, making the entire tax bill more progressive. Despite little interest from labor or business groups, these changes were passed as part of the Tax Reform Act of 1986. As Ventry (2000: 1002) argues, "the 1986 law reaffirmed the program's mandate as a tax offset for low-income families, and upheld Senator Long's 1972 desire to 'prevent the taxing of people onto the welfare rolls.'"

Policymakers were able to expand the EITC even under the retrenchment-hungry Reagan administration. Had the EITC been a traditional in-work subsidy like the FIS, it likely would not have been expanded in 1986. Defending the decision to exclude the working poor from Aid to Families with Dependent Children in 1981, David Stockman told reporters: "we just don't accept the assumption that the Federal Government has the responsibility to supplement the income of the working poor" (Pierson 1994: 126). Instead, it was framed as an offset against recent increases in payroll taxes. As such, the EITC fit perfectly with the Tax Reform Act of 1986. Rhetorically, it allowed the administration to target tax relief, rather than increased welfare spending, to working-class families—a key target population of competition for votes. This was especially important in the wake of the 1981 budget, which was widely criticized as too regressive. The inclusion of an EITC expansion helped make the overall budget progressive (Howard 1997: 145–149). Technically, the EITC had the advantage of being scored partially as tax reduction in order to conform to new deficit reduction budget rules (Ventry 2000).

According to Reagan, tax relief was poverty relief. Before signing the bill, Reagan remarked that "millions of working poor will be dropped from the tax rolls altogether, and families will get a long-overdue break with lower rates and an almost doubled personal exemption." He went so far as to call the 1986 tax reforms the "best antipoverty bill" to ever come out of Congress (Rimer 1995). Reagan's expansion of the EITC contrasts nicely with Nixon's earlier failed Family Assistance Plan. Whereas Nixon was accused of intending to increase the welfare rolls because the Family Assistance Plan proposed to expand Aid to Families with Dependent Children, Reagan could claim credit for taking people off the tax rolls through the expansion of the EITC and the dependent exemption. Only some of the EITC and none of the dependent exemption showed up in the budget as spending.

Rather than merely assuaging the desires of the various advocacy groups involved, the 1986 reforms encouraged them to push for more by demonstrating the power of family tax policy as a political winner. Whereas in the UK popular demands for tax relief eventually subsided after the Thatcher government included income tax cuts in their early budgets, the US demand for tax relief remained strong throughout the 1980s and into the 1990s. As continued economic pressure on families were traced to the tax system, the bipartisan solution remained tax relief for taxpayers.

Discussion

While treating chronic inflation and budget deficits as the proximate causes of the shift toward fiscalization, the evidence shows that the specific reactions of policymakers were intimately tied to the policy legacies available in each country. Policymakers in Canada and the UK diagnostically framed economic pressures on families as the result of the eroding value of family allowances. The solution, according to the logic of income supplementation, was to increase the value of child benefits to provide relief to all families with children. Whether this was done through fiscalization, as was the case in Canada with the introduction of the RCTC, or through traditional spending measures, as was the case in the UK with the Child Benefit and the FIS/Family Credit, policymakers built on the historical legacy of family allowances and interpreted their actions according to the logic of income supplementation. In the US, the absence of family allowances left policymakers with little choice but to trace the economic pressures on families to the tax system. Following the logic of tax relief, they built on the tax exemption for dependents. Rising payroll taxes led to the introduction of the EITC as a sort of dependent exemption for payroll taxes, while the eroding value of the dependent exemption itself led to its eventual expansion and indexation. In these cases, US policymakers interpreted their actions according to the logic of tax relief. This resulted in relief for a much more narrow subset of families with children.

This interpretation of the events of the 1970s and 1980s differs from alternative arguments that put conservative ideas (Blyth 2002) or resurgent conservative and business movements (Block 2009; Mirowski, and Plehwe 2009; Phillips-Fein 2009) at the center of their stories. Given the weight these approaches attribute to the antitax and antistate ideas and attitudes of these groups, it is worth discussing why neither can explain this period as well as my approach, which puts policy legacies at the center of the story.

Ideational-centered approaches argue that many of the broad shifts in policymaking we have seen since the 1970s can be traced to the popularity of conservative ideas among the public or political elites in the wake of the oil crisis. Blyth (2002) also argues that the crisis of inflation was open to interpretation. It is not that the right ideas won out but that the right people holding these ideas were in the right place at the right time. According to Blyth, ideas can be powerful because they provide certainty in uncertain times. Monetarism, for example, won the day in the US not because it was technically correct but because it was politically useful, in that it provided policymakers with a blueprint for action in times of uncertainty. One problem with this framework is that ideas can be "taken off the shelf" and used at will, making it hard to explain why some ideas won over others across countries (Prasad 2006). The same criticism applies to the cases of pocketbook politics in the US, UK, and Canada. While it is true that inflation created uncertainty in tax and social security policy, and that interpretation of the source of economic pressure on families was open to some interpretation by policymakers, it was policy legacies, not the ideas being pushed by business groups, that determined whether the pressures were traced to rising taxes burdens or eroding child benefits. The UK is a case in point. Although the election of Thatcher is often taken as evidence of the power of antitax ideas, child benefits were largely insulated from this backlash. Children, not taxpayers, were perceived as the most relevant target populations.

Similarly, approaches focusing on partisanship and the power of business groups (Block 2009; Mirowski and Plehwe 2009; Phillips-Fein 2009) have trouble explaining variation across countries. The antitax movement in the US is usually taken as a case in point, but a deeper evaluation of the historical record demonstrates that it was actually more moderate and liberal members of Congress who led the way on tax relief. Moderate and liberal Democrats, under the banner of tax relief, pushed the introduction and expansion of the EITC. As Prasad (2006) reveals, Reagan's 1981 income tax cuts came at the cost of business tax cuts. Business groups also opposed indexing for the same reasons. Shortly after the election, Reagan's transition team dropped indexing entirely from the platform in order to make room for deprecation allowances for tangible property. Indexing was only restored at the behest of Congress as a popular political issue (Brownlee and Steuerle 2004: 159). Indexation started with Republicans in the US but did not succeed until Democrats bought into it as a way to protect families from inflation. Far more than tax cuts, indexation was inadvertently responsible for "starving the beast" by reducing revenues. By 1990, indexation cost $180 billion in lost revenues annually, compared to only $80 billion for the 1981 tax cuts (Brownlee 1996: 101). The beast was starved as a way to lessen pressures on poor and middle-class families, not as an ideological attack. In Canada and the UK, it was left-leaning governments that introduced indexation in both cases. The shift toward fiscalization also began under Canada's Liberal government, with Conservatives simply continuing on the same exact path. Whether governments were dominated by the logic of income supplementation or tax relief, there was no sign of discontinuity between left-leaning governments in the 1970s and right-leaning governments in the 1980s.

Looking Ahead to the 1990s

The histories of the US, the UK, and Canada seem to be irrevocably intertwined. The same waves of reform periodically crash down on the shores of each country. In the 1930s, each country began to build a fledging welfare state. In the 1960s, each waged a "war on poverty." Like clockwork, policymakers in all three countries turned their attention to a new reform project in the 1990s. Spurred by both international and domestic events, child poverty became a major issue across the English-speaking world. Policymakers wrestled with how to best help low-income families battered by the social, economic, and political shifts that had begun two decades earlier. Moving in the same direction, the US continued on a parallel trajectory.

Fiscalization, which began in the 1970s, intensified and came to an apex as the US and the UK followed Canada in adopting a CTC. Similarly, Canada and the UK followed the US lead in adopting in-work tax credits. By mid-2000, the shift to fiscalization in family policy was complete. At the same time, the story of cross-national convergence on child and in-work tax credits in response to the issue of child poverty conceals important differences.

The next three chapters demonstrate the power of the logic of income supplementation to shape British and Canadian efforts to tackle child poverty using tax credits while, counterintuitively in many ways, taxpayers triumphed over poor children in the American effort to assist low-income families. Distinct logics of appropriateness, institutionalized in the 1940s and reinforced in the 1970s, determined whether policymakers decided that families needed income supplementation or tax relief.

4

Canada

TAKING CHILDREN OFF WELFARE

BECAUSE OF THEIR similarities, there is a long and fruitful tradition of analyzing Canada alongside the US in comparative research (Eidlin 2015; Leman 1980; Lipset 1990; Maioni 1998; Myles and Pierson 1997; Smith 2008). Nowhere is this truer than for the process of fiscalization in the 1990s. The reform efforts that led to convergence of child and in-work tax credits in the US and Canada were mirror images of each other. In addition to similar political cultures, Poor Law traditions, and renewed emphasis on child poverty and welfare reform, both countries saw the same exact confluence of political actors—specifically, an alliance of profamily conservatives and left-leaning think tanks—push for CTCs. The two countries' many similarities limit the factors that might potentially explain why they structured their tax credits so differently, thus providing the strongest test of my "logics of appropriateness" explanation. In addition, unexpected changes in the classification of child and in-work tax credits in the early 2000s offer insight into how the perception of tax credits as "revenues not collected" might influence whether certain policymakers see refundability as more or less politically attractive.

This chapter begins with an examination of the consolidation of various child-related benefits into the CTB in 1992 and then the Canada CTB in 1997 and concludes with an account of the nonrefundable CTC in the mid-2000s. For in-work tax credits, it examines the introduction of the WITB in 2007. As I will show, Canada follows the same trajectory as the US and the UK but differs notably from the former in terms of the logic of appropriateness used to decide who exactly was deserving of tax credits in each case. Like the US and UK, Canadian policymakers were driven by a desire to tackle child poverty. In contrast to the US efforts, both conservative and liberal policy could and did tap into an institutional legacy of income supplementation when shaping the country's tax credits. Policymakers still had to be careful not to expand "welfare" in their pursuit to help children. The logic of income supplementation provided policymakers with a way to "take children off welfare" by expanding the CTB.

In much the same way that the EITC in the US and the WFTC in the UK were part and parcel of larger shifts toward welfare reform, the CTB was also seen as part of a reform program aimed at encouraging welfare recipients to move into paid employment. Contra some accounts that argue being prowork necessitates distinctions in policy separating the welfare poor and the working poor (Bertram 2015; Steensland 2008), the Canadian case demonstrates that policymakers can craft prowork policies providing benefits to children regardless of their parents' employment status.

At the same time, the subsequent introduction of the new nonrefundable CTC and refundable WITB under the Conservative government of Stephen Harper, suggest that existing policy legacies remain available as a springboard for alternative logics. In this case, the Harper government easily designed a new CTC according to the logic of tax relief. Contributing to this shift was a decision by the auditor general of Canada to reclassify refundable tax credits as expenditures, while nonrefundable tax credits remained classified as revenues not collected.

"We Have to Put an End to Child Poverty"

As I showed in the previous chapter, policymakers became increasingly concerned about economic pressures on families beginning in the 1970s. By 1990, this concern shifted to an emphasis on child poverty in particular (Paterson, Levasseur, and Teplova 2004: 131–132; Wiegers 2002). The shift was an unexpected result of a speech in the House of Commons by outgoing New Democratic Party leader Ed Broadbent in 1989. In November 1989, the United Nations General Assembly adopted the Convention on the Rights of the Child, which Canada eventually ratified. Several days later, Broadband gave an impassioned speech on what he saw as troubling trends in Canadian child poverty. Not only was the child poverty rate higher in 1989 than it had been in 1973 but Canada's high poverty rate was second only to that of the US among industrialized countries.

Broadbent told his colleagues: "I am convinced that this will only become an issue in this country of ours when premiers from coast to coast and when the Prime Minister of Canada say, 'We have to put an end to child poverty'" (Canada. House of Commons Debates, 29 November 1989: 6176); he went on to introduce a motion in the House of Commons to "achieve the goal of eliminating poverty among Canadian children by the year 2000." The resolution passed unanimously with the support of all three of Canada's major parties. The debates that preceded the vote indicate that there was little consensus on how to achieve such a lofty goal, though. Some MPs mentioned increasing child benefits, but others spoke about raising the minimum wage, subsidized childcare, and early childhood education. The Senate subsequently released an interim report outlining the scope and depth of the problem but offered little in the way of recommendations (Canada Senate 1989).

The child poverty resolution soon took on a life as of its own as it was reinforced by a series of events over the next two years. In 1990, Prime Minister Mulroney cochaired the World Summit for Children in New York City. Instead of improving his image as child-friendly policymaker, the summit embarrassed Mulroney and the country by repeatedly highlighting the fact that Canada had one of the highest child poverty rates in the industrialized world (Guest 1999: 239–242). A national symposium on children in Ottawa in connection with the UN Convention on the Rights of Children the next year kept up the pressure on the Mulroney government to take action.

Activist groups began to capitalize on the issue as well. Taking their name from the 1989 resolution, activists formed Campaign 2000 in 1991 in order to garner support for a movement against child poverty. Members of that group viewed the focus on child poverty as "the most effective way to capture public attention in a short period of time." Ken Battle, who later played an instrumental role in the introduction of the CTB, admitted that child poverty was used as a "hook to talk about poverty generally" and as a "deliberate tactic to keep the heat on poverty" (quoted in Wiegers 2002: 19). The Child Poverty Action Group, formed in 1985, had long recognized the advantages of focusing specifically on child poverty: "The founding members of CPAG deliberately chose a child-centered advocacy strategy in an attempt to bring public awareness to the poverty being experienced by Canadian families. The identification of poor children allowed for a construction of the chronic social problem of poverty, which would hopefully resonate with the public and create support for more extensive and responsive policies than traditional anti-poverty arguments. The focus on children seeks to avoid the dichotomy of the 'deserving' and 'undeserving' poor, which has been part of social policy debates. Children cannot be seen to be responsible for their poverty" (quoted in Wiegers 2002). The Progressive Conservative government, under pressure from these groups and from within its own ranks, began to take action that same year. Subcommittees in both the House of Commons and the Senate each set up a series of hearings in 1990 leading to the release of comprehensive reports the following year. Each report represented the views of major actors involved in later policy reforms meant to tackle child poverty. In the House of Commons, the Standing Committee on Health and Welfare, Social Affairs, Seniors and the Status of Women was dominated by Progressive Conservative MPs. Barbara Greene, a member of the Progressive Conservative government's so-called Family Caucus, chaired the committee. In the unelected Senate, the Standing Senate Committee on Social Affairs, Science and Technology was still dominated by Liberal MPs. The committee's chair, Liberal MP Lorna Marsden, worked closely with Ken Battle of the new left-leaning Caledon Institute. Despite glaring differences in the political orientation of each committee, both diagnosed the problem of child poverty in similar ways and proffered a similar set of policy recommendations. Several themes emerged, including (1) the erosion of child benefits, (2) the need to ensure that reforms did not discourage work, and (3) the categorical distinction between welfare and child benefits.

The Erosion of Child Benefits

The rampant inflation of the 1970s and 1980s was still fresh in the minds of policymakers as they struggled to identify the source of the relatively recent rise in child poverty. Just as they had traced the increasing economic pressures on families to the erosion of child benefits in the 1970s, policymakers similarly traced the rise in child poverty to more recent changes in child benefits that had led to their erosion by inflation. The House report remarked on the consensus among those who testified: "most witnesses, in their appearance before the Sub-Committee, noted some manner in which they felt child benefits had been eroded by recent policies of the federal government" (Canada House of Commons 1991: 44). The Senate report included a technical report by Ken Battle tracing this erosion to the government's decision to partially deindex family allowances and the RCTC in 1986.

Battle called it "social policy by stealth." In chapter 4, I identified it as a strategy of policy drift. In much the same way that left-leaning governments in the US and UK allowed inflation to quietly increase revenues by eroding tax exemptions, the Progressive Conservative government allowed inflation to quietly decrease spending by eroding child benefits. In 1986, the government changed the indexation formula so it would only adjust benefits for inflation over 3% as a deficit reduction measure. Benefits would increase if inflation was particularly high, but their value could still erode by up to 3%, even in a low inflation environment. Battle estimated that this change removed $3.5 billion from the child benefit system between 1986 and 1991. "The antipoverty/income supplementation role of child benefits," he warned, "will weaken steadily over time, unless something is done to stem their erosion from inflation" (Canada Senate 1991: 101). Insofar as public policy was seen as one of the sources of child poverty, it continued to be traced to the child benefit system rather than to heavy tax burdens.

Ensuring Prowork Reforms

The second theme was a concern that the current mix of social programs had the effect of discouraging welfare recipients from moving into paid employment. Though the issue was typically associated with work-obsessed conservatives, it was left-leaning antipoverty advocates who raised it most often in Canada. The problem, as they saw it, was that the steep phaseout rate or "clawback" on social assistance benefits created implicit marginal tax rates of up to 90% in extreme cases. Parents who decided to move from welfare to work might find themselves no better off as the additional of wage income was offset by reductions in government benefits. In fact, the additional costs associated with work (transportation, clothing, etc.) might mean that they were worse off if they decided to work. Critics called this the "welfare trap" or "welfare wall" (Canada House of Commons 1991: 42; Canada Senate 1991: 25).

This was nothing especially new in Canada. Part of the original impetus for family allowances, after all, was to ensure that working families were as well off as families collecting unemployment benefits. The problem was that while child benefits were under federal jurisdiction, social assistance and other income support programs were set and administered by the provinces. Sometimes the federal government and provincial governments worked together to ensure that these distinct systems worked in sync, but there was an increasing perception that families were facing an increasingly complex and inefficient system that unwittingly penalized full-time work for those who most wanted and needed it.

Reinforcing Categorical Distinctions

Finally, the report reinforced the categorical distinctions between welfare programs and child benefits. The House of Commons (1991: 67) report, for example, discussed the "social assistance system" as distinct from the "tax-transfer system" for families. Clear logics of appropriateness governed how policymakers approached each, with welfare designated exclusively for income support and child benefits for income supplementation. As was the case in earlier periods, the existing RCTC was seen exclusively as providing income supplementation rather than tax relief, even by conservative policymakers on the committees.

It was the income support/income supplementation distinction that proved most important in the case of Canada, which was not exempt from the global trend toward workfare (Evans 1992). The increasing participation of women in the workforce also shifted expectations for single mothers on welfare, who were gradually coming to be perceived as employable. Women on welfare had always been subject to some stigma (Little 1998), but their perceived employability made it seem more like a choice now. New scrutiny led to new stigmatization. Within a few years, welfare recipients would become the target of conservative retrenchment efforts. On the other hand the children of welfare recipients were seen as perennially deserving of benefits. This created what Weaver (2000) calls a dual-clientele trap. How could policymakers separate their treatment of possibly undeserving parents from their deserving children? The child benefit system offered a creative alternative that satisfied the concerns of conservative profamily and liberal antipoverty advocates. The solution was to "take children off welfare" by shifting funding from social assistance to child benefits. The idea first took hold in Ontario.

In 1986, the Liberal-New Democratic Party coalition government in Ontario had created the Social Assistance Review Commission in order to examine the entire system of social assistance and make recommendations for reform. Two years later, the commission released *Transitions* (1988), a comprehensive report that fundamentally shaped welfare reform and child benefits in the 1990s. Among its authors' other concerns was their worry that the stigma attached to welfare adversely affected children at school. Earlier studies had found that the children of social assistance beneficiaries had more academic and psychological issues than similar children from low-income families not on social assistance. "It is reasonable to assume," they concluded, "that part of the explanation may lie in the continuing stigma of 'being on welfare,' which attaches also to children." They went on to recommend a "radical restructuring of the existing system of child benefits" in order to "remove children from the social assistance system entirely by using another program to meet their income needs" (Ontario Social Assistance Review Committee 1988: 115). This began a popular movement to "take children off welfare."

Echoing the 1988 *Transitions*, both committees emphasized "taking children off welfare" by increasing child benefits rather than social assistance—recommending funds from the latter be directed to the former. Doing so would "remove children from the social assistance rolls" and avoid the stigma attached to being on welfare (Canada Senate 1991: 29). The House of Commons report also assumed categorical distinctions between child benefits and welfare benefits, even though they often went to the same families.

The themes that emerged from these parliamentary hearings and reports were important not only because they guided subsequent policymaking processes but also because of what they tell us about the cultural legacies of public policies. First, policymakers continued to see the erosion of family allowances as a source of economic pressure on families—applying it specifically to child poverty now. For this reason, the logic of income supplementation for families—not tax relief—dominated the policymaking rationale. As I will show, this occurred even under a conservative government. Policy legacies, not the abstract ideology of conservative actors, determined whether the goal was income supplementation or tax relief in the 1990s.

Second, and relatedly, we also see an emergent trend toward "workfare" or general concerns with work incentives in social policy reform. This trend has been extensively documented elsewhere and has been assumed to be the reason for the popularity of in-work tax credits, such as the EITC in the US and the WFTC in the UK (Bertram 2015; Steensland 2008). The argument is that these tax credits were attractive precisely because they make categorical distinctions between the working poor and the welfare poor. As I will show, categorical distinctions separating welfare benefits from other family benefits are not necessarily predicated on making categorical distinctions between the families themselves. Canadians were determined to "take children off welfare" by shifting the source of children's cash benefits rather than by forcing their parents off social assistance and into paid employment. The presence of a third logic of appropriateness (income supplementation) meant that refundability, which was equated with welfare in the US, was seen as an alternative to the logic of income support rather than as being synonymous with it.

The Politics of the Child Tax Benefit

The Progressive Conservative government had made few changes to the country's system of child benefits since it had introduced a surtax on family allowances for upper-income families in 1989. By 1991, the federal government was providing $4.5 billion in combined child benefits through the family allowance, the RCTC, and the nonrefundable CTC. This created a maze of benefits each with different eligibility requirements. In the wake of the parliamentary child poverty reports, the DNHW issued its own report calling for child benefit reform as "a step toward focusing social policy and income security measures on families with the greatest need, while simplifying our system of family and child benefits" (Canada Department of National Health and Welfare 1992: 42). Like previous reports, it made a distinction between social assistance and child benefits. Finance Minister Donald Mazankowski touched on the same themes in the government's 1992 budget speech, in which he outlined broad goals for child benefit reform. In his speech, Mazankowski spoke of the need to help "families with children" rather than taxpayers with children (Canada. Commons Debates 1992: 7601). Tax relief was a major theme elsewhere in the speech, but it was totally unrelated to child benefit reform.

There was broad consensus on the need to rationalize and perhaps consolidate the different programs but little agreement on how exactly this should be done. Most antipoverty groups, welfare rights groups, and the New Democratic Party continued to push for a return to universalism but had since bought into the idea of "targeting within universalism" as a way to progressively target benefits toward the poorest families. These groups had little power because Canada's parliamentary system though. They had few, if any, veto points from which they could shape any reforms to the child benefit system. Instead, the entire process was shaped by a coalition of socially conservative profamily groups and economic conservatives in the Finance Department. This coalition was very similar to the US coalition that pushed for a nonrefundable CTC, skewing benefits away from the poor rather than toward them—the exact opposite of what we find in Canada. How do we explain the different results despite similar coalitions of advocates?

The key difference was not that Canadian conservatives were less conservative, nor was the Canadian public more prowelfare. Instead, we can attribute continued divergence to differences in the cultural legacies of public policies in each country. The historical absence of family allowances and the concomitant logic of income supplementation in the US meant that beneficiaries fell into one of two categories—either you were a taxpayer appropriately receiving tax relief, or you were a welfare recipient appropriately receiving income support. Family allowances offered a third option for Canadians. Children did not have to fit into either the taxpayer or welfare recipient categories—they could be seen as distinct beneficiaries in and of themselves. The policy legacy of family allowances provided a springboard from which children could make claims on the government. This was the "symbolic bridge" that policymakers could build on and that enabled them to target benefits at the poorest children (Myles and Pierson 1997). This is most clear when we examine Canadian profamily groups, who held otherwise similar socially conservative views on a range of issues, including animosity toward welfare under the belief that it undermined family life.

Smith (2008) argues that Canadian political institutions, relative to American institutions, are less conducive to profamily activism, but evidence suggests that the Progressive Conservative government under Mulroney was the exception to this general rule. It was during this period that the Family Caucus gained power within the broader Progressive Conservative caucus. The Family Caucus identifies itself as profamily in the social conservative sense and as a "defender of Christian values" (Erwin 1993: 416). According to journalist Geoffrey York (1992), "the family committee can trace its origins to a Tory caucus meeting in the spring of 1989, when [Progressive Conservative MP Al] Johnson gave a rousing speech about the Canadian tax system and its alleged biases against married couples. After his speech, he found himself surrounded by Tory MPs who agreed with his concerns about the weakening of the traditional family unit." Like their American counterparts, the Family Caucus had the initial worry that what they saw as marriage penalties in the tax system encouraged single parenthood and cohabitation over traditional marriage (Ries 1992). Despite tracing its original grievances to the tax system, the caucus saw its orientation as decidedly profamily rather than antitax when it came to child benefits. By 1992, Family Caucus members made up about 20% of the entire Progressive Conservative caucus, with several members in key cabinet and committee positions (York 1992). This clout was enough for them to successfully push the government to remove tax advantages for unmarried common-law couples. They then turned their sights on child benefits.

Fortunately, one of their members was MP Barbara Greene, who had chaired the Senate committee that had published the 1991 report *Child Poverty*. Greene and other Family Caucus members used the renewed focus on child poverty to push for reforms to the child benefit system. "We'd like to see a guaranteed annual income for children to take them out of poverty," she told reporters; "we want them off welfare. You would remove a lot of the disincentives to work. As a person earns money, they would not have their benefits disappear to the same degree." MP Al Johnson, the informal leader of the caucus, similarly agreed that the focus needed to be on targeting benefits to poor children: "we've got to get it visible and focused on the child. It's an issue that has very broad support in our caucus" (York 1991c). *Child Poverty* had recommended a consolidation of the three child benefit programs, as had been expected. The Senate committee had seen the proposal as profamily, prowork, and antiwelfare but not antitax. Family Caucus members followed up with strong pressure on Mulroney and Mazankowski to follow through on the recommendations (York 1991b).

Family Caucus members saw these child benefit reforms as a way to strengthen the traditional family because they offered economic stability, helping prevent family breakdown (unlike social assistance, which they saw as contributing to family breakdown). They also viewed child benefits as an alternative to the childcare proposals floating around the DNHW at the time. Such proposals disfavored mothers who chose to stay at home with their children. Family Caucus members saw this as an unwarranted intrusion into family life (Hale 2002: 242). Unlike childcare subsidies, an increase in child benefits would go to mothers whether or not they worked. "The new child benefit," Johnson said, "is a tiny step toward the goal of giving women a greater opportunity to stay at home with their children" (York 1992). Despite the same antichildcare, antiwelfare bona fides, this approach stands in stark contrast to that of the US profamily groups who, using the work of Eugene Steuerle on the erosion of the tax exemption for dependents, focused exclusively on taxpayers with children.

The Family Caucus was able to form a coalition with the Finance Department under Mazankowski, who had replaced Wilson in 1991. Proposals to consolidate all three child benefits into one program would help rationalize the system and bring it all under the control of the Department of Finance if it was introduced as a tax credit. This would give Mazankowski more control over child benefits, so he could adjust them based on the fiscal situation. The government continued to struggle with keeping the budget under control as the deficit persistently grew. Whereas the Family Caucus opposed childcare proposals on moral grounds, Mazankowski opposed them on economic grounds. The government simply could not afford a new social program that could grow beyond his control (Hale 2002: 242). A CTC program would have the important advantage of reducing spending on the books. The cost-conscious federal government could, as previous governments had done, categorize an expanded CTC as "revenues not collected" rather than spending (Battle 1999: 1221). The Department of Finance announced that it would be consolidating the family allowance and both CTCs into the CTB in the 1992 budget.

The proposal was introduced in Bill C-80 as a tax measure to amend the Income Tax Act, but Mazankowski and the Family Caucus did not want it framed as a fiscal measure (Phillips 1999: 219–220). It was to be part of the government's effort to fight child poverty. For this reason, it was left to DNHW minister Benoît Bouchard, who had not previously been consulted on the proposal, to lead the public debate on the CTB as a social security measure (Blake 2009: 269). In February 1992, the DNHW released a child benefit white paper outlining the proposal for the new CTB. The white paper traced the idea for a consolidated child benefit back to welfare groups' emphasis on child poverty and the recommendations of House and Senate committee reports on child poverty.

The importance of the cultural legacy of family allowances became clear when Bouchard introduced the legislative proposal before the House of Commons. He began by extensively quoting excerpts from the 1944 speech by Prime Minister King in which he first proposed family allowances. Bouchard then traced their evolution to the 1978 decision to shift funds to the RCTC. In doing so, he framed the changes as the inevitable evolution of family allowances adapting to the circumstances of the day. The new CTB was simply another step in this long evolutionary process (Canada. House of Commons Debates, 25 February 1992: 7636–7637). As such, the rhetoric around the proposal was completely child-centered rather than being framed as tax relief. The new CTB would increase benefits, target them more toward poorer families, and consolidate fragmented programs. The total cost of child benefits increased from $4.5 billion under the old system to $4.9 billion under the new one (Canada Department of National Health and Welfare 1992).

The government held a series of hearings on the CTB proposal in the House of Commons over the next several months. Although critics correctly pointed out that these hearings were mere formalities and unlikely to change the government's handling of the reforms, they offer a glimpse of stakeholders' motives, as hearings are the place where the "reasoning behind particular policy proposals is made most explicit" (Guetzkow 2010: 179). Throughout the hearings, there was no talk of taxpayers or tax relief. The CTB was perceived wholly as income supplementation for low-income families. Critics focused on two issues they saw as major shortcomings of the reform. The first was the government's continued insistence on only partially indexing the new CTB, so that it automatically increased to account for inflation rates above 3%. Ken Battle called this the "Achilles heel" of the proposal (Canada House of Commons 1992: 2–10). The government, still concerned with growing deficits, largely ignored these criticisms. Instead, they promised to raise benefits as the fiscal situation allowed it but objected to indexation tying their hands. This ensured that child benefits would remain a prominent issue for years to come.

Second, critics pounced on what they saw as a conservative attempt to stigmatize the welfare poor by adding a special Working Income Supplement (WIS) for working poor families that was unavailable to families receiving social assistance. Part of the CTB, the WIS was an additional $500 credit for working families earning at least $3,750 per year. One official representing the Canadian Labour Council captured the sentiment of most left-leaning antipoverty advocates when he accused the government of making an "offensive distinction between children in families whose parents work and those whose parents do not have a job" (Canada House of Commons 1992, 6: 62). Almost all the other critics who testified echoed this concern. There is no doubt that the WIS had the *effect* of making distinctions between those in work and those on welfare. The question remains whether this was part and parcel of the larger trend toward workfare premised on Poor Law policy legacies, as analysts of the US changes (Bertram 2015; Steensland 2008) and contemporary Canadian critics have argued.

Evidence from the same hearings conclusively shows that this is not the case. The introduction of the WIS as part of the CTB was indeed a measure intended to help families move from welfare into work. There was a consensus among policy experts, discussed in the child poverty reports, that the structure of social assistance and child benefits created a "welfare trap" or "welfare wall" that prevented families on welfare from moving into paid employment, as was their preference. Progressive Conservative policymakers saw the WIS as the best technical solution available to address this problem. Mazankowski took on the accusations of making deserving/undeserving distinctions head-on in his testimony: "In our minds there's no question of distinguishing between deserving and undeserving families. Rather, it is a question of directing limited extra resources to where they will have the greatest effect in assisting lower-income families. The extra expenses, lost social assistance benefits, and other challenges facing low-income parents who seek to enter or re-enter the workforce have long been identified as a pressing problem. The parliamentary committee on child poverty has recently emphasized this problem. The earned income supplement of $500 payable to low-income families with earnings of $3,750 provides a novel and substantial response to this problem" (Canada House of Commons 1992, 1: 21–22). MP Johnson of the Family Caucus was similarly taken aback by the accusations, countering them each and every time they were brought up by witnesses. He was particularly upset by the accusation suggesting that the government was portraying those on welfare as lazy:

> one comment was made in the presentation that the federal government was somehow insinuating that people did not want to work by providing this benefit. I did not understand that from the white paper at all. I felt it was an indication that the basic problem under the welfare system is we have marginal tax rates of 100% or more if people go to work. We are trying to alleviate that problem. I saw no suggestion that people did not want to work. In fact people do want to work, but under the present situation it is virtually absurd in some cases for them to go to work. The assistance was needed to help in that area. (6: 12)

When he was confronted with the same accusations from a university professor at a later hearing, he responded in the same manner:

> I listened to your comments about the motives or imputed motives of people worrying about the implication of deserving poor versus non-deserving poor and so on, because of working or not working. I would comment as far as what I know about the development of this bill that those ideas were not part of the development.... As I see it, this $500 is simply, as you say, $40 a month. It pays for things like bus fare and things like that. It is not a case of whether they are deserving or not. It is a reimbursement of what are assumed to be real costs of change the status from work to non-working. There was not this imputation of deserving or not deserving in people's minds that I know of. It may be there but I don't see it there. As many witnesses have said here, and I agree profoundly, almost everybody wants to work. There is no such thing as people being undeserving because they are unemployed or on welfare. People want jobs if there is any possibility to get them. The big problem I see we have in the welfare system, the CAP [Canada Assistance Program] program—and I have mentioned it a couple of times—is this barrier that we have of 100% or more than 100% tax when people want to get off welfare or off unemployment insurance. They can't just take a job because they are on welfare or unemployment insurance and it is reduced 100% or more than 100%. The issue is to find a way to assist people in moving across that line. It is not a question of whether they are deserving or not deserving. (7: 27–28)

The Progressive Conservative government could not make it any clearer. The WIS component was in no way meant to convey symbolic boundaries between the welfare poor and the working poor. If that was the case, then what prevented the government from pursuing their goal of "taking children off welfare" by redirecting social assistance benefits to an enlarged CTB, as was recommended by several reports?

Comments from Johnson during the hearings point to difficulty coordinating changes with the provinces. Child tax credits were under the complete jurisdiction of the federal government, where a parliamentary system left no veto points for the Progressive Conservative government. Social assistance on the other hand was partially funded by the federal government and administered by the various provinces. Redirecting funds from social assistance to the CTB risked upsetting provincial leaders, who had a de facto veto over any policy change in this area. Johnson told one witness: "we didn't go into the welfare side of the thing right now because of the constitutional negotiations and the problem of having to renegotiate" with the provinces (Canada House of Commons 1992, 5: 15). He explicitly told representatives of the Canadian Labour Council: "oh, we would [give more to the poorest families through the CTB] if I had my way, but this is the problem with jurisdiction" (6: 98). Johnson's frank talk strongly suggests that state structures, rather than cultural legacies, explain the Progressive Conservative decision to introduce the WIS within the CTB. Subsequent changes reinforce this conclusion. Foreshadowing changes to come, Battle said to MPs that the "only solution I know to that dilemma is a combined federal-provincial child benefit" (2–18). Battle and the left-leaning Caledon Institute continued to play a key role in the evolution of the CTB in 1998.

With a strong majority in Parliament and broad public support, the Progressive Conservative government passed Bill C-80 by the end of the year, and the CTB took effect in 1993. The introduction of the CTB replaced the forty-seven-year-old universal family allowance program with an income-tested tax credit. In converting the remainder of the family allowance into a tax credit, the government was also able to shave $2.2 billion off the spending side of the budget. The deficit-weary Department of Finance proudly announced that it was able to constrain program's spending to 0.9% in 1993–1994 through "restraint measures" as well as the "restructuring of the child benefit system." Unlike family allowances, the new CTB, the Department said, "represents a reduction in income taxes that would otherwise be payable and is set off against personal income tax revenues rather than being included as part of program spending" (Canada Department of Finance 1993: 66).

The full fiscalization of child benefits was complete. The popularity of the new CTB could not save the Progressive Conservatives in the 1993 election, though. A recession, combined, ironically, with an antitax backlash against the government's introduction of an unpopular federal VAT, led to the decimation of the Progressive Conservative Party in the election and the beginning of thirteen years of federal rule by Liberal governments. The steady march of fiscalization continued unabated under the Liberals.

Expanding the Child Tax Benefit

The introduction of CTB marked a shift in focus on child poverty but no increased benefits for families on social assistance, which meant that policymakers had yet to make progress on their goal of "taking children off welfare." This, along with the issue of child poverty in general, remained a primary goal of policymakers throughout the 1990s. Despite the change in political parties, there was little change in strategy between the outgoing Progressive Conservative government and the incoming Liberal government of Prime Minister Jean Chrétien. Like Mulroney before him, Chrétien was constrained by a stubborn deficit. Rivals in the cabinet, representing the old-guard left wing of the party and the new "Third Way" approach, would determine the direction of policy change.

Lloyd Axworthy, who was appointed as minister of the new Department of Human Resource Development, represented the old guard.[1] Shortly after taking office, he was given the green light to establish the Social Security Review, in consultation with the provinces. Axworthy's rival was Finance Minister Paul Martin. Like previous finance ministers, Martin was more concerned with whittling away at the deficit before undertaking any comprehensive reforms to Canada's social security system.

The launch of the Social Security Review made it seem like Axworthy would be taking the lead in the cabinet. Subsequent events quickly made clear that the power actually lay in the Department of Finance. Martin himself had also begun undertaking a budget review of all spending when he became finance minister. With the support of Chrétien, Martin was able to undercut Axworthy in one swipe with the announcement of the 1994 budget. That budget put reducing the deficit at its center (Canada Department of Finance 1994). Axworthy already knew that any proposed reforms would be constrained by the Finance Department's reluctance to allow new spending programs, but the 1994 budget went beyond this. It was widely expected that Canada's federal unemployment insurance program would be reformed at a substantial cost savings to the government. Instead of freeing up funds for other social spending priorities, Martin dedicated most of it to balancing the budget. The next budget went one step further and introduced substantial spending cuts in transfers to the provinces, which administered most of Canada's social programs (Battle and Torjman 1995: 7).

The Liberal government pursued new austerity measures with a vigor that would have made conservatives blush. Pressure from interest rate hikes in the US and a peso crisis in Mexico gave new urgency to the need to bring down the deficit (Greenspon and Wilson-Smith 1996: 160, 235–236). Echoing President Clinton's assertion that the era of big government was over, Martin announced in his budget speech: "Canadians have told us that they want the deficit brought down by reducing government spending, not by raising taxes, and we agree. The era of tax and spend government is gone" (Canada. Commons Debates 1994: 1704). He went on to promise $5 in spending cuts for every $1 the government raised in revenues. The rationale was influenced by what had recently happened in Sweden, whose government had primarily used tax increases to deal with their deficit. The subsequent drop in the kronor and an increase in interest rates scared Canadian policymakers. According to Martin, "what Sweden was important for was that the markets would not give you credit for tax actions. A year earlier, the markets didn't seem to care how you reduced your deficit. Sweden demonstrated the market had evolved" (Greenspon and Wilson-Smith 1996: 255–256). The need to cut spending made the CTB even more politically attractive to the Liberal government.

Axworthy proceeded with the Social Security Review anyway but without any resources to offer provinces for shared programs and no additional funding for the programs fully under federal jurisdiction. The review process was plagued by endless conflicts between the federal MPs of different parties and between the federal representatives and their provincial counterparts. The Department of Human Resource Development was supposed to release two reports but was dismantled before it could release the second one (Greenspon and Wilson-Smith 1996: 137–152; Rice and Prince 2004: 116–117). There was a wide consensus that the review was a total failure insofar as it led to no direct policy reforms. The review was important insofar as it continued to keep the discussion on reforming the CTB alive though. The first report brought attention to the "welfare wall" faced by social assistance beneficiaries as well as the concept of "taking kids off welfare" by expanding the CTB or some other provincial program (Canada Department of Human Resource Development 1994).

The failure of the federally led Social Security Review did not stop the provinces from acting on their own, independently of the Department of Human Resource Development. Later the same year, the provinces (with the exception of Quebec) formed the Ministerial Council on Social Policy Reform and Renewal in order to devise a unified provincial strategy for dealing with the federal government's draconian cuts in intergovernmental transfers. One of the areas that received focused attention was the continued demand for some sort of integrated federal-provincial child benefit to build on the federal CTB. The provincial report noted that "forty per cent of all social assistance beneficiaries in Canada are children" and went on to recommend a "possible consolidation of income support for children into a single national program, jointly managed by both orders of government, with options for either federal or provincial/territorial delivery of benefits" (Ministerial Council on Social Policy Reform and Renewal 1996: 14).

While the Ministerial Council provided the initial impetus for federal action on an integrated child benefit, British Columbia provided a concrete model. In 1996, the province introduced the Family Bonus for low-income families with children. The Family Bonus was an income-tested provincial benefit of up to $1,236 per child delivered by Revenue Canada on behalf of the province. The amount was equal to what had previously been provided per child on social assistance, which was reduced when the Family Bonus was introduced. Unlike social assistance benefits, the full Family Bonus went to all families with incomes lower than $18,000 and then gradually phased out thereafter (Battle 1999: 1231). In essence, British Columbia succeeded in taking children off welfare. These events led to the formation of a federal-provincial working group for further exploration of the idea of creating an integrated provincial-federal child benefit.

In the working group, Saskatchewan premier Roy Romanow pushed the idea hard and found a positive reception with new Department of Human Resource Development minister Pierre Pettigrew. Prime Minister Chrétien also endorsed the concept at the First Ministers Conference that summer (Greenspon 1996). Support for the initiative was based on two rationales, both of which would be fulfilled by an integrated tax benefit. The first was policymakers' concern with the "welfare wall" faced by social assistance beneficiaries as they moved from welfare to work. The second was continued concern with child poverty among the public.

The increased emphasis on moving social assistance beneficiaries back to work brought increased attention to the problem of "welfare walls" or traps within the welfare system. Reports from the Department of Finance (1994), the Ontario Social Assistance Review Commission (1988), the Department of Human Resource Development (1994), and the National Council of Welfare (1993) all recognized that taking a job could actually result in less income for social assistance beneficiaries because benefits were withdrawn at a prohibitively high rate as one's income from wages increased. In much the same way that President Clinton sought to "make work pay" in the US, policymakers in Canada sought to "break down the welfare wall" (Battle and Torjman 1993).

Ken Battle, the former head of the National Council of Welfare and then director of the Caledon Institute, had a hand in almost all of the reports discussing the welfare wall (Hale 2002: 242–243). In a political system not very conducive to policy entrepreneurs (especially from outside think tanks), Battle was able to work his way into the inner circles of government in order to press for action on the welfare wall issue. By the summer of 1996, he had been appointed a senior advisor in the Department of Human Resource Development. According to Battle (2003: 15), "in that capacity, I wrote the basic document making the case for the National Child Benefit; the paper was circulated, probably also outside Ottawa. I would characterize Caledon's work at this point as (small p) political work, as I functioned as a temporary pseudo-official/political aide in an informal coalition of line department and central agency officials working to bring the National Child Benefit idea to life." Battle went on to become one of the few non–civil servants ever to make a presentation before the prime minister's cabinet. With new support from the provinces, he could push for shifting social assistance funds into an integrated CTB to replace the WIS as a supplement the CTB.

The issue of child poverty also bolstered support for the proposal. Pettigrew spoke frequently about fighting child poverty, considering it a major priority. Prime Minister Chrétien also saw it as an advantageous political issue ahead of the 1997 elections. The public continued to see child poverty as an important issue as well, but their support depended on how policymakers sought to tackle it. Social assistance and those who received it were highly unpopular. In anticipation of the 1995 provincial election in Ontario, the Progressive Conservatives released an election pamphlet under the banner of the "Common Sense Revolution." Much like the US Republicans' "Contract with America," the pamphlet was highly critical of welfare programs, promising to slash "Cadillac" welfare benefits by 20% and eliminate fraud and abuse in the system (Progressive Conservative Party of Ontario 1995). It helped the Progressive Conservatives win the election, and they soon followed through on their promise. Most other provinces followed suit in cutting benefits and introducing harsh new workfare requirements (Little 1998). The antiwelfare backlash hit Canada just as hard as it did the US.

Federal policymakers were well aware of this fact and used extensive public opinion polling to craft their strategy for tackling child poverty. It was important for the government to be perceived as increasing benefits for children rather than for welfare. This fit in nicely with the strategy of taking children off welfare. As one pollster bluntly put it, "you present it by talking about child poverty and not talking about giving more money to people on welfare." Another Liberal communications strategist told reporters: "we are talking about poor kids, not just poor people." One influential focus group found that the public reacted negatively to talk of the welfare poor, single mothers, and handouts. They reacted very positively on the other hand to talk of children, the working poor, and tax credits (Greenspon 1997b, 1997c).

British Columbia's Family Bonus model solved both of these problems. By extending benefits to families making upward of $18,000 per year, it ensured that a single mother on welfare would keep at least some of the family's benefits, lowering the welfare wall, as she moved from welfare to work. It also enabled policymakers to increase benefits for the poorest children without necessarily increasing "handouts" for "single mothers" or the "welfare poor." In fact, it had the added effect of "taking children off welfare" by subtracting the Family Bonus from the mother's social assistance check. Instead, benefits would only be increased for the "working poor" through the use of "tax credits." This eliminated the dual-clientele trap that plagued efforts to help children through social assistance.

In their platform for the 1997 election, the Liberals argued that these changes would "remove children from the welfare system entirely, significantly reduce the depth of child poverty, reward low-income families for working, and go a long way towards eliminating the 'welfare wall'" faced by poor families: "Over time, the new enriched Canada Child Tax Benefit will gradually replace provincial welfare benefits for children" (Liberal Party of Canada 1997: 60).

One potential obstacle remained. Despite the consensus among provincial leaders, Pettigrew, Chrétien, and the public, the proposal did not have the blessing of Finance Minister Martin, who remained silent on it throughout this time. Still wary of the budget deficit, Martin did not want to make any promises for new spending that could hamper the progress they were making on balancing the budget. A sudden change in luck finally brought Martin on board. Falling interest rates and an improved economic outlook meant that Martin was going to reach his goal of balancing the budget a full year earlier than expected (Little 1997). Under these conditions, Martin's earlier retrenchment strategy was finally beginning to pay fiscal dividends. The Liberal government promised that any surplus would go toward a "down payment" toward fighting child poverty by increasing the CTB.

Pettigrew met with his provincial counterparts in January 1997 to discuss concrete proposals for what would become the National Child Benefit. The group quickly came to the consensus that a benefit similar to British Columbia's Family Bonus was the best policy. The proposal that emerged was that the federal government would replace the WIS with a National Child Benefit that went to all low-income families regardless of work status (Greenspon 1997a). The provinces would then be able to subtract this amount from their social assistance payments if they chose, as long as they "reinvested" it in other provincial services directed at poor children (i.e., childcare, school lunches, wage supplements, etc.). The only aspect left open to discussion was the price tag. The fiscally conservative Liberal government considered $300 million to be a safe "down payment," which would be increased as the fiscal outlook improved, while the cash-starved provinces asked for a $1.2 billion down payment. The Department of Finance initially agreed to contribute $600 million, which was subsequently raised to $850 million under pressure from an impending election.

In February 1997, the Finance Department released a budget paper announcing that the Canada CTB would replace the current CTB in 1998 (see Figure 4.1). The CCTB was made up of two different tax benefits. The first was a base benefit of $1,020 per child for families earning up to $25,921 per year, which then phased out gradually until it reached a family income of $66,700. This base benefit was supplemented by the $605 National Child Benefit for families earning up to $20,921, which then phased out gradually until it reached an income of $25,921.

The Liberal government passed the changes into law by the end of the year and began paying out the Canada CTB in 1998. Like the previous child benefit, the Canada CTB was not indexed to inflation to allow the federal government room to adjust it based on the fiscal situation, but the government's "down payment" was accompanied by promises to increase the benefit until it totally displaced the children's portion of social assistance. As the fiscal situation improved, with the federal government recording budget surpluses for the first time in decades, the Liberals made upward adjustments accordingly.

Finally, the increase in the Canada CTB, along with other federal and provincial tax credits, allowed the government to claim that it was successful in its goal of "taking children off welfare." In 1989, social

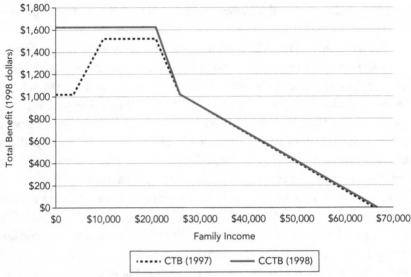

FIGURE 4.1 CTB/Canada CTB for parent with one child.

Source: National Council of Welfare. (1997). Child Benefits: A Small Step Forward. Ottawa: National Council of Welfare.

assistance accounted for 86.2% of total income for a single parent with one child receiving welfare in Ontario. By 1999, this dropped to 78.7%, and to 63% by 2009. Some of this is a result of absolute cuts in social assistance, but much of it is a shift of income from welfare to various federal and provincial tax credits. The total amount of benefits as a percentage of Canada's low-income cutoff, a measure of poverty, dipped down in the 1990s before rising back above its 1980s average (see table 4.1).

The Canada CTB continued to grow even after the victory of the newly reborn Conservative Party under Harper in 2006. The Canada CTB's success, relative to social assistance, stems from its symbolic distinction

Table 4.1 Changes in social assistance and benefit income in Canada, 1989–2009

Year	Social assistance as % of total benefit income (Ontario)	Total benefit income as % of low-income cutoff
1989	86.2	68.5
1999	78.7	60.3
2009	63.0	77.5

Source: Author's calculations from National Council of Welfare, 1989, 1999, 2009.

as a program specifically for children separate from stigmatizing "welfare." The Canada CTB/National Child Benefit was everything to everyone: prowork, anti–child poverty, antiwelfare, and antispending all in one. Its general growth overall stems from the tax credit's classification as revenues not collected. Even as both Progressive Conservative and Liberal governments sought to cut other popular spending programs in order to reduce the deficit, the Canada CTB/National Child Benefit never became a target, because shrinking it would only be seen as raising taxes rather than constraining spending. Though the Canada CTB's classification advantage was successful in the 1990s, it underwent significant changes around 2005. This had a profound impact on the trajectory of refundable tax credits in Canada. For the first time, nonrefundable and in-work tax credits became more politically attractive to policymakers and ushered in a shift to the logic of tax relief.

Fiscal Dividends and Tax Relief

By the end of the 1990s, decades of austerity under both Progressive Conservative and Liberal governments finally brought Canada its first balanced budget since 1974. Policymakers and the public began to talk about "fiscal dividends" as lower debt payments led to budget surpluses by 1999. The Liberal government won reelection in 1997 by promising to split the benefits of the fiscal dividend fifty-fifty between increased funding for social programs and tax relief. Public demand soon shifted decisively toward tax relief.

As part of their earlier austerity strategy, the Liberal government deindexed personal income taxes, raising revenues through bracket creep, and introduced income tax surcharges. As a result, tax burdens rose faster than incomes throughout the 1990s and led to stagnating incomes for many middle-class Canadians. With an election planned for 2000, the Liberal government tapped into latent public demand to make middle-class tax relief a major issue. A tax bidding war ensued, with three of the four major parties proposing at least $100 billion in tax relief (Hale 2002: 264, 281–282). The Liberals retained power and enacted major tax relief measures in their 2000 budget. In his budget speech, Finance Minister Martin told Parliament: "while tax reduction must benefit all Canadians, it must primarily benefit those who need it the most: middle and low income earners, especially families with children" (Canada. Commons Debates 2000: 4105). Children and families remained central, but a new identification of the source of pressure on them led to a shift to the logic of tax relief. The budget restored full indexation of the tax system, increased personal exemptions, and cut tax rates on the middle class.

The government also included changes to the Canada CTB. In addition to increasing the maximum benefit to adjust for inflation, they extended the income threshold at which the Canada CTB begins to phase out from $25,921 to $35,000 and cut the phaseout rate in half (Canada Department of Finance 2000). In doing so, they ensured that the majority of increased benefits would go to working- and middle-class families with children. By including these changes in a broader package of tax relief, policymakers were drawing on multiple logics of appropriateness to justify it. While official documents referred to other tax changes explicitly as tax relief, the Canada CTB changes were kept at arm's length. In isolation, policymakers discussed the Canada CTB as a child benefit that should be allocated according to the logic of income supplementation. At the same time, they recognized that its categorization as "revenues not collected" made it politically advantageous to aggregate it together with other tax measures in order to maximize the total amount of tax relief perceived. Total personal income tax relief from indexation, exemption increases, and rate cuts over four years amounted to $13.3 billion but jumped to $16.1 billion when the Canada CTB was included.

Even as the Liberal government took advantage of the Canada CTB's classification, first to constrain spending in the face of deficits and then to accede to demands for tax relief, issues lurked behind the scenes. As early as 1992, the independent auditor general of Canada began to take issue with the classification of the RCTC and then the CTB as "revenues not collected" rather than as expenditures. Other issues took priority over the next several years, but the auditor general returned to it beginning in 1999 (Auditor General of Canada 1999). Further reports charged that the accounting practice of netting the CTB against income tax revenues was "inappropriate" and "obscures the true size of government revenues and expenditure" (Auditor General of Canada 2000: 14) The government, much to the chagrin of the auditor general's office, resisted even visiting the idea of any changes until 2004. That year the Treasury Board Secretariat put together a working group of interested stakeholders, including the auditor general (Canada Department of Finance 2005: 334–335). As expected, the working group recommended, among other things, that the Canada CTB be reclassified as spending in government accounts in accordance with professional accounting standards.

An election in early 2006 ousted the Liberal government and replaced it with a Conservative government under the leadership of Stephen Harper. Under Harper's leadership, the Conservatives began running on a platform centered on tax relief. This platform helped them win ninety-nine seats in the 2004 election. Harper continued to campaign on an antitax platform, making a promise to cut the hated goods and services tax, a central part of his 2006 election campaign. It paid off. The Conservatives increased their share of seats and were able to form a minority government with Harper as prime minister and Jim Flaherty at finance minister (McCabe and Major 2014).

In contrast to the previous government, the Conservatives adopted the auditor general's recommended accounting standards immediately in their first budget. The reclassification fundamentally altered the Conservatives' approach to the use of tax expenditures. With the Canada CTB reclassified as spending, it no longer fit into a conservative agenda as it had under the Mulroney government. Finance Minister Flaherty's 2006 and 2007 budgets embodied the continued public demand for tax relief: "This government believes that Canadians pay too much tax. It believes they should have greater opportunity to reap the rewards of joining the workforce and, once in the labour market, to keep more of their hard-earned tax dollars, so that they can invest in the things that matter most to them and their families" (Canada Department of Finance 2006: 64). It is important to recognize that the emphasis on tax relief did not represent a move to the right by the Conservative Party of Canada. The antiwelfare, profamily, prowork themes that ran through earlier policy changes remained important to the Conservative government. The concern for tax relief was a reaction to earlier Liberal campaign promises for it. Even in opposition, the Liberals sought to attack the Conservative government as not going far enough with their tax relief proposals. The problem, in the words of one Liberal MP, was that they were "small potatoes" relative to the Liberals' own proposals (Canada. Commons Debates 2007: 2628). Both parties simply changed their views on the sources of economic pressure on families. Families had sacrificed through austerity, and it was time for them to reap fiscal dividends through tax relief.

Flaherty made this explicit in his 2007 budget speech, in which he tied the introduction of two new tax credits to lower debt levels. He told the House of Commons: "lower debt will mean lower interest payments which will mean lower taxes . . . . There were many personal tax relief options we could have pursued in this budget. We made a choice. We chose to support hardworking families . . . . For personal income tax relief, we chose to focus on helping families" (Canada. Commons Debates 2007: 7621). Rather than further enriching the Canada CTB, the government introduced two entirely new tax credits: the WITB and a distinct *nonrefundable* CTC.

The WITB had actually been initially proposed as part of the previous Liberal government's 2005 minibudget, which the Liberals had failed to pass before the 2006 election. It was a refundable tax credit modeled after the US EITC and Quebec's Work Premium. Its purpose was to further lower the welfare wall for social assistance beneficiaries with or without children. Like the EITC, policymakers framed it as helping "make work pay," in order to help people overcome the "welfare wall" and move into paid employment (Canada Department of Finance 2007; Good 2013). The WITB, which had been framed as a work subsidy in earlier Liberal proposals, was now framed as tax relief under the Conservatives. Although refundable, the WITB was technically classified as "revenues not collected" under the new standards. Moreover, by limiting it to the working poor, the government could credibly claim that it was only going to taxpayers.

The budget also proposed a new nonrefundable CTC worth $310. The new CTC would overlap, but exist separately from, the existing refundable Canada CTB. Unlike the Canada CTB, which was governed by the logic of income supplementation, the new CTC was wholly governed by the logic of tax relief. This enabled the government to justify excluding the lowest-income families with children (parents making less than $19,000 received nothing), on account of the fact that they paid no federal income taxes and therefore were not "taxpayers" deserving of tax relief, while benefiting many middle- and upper-income families who were excluded from the full benefits of the income-tested Canada CTB. It is clear that the government could have achieved the same result by simply extending the Canada CTB further up the income distribution but instead chose to introduce a new separate tax credit. The key differences were that introducing a nonrefundable CTC, unlike expanding the Canada CTB, was perceived as tax relief and would not count as spending. The logic of tax relief emanated from Flaherty's discussion of the CTC: "the new child tax credit will benefit about 3 million taxpayers, taking up to 180,000 low-income Canadians off the tax rolls and providing more than 90 per cent of taxpaying families with the maximum benefit of $310 per child. Given the average number of children per family, the measure will provide tax relief of about $430 on average for those with incomes less than $37,000 and about $505 on average for those with incomes between $37,000 and $74,000" (Canada Department of Finance 2007: 227). The government touted the new CTC and WITB as accounting for $2 billion out of $9.7 billion in tax relief in the 2007 budget (139). Despite their status as a minority government, the Conservatives were able to pass the 2007 budget without issue. Both the New Democratic Party and the Liberal Party were opposed but abstained, for fear of going on record as opposing popular tax relief. This strategy allowed policymakers to target tax credits at "deserving" populations that appeared to cost nothing in terms of spending under the new accounting standards. As a result of this early success, the use of targeted nonrefundable tax credits has exploded under the Harper government (Sand and Taylor 2011), demonstrating the versatility of tax credits as the new social policy tool of choice and the power of classification schemes for shaping policy.

Discussion

At first glance, the early 1990s seems like an inauspicious time to undertake a campaign to tackle child poverty in Canada. A Conservative government held power at the federal level and had made deficit reduction through spending cuts a major priority. The election of a Liberal government had brought no hope, as their zeal for austerity was even deeper. Across the provinces, antiwelfare forces were pushing for reforms to social assistance programs that emphasized cutting benefits and pushing welfare recipients into work. Despite these obstacles, child poverty had declined, and spending on cash programs for families had increased by the end of the 2000s. How is this possible? Tax credits turned out to offer policymakers the solution to all of these problems, for two reasons.

The first was their unique classification as revenues not collected. In the case of Canada, it was tax credits' technical dimension (Carruthers and Espeland 1991) that proved most politically advantageous. The same nagging deficit that plagued policymakers in the 1980s continued to constrain their actions well into the 1990s. Austerity measures to close the deficit partly took the form of revenue increases (i.e., goods and services tax and deindexation), but the expectation was that spending restraint was the primary way to bring it under control. Unlike family allowances or social assistance, tax credits were not classified as spending. This made them politically attractive as a vehicle for family benefits.

The Progressive Conservative government was able to increase the total amount of cash benefits for families with children by converting family allowances (combined with existing child-related tax benefits) into the refundable CTB. This appeared as a $2.2 billion spending reduction in the budget. The subsequent Liberal government followed this strategy by repeatedly increasing the value of the CTB. The introduction of the National Child Benefit portion shifted funds out of provincial social assistance programs and into the newly expanded Canada CTB. In doing so, it removed social assistance spending from the budget as well. Fiscalization was a successful strategy for obfuscating the true costs of new spending on children in an environment hostile to any new spending initiatives.

Even as new public support for tax relief made the Canada CTB's logic of income supplementation less attractive, policymakers could still count Canada CTB expansions as revenues not collected. Though not seen as tax relief itself, these revenue losses were packaged as part of the aggregate value of larger tax relief measures elsewhere in the budget. The relatively obscure changes in the classification scheme after 2006 changed the political calculus for policymakers in unexpected ways. By moving the Canada CTB back to the spending side of the budget ledger, the reclassification made expansion even less attractive to the new government. The Conservatives gave up on Canada CTB expansion altogether in favor of introducing a new nonrefundable CTC.

The nonrefundable CTC, along with the new WITB, also highlights the political advantage of tax credits' rhetorical dimension. The Conservative government was still able to narrowly channel cash benefits to families by providing tax relief via tax credits rather than broad-based reductions in tax rates. The WITB in particular, initially envisioned as a traditional in-work subsidy by the previous Liberal government, was reimagined as providing the rhetorical benefit of tax relief under the Conservatives. Together, the rhetorical and technical dimensions of tax credits explain much of their increasing use during this period.

Whereas classification explains the use of tax credits, it is the cultural legacy of public policies that explains their distribution relative to what I will describe in the US in chapter 6. Tax credits are unique, in that two distinct logics of appropriateness can apply to them. When viewed as relieving the tax burden on families and workers, the logic of tax relief seems most relevant. When viewed as benefits for children or low-income workers, the logic of income supplementation seems most relevant. As I have shown, in Canada each of these two logics was dominant at different times during this period. The dominant logic at any given time depended crucially on how cultural legacies interacted with contemporary political environments.

Unlike the US, which had only institutionalized logics of tax relief and income support, Canada, in addition to these two logics, had also institutionalized the logic of income supplementation through the introduction of family allowances. Although Canadian policymakers had access to multiple logics, they did not necessarily have the freedom to choose the one that best fits their ideological proclivities. Indeed, conservatives used the logic of income supplementation to introduce the refundable CTB and then used the logic of tax relief to introduce the WITB and the nonrefundable CTC.

The key factor explaining the difference was the perceived source of economic pressure on families at the time. In the 1990s, when concern for child poverty was strongest, the consensus among policymakers was that the erosion of child benefits due to partial deindexation was the primary source of economic pressure on families. If all families were suffering as a result, then it was logical to increase benefits for all families. In the 2000s, after years of austerity, the new consensus among policymakers was that rising taxes, due to partial deindexation of the tax system, was the more pressing source of economic pressure on families. In this case, only taxpaying families were suffering as a result, so it was logical to limit tax relief to taxpayers—even if it meant excluding the poorest children.

Looking ahead, it is worth noting the key similarities and differences that make Canada's trajectory distinct from the US's comparable one toward the use of child and in-work tax credits as favored social policy. As I mentioned at the beginning to this chapter, the Canadian case parallels the US case in that policymakers in both countries were motivated by the goal of tackling children poverty in a manner that was antiwelfare, prowork, and profamily. The constellation of critical players was, similarly, made up of conservative profamily groups and liberal antipoverty groups pushing for tax credits. The threat of deficits loomed large in both cases. The crucial difference was the historical absence of a legacy of family allowances in the US. As I will show, this prevented US policymakers from tapping into the logic of income supplementation to advocate for fully refundable tax credits.

The Canadian approach to welfare reform is most informative here, in that it was really no different from what occurred in the US. In both countries, public opinion was decidedly in favor of workfare-type reforms, and policymakers obliged (Bashevkin 2002: 169). The ability to tap into the logic of income supplementation gave Canadian policymakers a third option distinct from tax relief and, most important, income support. It was logically possible to "take children off welfare" by redirecting cash benefits through refundable tax credits, because they had always been seen as separate benefits with alternative logics of appropriateness. As I will show in chapter 6, the absence of the institutionalization of the logic of income supplementation meant that US policymakers could not offer benefits for children outside the framework that was limited by the logic of tax relief.

5

The United Kingdom

THE CHILDREN'S BUDGET

THE UK WAS the last of this book's three countries to shift to fiscalization but did so quickly and fully in a short four-year period. This chapter examines the introduction of the WFTC in 1999 and its subsequent split into the refundable WTC and the CTC in 2003, all under the "New Labour" government of Prime Minister Tony Blair and Chancellor of the Exchequer Gordon Brown. Why did fiscalization finally emerge during this period and why did the British follow Canada in using refundable tax credits that extended benefits to the poorest families with children?

First, the shift to fiscalization occurred much later because, as Myles and Pierson (1997) and Levy (1999) might predict, policymakers first turned to income-testing at the top. Thatcher's decision to shift to the more stable VAT as a revenue source lessened (but by no means eliminated) pressure for austerity. This is only half the story, though. When the Labour government reached the limits of this strategy in the late 1990s, the Treasury quietly turned to fiscalization as the solution for further expansion of the welfare state in the face of continued pressures for austerity. By converting the Family Credit, a traditional spending program, into the WFTC, a tax credit, the Labour government hoped to obfuscate the effects of this expansion in the budget. The limits of fiscalization as an obfuscation strategy to mask the true effects on the budget were soon tested, as the Office of National Statistics (ONS) called the government's reclassification into question. The ensuing battle shows what can happen when the technical dimension of tax credits as revenues not collected comes into conflict with its rhetorical dimension.

Second, much has been made of the close relationship between Blair and US President Clinton during this period, leading us to expect the UK to emulate the US reforms that took place several years earlier based on the logic of tax relief. While UK policymakers pursued the same goals of welfare reform and making work pay, they continued to do so according to the dominant logic of income supplementation that had been reinforced in the 1970s and 1980s. Although the government sometimes referred to the WFTC as a tax cut for families, in order to reinforce the rhetorical dimension of tax credits as revenues not collected, policymakers and the public clearly traced its policy legacy to the FIS, discussed in the previous chapter. Opponents of the change took issue with several aspects of the proposed WFTC, including the administrative burden on employers and the possible shift "from purse to wallet," but there was never any criticism that it was not true tax relief, as was the case in the US, as I will show in the next chapter. The logic of income supplementation was firmly institutionalized in the WFTC from day one.

The logic of income supplementation behind British tax credits became most clear after Prime Minister Blair made a very unexpected and very public pledge to end child poverty in 1998. Even when policymakers were initially proposing the introduction of nonrefundable tax credits (for the same classification purposes mentioned above), their rhetoric had been infused with the logic of income supplementation, not tax relief. Just as the WFTC traced its legacy to the FIS, the new nonrefundable Children's Tax Credit traced its legacy to the Child Benefit. In both cases, the government repeatedly stressed that the initial structure of these tax credits was only a short-term response to the problem of poverty traps and that they were working on reforming them as soon as possible so as to extend them to more families, including those on social assistance. Nonrefundability was a short-run reaction to classification issues, not a constraint imposed by the logic of tax relief.

In addition to bolstering chapter 4's findings on the role of family allowances in institutionalizing the logic of income supplementation, the UK case is important because it acts as a crucial test case for theories of the institutionalization of cultural categories. Some scholars have argued that the US's introduction of the EITC in 1974 institutionalized the working poor as a distinct target population, further entrenching Poor Law distinctions between the "deserving" working poor and the "undeserving" welfare poor (Bertram 2015; Steensland 2008).

Whereas Canada introduced its CTC before introducing its in-work tax credit, the UK followed the same sequence as the US in introducing the predecessor to its in-work tax credit before its CTC. Because the UK also introduced a wage subsidy for the working poor in 1970, the FIS, we might expect it to similarly institutionalize and entrench categorical distinctions based on work, with the WFTC for the working poor and workfare for the welfare poor.

The subsequent split of the WFTC (the successor to the FIS) into the re-fundable WTC and the CTC suggests that the effects of the cultural legacy of the Poor Law have been much more limited than many have assumed. Not only did the UK take a program ostensibly aimed at the working poor and extend it to the welfare poor, they did so by redirecting a portion of welfare benefits into the refundable CTC, introduced in 2003. Rather than being perceived as contamination through symbolic pollution, the CTC was perceived the same way it had been in Canada—as taking children off welfare. Instead, these changes were predicated on the ability of policymakers to tap into the logic of income supplementation stemming from the UK's legacy of family allowances decades earlier.

New Pressures, New Labour

Whereas policymakers in the US and Canada were constrained by concrete budget deficits, policymakers in the UK were constrained by the mere threat of deficits. For most of the post-1970s era, a series of Conservative governments controlled spending by shifting expenditures from universal to income-tested programs in a manner consistent with Myles's (1998) and Levy's (1999) argument that these programs were best suited for expansion in austere environments. While Conservatives thrived in this new environment, the Labour Party struggled. Labour's image as a tax-and-spend party wedded to universalism, which became increasingly untenable after the 1970s, was partly responsible for their seventeen-year exile from power. Under the leadership of Tony Blair, Labourites endeavored to shed their socialist image and rebrand themselves as the more fiscally moderate New Labour in the 1990s.

Under Blair's leadership, they were able to return to power in 1997 based on election promises that they would not raise taxes or increase spending beyond plans already set in place by the outgoing Conservative government (Connell 2011: 53). This simple election promise had major ramifications for the kinds of policy reforms the Labour government could enact. Much of the room they did have for spending increases was absorbed by perennially popular demands for increases in the health and education budgets. Taxing universal benefits to redistribute funds to lower-income beneficiaries ran counter to their efforts to avoid the perception that they were raising taxes. Further income-testing of Family Credit (the successor to the FIS), which already had a 70% withdrawal rate, would undermine efforts to encourage work, while expanding it and lowering the withdrawal rate would involve substantially increasing spending. The number of politically acceptable solutions looked severely limited.

The Treasury Department under Gordon Brown found a solution in fiscalization. In public, Brown earned the title "Iron Chancellor," for the tight control he kept over the public purse. In private, colleagues knew him as "Red Gordon" because of his preferences for increased redistribution to poor families. Officials at the Treasury spoke of "redistribution by stealth" via the tax system (Grice 1999). Did the election of the New Labour government in 1997 necessarily ensure that fiscalization would follow, though? Internal party divisions over the best approach to fight poverty might have remained strong enough to hamper early efforts to re-shape social policy. It was only because the Treasury Department took the lead that the opportunity for fiscalization developed.

The fault line was between an old guard wedded to traditional Beveridge plan principles and New Labour reformers looking to build a Beveridge plan "for the twenty first century" (Blair 1999). Both factions had the same goals of expanding the welfare state, initiating welfare reform, and tackling child poverty. Both saw the primary problem as stemming from barriers to work. Policy papers during this period were filled with discussions of "poverty traps" and "benefit traps" in the welfare system. The two factions differed fundamentally in their approaches to solving these issues and reaching these goals. These differences manifested themselves in a battle between Frank Field and Gordon Brown for control over the direction reforms.

As the former director of the Child Poverty Action Group in the 1970s, Frank Field had the professional bona fides to lead a new fight against child poverty. At the same time, his reputation as an advocate of welfare reform gave him leverage with moderates in the party. Aside from his position on welfare reform, he very much represented the old guard of the Labour Party. Field sought a "return to Beveridge" approach entailing a staunch opposition to further income-testing of social security benefits. Field voiced his opposition to the FIS in the 1970s and continued to voice opposition to any expansion of its successor, Family Credit. Instead, Field pushed for renewed emphasis on contributory social insurance programs (Connell 2011). Universal social insurance programs, he argued, did not discourage work, like income-tested programs, nor were they stigmatizing, because workers felt as if they had paid into the system to earn their benefits. Field was tapped to be minister of state for welfare reform after 1997 and given the green light to write a green paper on what many thought would be the blueprint for the new government (*Economist* 1998).

In contrast to the approach proposed by Field and officials at the Department of Social Security, Gordon Brown and officials at the Treasury Department saw the need to move away from Labour's traditional universalist principles. Like Blair, Brown was part of the New Labour movement, hoping to shed the party's tax-and-spend image. Field's vision would require increased taxation and spending at a time when there was immense pressure to constrain both. Brown believed in the need for *more* income-testing, or what he called "progressive universalism," as a way to keep taxes and spending low (*Economist* 1998; Waldfogel 2010).

What looked like a battle for the soul of the Labour Party ended up being something like a foregone conclusion. Events in 1994 shifted the power to Brown even before Labour formed a government in 1997. That year, it was expected that both Brown and Blair would run for party leadership. Since both men were "modernizers," there was a chance they would split the ticket and both lose. In what became known as the "Granita pact," they agreed that Blair would run for the leadership and Brown would be appointed chancellor and given control over economic and social policy in this capacity (Connell 2011: 94–95; Glennerster 2007: 225). Field's appointment as minister of welfare reform actually left him with very limited power in the government. Fiscalization did not simply hinge on this small contingency of internal party politics. The fact that both of the frontrunners were "modernizers" suggests that adaptation to the new austere environment had moved the party in this direction and that dispensing with Field was a perfunctory move more than anything. Blair never intended to empower Field.

Field first became aware of this during the cabinet meeting where the idea of using tax credits was originally brought up. As had been the case with a 1995 working group, Field quickly dismissed the idea as "unworkable" (Bochel and Defty 2007: 37). Little did he know that the Treasury Department was already developing plans to introduce both child and in-work tax credits. The Treasury Department had independently crafted and would eventually introduce these proposals without ever consulting Field or any officials at the Department of Social Security (Bower 2005: 234; Connell 2011: 153). Field became furious when he finally realized he was being sidelined from the reform process, resigned from his minister position in protest, and went on to attack Brown's proposals from the backbench (Waugh 1998). Field's resignation and Blair's continued support of Brown signaled the triumph of the Treasury Department over the Department of Social Security. Once firmly in control of the reform agenda, the Treasury Department set out an ambitious program for reform of the entire tax and benefit system.

The Late Turn to Fiscalization

The Labour government's full-fledged attack on child poverty had not yet been declared when they took office in 1997. Their initial agenda focused more broadly on undertaking reforms to "promote work incentives, reduce poverty and welfare dependency, and strengthen family and community life" (HM Treasury 1997: 36). This included workfare-style reforms to social assistance like the ones seen in the US and Canada. The government was also concerned with "unemployment traps" and "poverty traps" that made welfare more attractive than work for many low-income families. A number of reports showed that families on social assistance identified the sudden and steep loss of benefits as one of the major reasons they were not moving into paid employment. Families faced implicit marginal tax rates of over 50%, with some even reaching higher than 100% (HM Treasury 1997). Family Credit, the expanded and renamed successor to the FIS, was the perfect candidate for achieving the government's goals—but only if the government could reform it in a way that didn't increase total spending.

In May 1997, Brown asked Martin Taylor, chief executive of Barclays, to write a report on possible reform of the tax and benefit system. At Brown's request, Martin looked into replacing the Family Credit with the American EITC as the model. Unsurprisingly, Martin's report recommended expanding the Family Credit by lowering its withdrawal rate from 70% to 55%, as a way to reduce work disincentives and make it available to more working-class families. Furthermore, the report recommended converting the Family Credit, which was a traditional social security benefit administered by the Department of Social Security at the time, into a tax credit administered by Inland Revenue (HM Treasury 1998a). Martin's recommendation would become the proposal for the WFTC.

The official rationale for conversion into a tax credit was fourfold: (1) it would reduce the stigma associated with claiming in-work benefits; (2) it would be more politically acceptable to claimants and taxpayers; (3) administering it through paychecks would reinforce the rewards of work; and (4) it would reduce disincentives to work. However, there's reason to doubt that these public rationales took precedence over more private rationales within the Treasury Department. There's little evidence that stigma or public acceptance was limiting the Family Credit. In fact, a strong majority of the public supported increasing benefits for "parents who work on very low incomes" (Hills 2002: 554). The stigma, exemplified by the Family Credit's less than full take-up rate, really stemmed from the policy's complex structure (as is the case for the EITC and in-work benefits in general). There was little reason why the government could not have retained a reformed Family Credit with a lower withdrawal rate and shifted administration to employers.

The structure of the proposed WFTC was very similar to that of the Family Credit, which the government planned to replace. Broadly, the WFTC kept the same eligibility requirements in place; it was merely more generous than the FIS and encompassed more families. The maximum value of the benefit was increased, the threshold at which the benefit began to be withdrawn was extended, and the withdrawal rate was significantly reduced (Duncan and Greenaway 2004). These changes came with a heavy price tag. The cost of expanding the Family Credit to another 400,000 families raised the cost of the program from £3.5 billion to £5 billion (HM Treasury 1998b). Expanding it would mean increasing spending well beyond the bounds set earlier in the election promise to limit spending.

The ulterior motivation for converting the Family Credit into a tax credit was obfuscation. The WFTC was similar in almost all respects to the Family Credit, except that it would be classified as revenues not collected rather than as spending. By converting the Family Credit into the WFTC, the government could substantially expand the program while appearing to cut taxes and spending. Reflecting the rhetorical dimension of fiscalization, Brown announced the WFTC as a "tax cut for hundreds of thousands of working families on low income" in his 1998 budget speech (Brown 1998). Reflecting the WFTC's technical dimension, the Treasury Department "lopped some pounds 2.5bn off what is conventionally called 'welfare spending' yet was able to claim credit for more than doubling the amount of financial help the Government is offering families in low-paid work," according to one observer (Walker 1998).

Brown faced some pushback from senior officials in the Treasury Department, with some reportedly calling the reclassification "pure Orwellian Animal Farm" in character (Bower 2005: 234). The Conservative opposition pounced on it as redistribution by stealth, while the Liberal Democrats welcomed it. Business groups opposed the reform because they would be tasked with administering it in employees' paychecks. Their opposition had led Conservatives to nix similar plans to convert the Family Credit into a tax credit in 1988 (Coyle 1998). The Labour government ignored these criticisms and went ahead with their plans to introduce the WFTC anyway.

The change came with two targets in mind, one concerned with spending and the other with taxation. On the spending side, the government was constrained by the Bank of England. In order to meet its inflation targets for monetary policy, the Bank of England Monetary Policy Committee needed to ward off inflationary pressures from increased government spending. This meant that the government was limited in how much it could increase spending (*Independent* 1998). In classifying the WFTC as revenues not collected, the government hoped to leave more room for spending elsewhere in the budget without exceeding spending limits. On the revenue side, the government was constrained by election promises not to raise the overall level of taxation. By offsetting the WFTC against total tax revenues, the government could raise taxes elsewhere in the budget while leaving the overall tax level unchanged.

The Treasury Department, which was careful not to publish any data that might make it look like spending had risen, ran into problems when the ONS released figures classifying the WFTC as a traditional expenditure. Such a classification would push the Labour government well over their promised limit on spending. This led to a public dispute between Brown and the head of the ONS, Tim Holt, who refused to back down when questioned on the decision. Holt was eventually forced out, ostensibly for unrelated reasons, but not before damage was done (Bower 2005: 305). The Conservative opposition quickly seized on the ONS statistics and accused the Labour government using "fiddled figures." Shadow chancellor Francis Maude accused the government of raising taxes "by stealth" and breaking their "pre-election promise not to 'increase tax at all' " (Grice and Coyle 1999).

The Treasury Department responded by releasing its own figures showing the WFTC as offsetting taxes, and thus a decrease in taxes and spending as a proportion of GDP, since they took office (Schaefer 1999). In addition, the government subsequently introduced the Children's Tax Credit. As a nonrefundable tax credit, the Children's Tax Credit (discussed in more depth later in this chapter) was classified by the ONS as revenues not collected, but it redistributed less income to poor families (HM Treasury 1999b). The government was able to ride out criticism of the WFTC for several years in part because the multiplicity of measures obfuscated the real cost to stakeholders.

Eventually, increased pressure from the IMF about the budget's "lack of transparency" (Coyle 2000) and the opposition led the Treasury Department to address the classification issue. The Labour government, in an effort to blunt criticism about the WFTC's classification, as well as address issues with their administration, announced that they would be splitting the WFTC into two separate tax credits and replacing the Children's Tax Credit. The WTC was based on the US's EITC model, and the CTC was based on Canada's CTB model (UK Inland Revenue 2001). Both tax credits were refundable. The government announced in the 2002 budget that they would continue to count the tax credit as "negative taxation for the purposes of calculating net taxes and social security contributions, as used in the tax–GDP ratio," and that the ONS would classify the WTC and the CTC as "negative taxation to the extent that credits are less than or equal to the tax liability of the household, and as public expenditure where credits exceed the liability" (HM Treasury 2002a: 216). The change was a partial victory for the Labour government. Using the partial classification, almost 20% of the tax credits appeared as revenues not collected, substantially lowering the appearance of spending (Brewer et al. 2002: 533).

Both the rhetorical and technical dimensions of tax credits enabled the government to expand social benefits in an otherwise austere environment. By framing the tax credit as offsetting tax revenues broadly conceived, the government successfully used this rhetorical dimension to deflect criticism that they were raising taxes on the middle class. The technical dimension of the tax credits proved more complex, as is shown by the battle between the Treasury Department and the ONS. Initial statistics used by the Treasury Department were undermined by more "legitimate" statistics from the ONS. While the public had little idea about which set of numbers to trust, more interested stakeholders, such as the Bank of

England and the IMF, gave legitimacy to the ONS numbers. The government, forced to back away from their initial ambitious plans, nonetheless achieved a partial victory after reforming their programs to satisfy the number crunchers at the ONS.

Budget dynamics help us understand the shift to the use of child and in-work tax credits between 1999 and 2003, but we must look to the increasing attention to child poverty during this period to understand why the UK's tax credits ended up looking like those in Canada rather than the US.

The Pledge to End Child Poverty

As was the case in the US and Canada, child poverty became a major component of the reform agenda in the UK. There had been little discussion of child poverty under previous Conservative governments. Part of this paucity of discussion stemmed from the fact that the UK did not have an official poverty measure against which to gauge the problem. Statistics did exist and were in circulation, but the lack of an official measure meant that policymakers could use whichever measure they found best suited their agenda (Piachaud and Sutherland 2001: 97). When Labour took over in 1997, they officially adopted the relative poverty measure (50% of median income) used by the OECD and most European countries. Child poverty could officially be quantified.

When this measure was used, the findings shocked many Britons. Throughout the 1960s and 1970s, the child poverty rate had hovered around 10%. Beginning in the 1980s, it had climbed rapidly until it settled around 25% in the early 1990s. Statistics from the OECD showing the UK with one of the highest child poverty rates in Europe, and just below that of the US, added urgency to the matter (Waldfogel 2010: 24). A number of influential reports and the continued work of the Child Poverty Action Group nudged the issue onto the public's radar, but it was a major speech by Prime Minister Blair that put child poverty center stage. Standing in Toynbee Hall, a famous settlement house in east London, Blair spoke about the various social problems stemming from child poverty in March 1998. Most important, Blair (1999: 17) made a public, and very ambitious, commitment to end child poverty in the UK: "our plans will start by lifting 700,000 children out of poverty by the end of the Parliament. Poverty should not be a birthright. Being poor should not be a life sentence. We need to sow the seeds of ambition

in the young. Our historic aim will be for ours to be the first generation to end child poverty, and it will take a generation. It is a twenty
year mission but I believe it can be done." Blair had not consulted with
his cabinet before making the speech. The promise surprised many,
given the fiscal constraints the government faced. The speech, and the
poverty pledge in particular, received wide coverage in the newspapers
(Cross and Golding 1999). Blair could not backtrack even if he wanted
to. According to Waldfogel (2010: 1), "once the pledge was made, it took
on a life of its own." Luckily for Blair, it never became an issue, because he had the backing of Gordon Brown at the Treasury Department.
Brown, a devout Christian, considered child poverty to be a "scar on the
nation's soul" and fully supported the ambitious pledge (Piachaud and
Sutherland 2001: 96). This was crucial, as the tight budget constraints
gave the Treasury Department effective veto power over any new social
programs aimed at tackling poverty.

Unlike US policymakers, who would use the EITC and the tax exemption for dependents as springboards for tacking child poverty, British
policymakers used the Child Benefit and the Family Credit as their
springboards for action. As such, they built on the longstanding logic of
income supplementation that was institutionalized in these programs.
Policymakers perceived child poverty as stemming from the erosion or
stagnation of these income supplements. Insofar as this erosion was
traced to rising tax burdens at all, the government responded by lowering
national insurance contributions (payroll taxes) for the working class.
Little to no connection was made to the new tax credits. The WFTC and
CTC/WTC split that followed were governed wholly by the logic of income
supplementation. Reflecting this logic in his speech, Blair was specific
that the government's reforms would "help more than the poorest children. All parents need help. All children need support" (Blair 1999: 15). As
a result, broad-based benefits were increasingly targeted toward children
in the poorest families.

Public opinion polls and surveys of MPs showed consistently high
support for spending on child benefits and parents working at low
incomes, even while spending on the unemployed and single parents
remained low (Bochel and Defty 2007: 119; Hills 2002: 543; Taylor-Gooby
and Martin 2008: 237). This support remained high even when it came at
a cost to competing social groups, such as taxpayers. The focus on child
poverty led the government to first look to the country's family allowance
program, the Child Benefit. Stemming from the cultural legacy of family

allowances, there was broad consensus among policymakers of all parties that direct cash benefits for families with children were a legitimate mechanism for alleviating child poverty. Unlike policymakers in the US, UK policymakers assumed that giving more money to parents would result in poverty reduction among children (Waldfogel 2010: 64–65). Channeling new funds into the Child Benefit was not without its problems, though.

The last time the Child Benefit had seen an increase in real value was when it had been doubled between 1977 and 1979 as a response to inflation-induced erosion. Despite deindexation under Thatcher, the real value of the Child Benefit had hovered around £17 per week for the first child throughout the 1990s. The Labour Party made increasing it part of its platform in every election between 1979 and 1992, as part of a longstanding commitment to universal benefits. Just as the loss of the 1992 election had pushed reformers in the Labour Party to rethink welfare reform, it had also pushed them to rethink their commitment to universalism. The cost of principled commitment to universalism was much higher in the age of permanent austerity. The growth of the FIS/Family Credit under both Labour and Conservative governments made this apparent.

In contrast to Canada, the UK had resisted income-testing the Child Benefit up until this point. After 1992, concern was growing that universalism in child benefits was just becoming much too expensive to maintain (Wickham-Jones 2003: 30). Some members of the Labour Party began to look into the possibility of income-testing it. In March 1995, the Working Party on Social Justice considered taxing the Child Benefit for upper-income families but ultimately rejected the idea as too administratively problematic (Connell 2011: 38).

There was considerable public support for such a shift. A 1998 public opinion poll found that 52% of respondents thought that the Child Benefit should be lowered or withdrawn altogether for upper-income families (Hills 2002: 556). The issue for the Labour government was translating this support into concrete policy changes. Chancellor Brown continued to support taxing the Child Benefit, despite possible administrative issues, but faced opposition from within the party. The old guard clung to universalism on principle, while others, including Blair, worried that it would cost votes in "middle England" after early proposals for taxing the Child Benefit were leaked and received negative public attention (Grice 1999). Plans for an income-tested CTC emerged as part of what was dubbed the "children's budget."

The Children's Budget

In the "children's budget," the Treasury Department undertook a series of policy changes in 1999 and 2000 aimed at tackling child poverty. This agenda included increasing the Child Benefit and introducing the WFTC as well as a new Children's Tax Credit. The logic of income supplementation permeated all of these changes. Together, increases in the Child Benefit and the introduction of the WFTC and Children's Tax Credit amounted to £6 billion in new spending (or rather, revenues not collected for much of it) on children between 1998 and 2001. Tax credits took up the bulk of this (see Figure 5.1).

First, the Treasury Department increased the value of the Child Benefit by 20%, while leaving it untaxed, with the caveat that they would reexamine the possibility in the future. This was the largest increase since the 1970s (Greener and Cracknell 1998). Reflecting the logic of income supplementation, government framed the Child Benefit as the "fairest, most efficient and cost effective way that society can recognise the extra costs and responsibilities borne by all parents" (UK Home Office 1998). Higher spending for children proved popular, despite the austere environment in which the government found itself. Brown grudgingly went along with the continuation of universalism, knowing that this left less

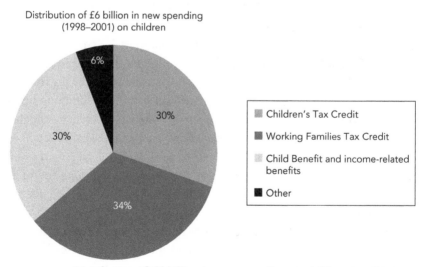

Distribution of £6 billion in new spending
(1998–2001) on children

- 6%
- 30%
- 30%
- 34%

- ▨ Children's Tax Credit
- ▧ Working Families Tax Credit
- ▧ Child Benefit and income-related benefits
- ■ Other

FIGURE 5.1 Distribution of £6 billion in new spending on children (1998–2001). *Source*: HM Treasury, *Supporting Children through the Tax and Benefit System*. The Modernization of Britain's Tax and Be nefit System 6. London: HM Treasury, 1999.

room for other spending priorities. Fiscalization would soon prove most advantageous here.

Second, as discussed above, the Treasury Department introduced the WFTC, as a replacement for the Family Credit, and a new nonrefundable children's tax credit. Because both tax credits initially excluded the poorest families, it is tempting to see them as reflecting the logic of tax relief or reinforcing Poor Law distinctions between the welfare poor and the working poor. Government documents make it clear that this is not the case. The perception of tax credits as revenues not collected partly pushed the government toward fiscalization, but we must still explain the WFTC's shifting distribution of benefits. Whereas the Treasury Department's rationale for the decision to convert the Family Credit into a tax credit was largely kept out of the public discussions, the rationale behind the reforms in general was laid out explicitly and very much debated in public. As Blair's historic speech makes clear, the government was driven by their promises to end child poverty in the UK. It was left to Brown at the Treasury Department to translate this goal into concrete policy proposals.

Following the logic of income supplementation, the government emphasized that the "tax and benefit system needs to support all children, recognising the extra costs and responsibilities that parents face, and the importance of children for the future of society" (HM Treasury 1999a: 39). Without explicitly admitting that the initial nonrefundable structure of these tax credits was part of a larger strategy of obfuscation, the Treasury Department assured the public that their "long-term goal is to create an integrated and seamless system of financial support for children" with a future refundable CTC that would "bring together the different strands of support for children in the Working Families' Tax Credit, in Income Support and in the Children's Tax Credit" and explicitly "building upon the foundation of universal Child Benefit." Eventually, the refundable CTC would make no distinctions based on taxpayer or worker status, as it would be "paid to families in and out of work, direct to the main carer, and complemented by an Employment Tax Credit paid through the wage packet to working households with and without children" (39). Rather than using the US CTC and EITC as models, the Treasury Department looked to Canada's CTB and Australia's family tax benefit as models for how to structure what would eventually become the CTC and the WTC.

Between 1997 and 2005, the government released a series of reports, *The Modernisation of Britain's Tax and Benefit System*, in which they laid out their plans for reaching these goals. The series provides us with a comprehensive overview of the Labour government's vision for the new tax credits as they evolved from the WFTC to the CTC and WTC. Of the eleven papers in the series, eight focus primarily on the Treasury Department's tax credit proposals. By examining these eight papers, we can map out the logics of appropriateness that policymakers had in mind as they crafted the new tax credits.

As a late fiscalizing country, it is possible that the UK could have followed either the logic of tax relief reforms of the US or the logic of income supplementation reforms of Canada. In order to uncover which was the dominant logic of appropriateness in the UK case, I coded these eight papers focusing on tax credit proposals for the relevant target population, as well as the goal.[1] Together, these eight papers give us a good picture of which logics of appropriateness dominated discussions of child and in-work tax credits. This coding was straightforward. The government discussed each proposal in very explicit terms, because neither population/goal suffered from any sort of stigma, unlike content analysis of welfare reform (e.g., Hancock 2004).

In regard to the target population, I searched for two alternative phrases ("children" and "taxpayer" or "taxpaying") to assess the salience of each cultural category. I excluded all references to "children" that were part of the phrase "children's tax credit" so as not to bias the results simply because of repeated reference to the proper name of the policy in question. In regard to reform goals, I searched for two additional phrases ("child poverty" and "tax relief" or "tax burden") to assess how these target populations might be connected to particular logics of appropriateness. The discourse behind the Labour government's agenda was overwhelmingly one of income supplementation. "Children" were mentioned 763 times, compared to 22 mentions of "taxpayers"—a 34.7-to-1 ratio (see table 5.1). "Child poverty" received 81 mentions, compared to 19 for "tax relief"—a 4.3-to-1 ratio. In simple quantitative terms, the Modernisation series clearly followed the logic of income supplementation.

In keeping Blair's pledge, the reforms were aimed at tackling child poverty via income supplementation. The government was most worried about the long-term increase in child poverty. Not only was it higher in the UK than in other European countries, it had also been rising faster than in other countries since the late 1970s. It was also noted that the UK had a much higher rate of lone-parent families, as well as "workless" households. Whereas in 1968 only 4% of children lived in households where their parent(s) did not work, this number had climbed to 20%

Table 5.1 The logics of appropriateness in The Modernisation of Britain's Tax and Benefit System

Target populations			
"Children"	"Taxpayer/ing"	Total	Ratio
763	22	785	34.7:1
Policy goals			
"Child poverty"	"Tax relief/burden"	Total	Ratio
81	19	100	4.3:1

Source: Author's calculations from HM Treasury, *The Modernisation of Britain's Tax and Benefit System*, nos. 1–11. London: HM Treasury, 1997–2005.

by 1998 (HM Treasury 1999a: 10). These particular circumstance led to a three-pronged strategy to (1) "ensure that parents have the help they need in finding work," (2) "ensure that tax and benefit policies support and reward work," and (3) "provide direct financial support to all families recognising the extra costs of children" (24).

The first goal was achieved through the "New Deal" welfare reforms, which were similar to workfare reforms undertaken in other countries. The WFTC was initially proposed as a part of a broader strategy to reach the second and third goals. Because policymakers saw a link between workless households and child poverty, it made sense for them to tackle child poverty by making work pay for parents. Like policymakers in Canada, they perceived the biggest obstacle as a series of employment traps and poverty traps that were built into the tax and benefit system. On the tax side, the Treasury Department created a new 10% rate tax bracket for low-income workers and continued to increase the progressivity of National Insurance Contributions, so that the lowest-income workers became exempt altogether.[2]

As discussed, the decision to convert the Family Credit into the WFTC was driven by Brown's desire to take spending off the books. Changes in the structure of the tax credit on the other hand were driven by desires to "reward work" as part of this three-pronged strategy. The WFTC did this by increasing the maximum possible benefit while decreasing the rate at which the benefit was withdrawn as wage income rose. By directing the increased benefits toward the working poor, the government was targeting funds in a way that maximized their effect on the reduction of child poverty. The WFTC was more cost-effective than universal programs and went to families already close to the poverty threshold, making it easier to push them above the line. Children of working parents were not necessarily seen as more deserving. It was simply easier to target them, given already existing program structures. Decreasing the withdrawal rate added more expense but was necessary in order to eliminate the employment traps inherent in the old Family Credit system, which contained implicit marginal tax rates of up to 100% as the withdrawal rate interacted with other programs.

The third goal, providing support for children, saw its trajectory constrained mostly by budget pressures. This issue was so important that the government made it a priority to increase the value of the Child Benefit as part of the "children's budget" in 1998 and 1999. While doubling the Child Benefit's value, the increase barely brought it above its historical value, after adjustment for years of erosion by inflation. Pressures for cost containment left no room for further increases in the expensive universal Child Benefit. Brown first tried to turn to income-testing at the top by proposing to tax the Child Benefit. This quickly ran into opposition from Conservatives, who reminded the Labour government of their election promises not to raise taxes, leading Brown to back away from his initial proposal.

Brown turned to fiscalization as an alternative solution. In October 1999, the Treasury Department announced a plan to introduce a Children's Tax Credit worth up to £416 per year as a way to support all children (HM Treasury 1999a: 35–37). Much like the American CTC, the Children's Tax Credit was initially nonrefundable and thus excluded the poorest children. Unlike the case of the US, though, this decision stemmed from classification issues rather than from the perception of the target population. The government very much saw the new credit as in the same vein as the Child Benefit—as a benefit for children in general. In fact, it came at the cost of other taxpayers. The new credit, when introduced in 2001, replaced tax allowances for married couples and mortgage holders. Whenever officials discussed the proposal, they spoke of it as a benefit for children or as a way to reduce child poverty.

The introduction of the Children's Tax Credit served three purposes. The first stemmed from short-term electoral considerations. The opposition Conservatives were making tax reduction a central component of their platform for the upcoming election. By redirecting funds to the Children's

Tax Credit instead of the Child Benefit, the government could credibly claim to be providing tax cuts, thereby outflanking the Conservatives on the issue (Grice 2000).

The second advantage was that the Children's Tax Credit allowed Brown to introduce income-testing of benefits for children in a less salient manner than by directly income-testing the Child Benefit. The Children's Tax Credit was phased out for upper-income families, tapering off for those making above £40,000 per year. Unlike taxing the Child Benefit, which was seen as a tax increase, the Children's Tax Credit was simply seen as a targeted tax reduction. According to one official, "the children's tax credit is a very clever way of getting round the problem of taxing [the] child benefit, which would have been very difficult technically" (Brown 1999). The opposition accused the government of imposing a "stealth tax" on child benefits, but the claim fell on deaf ears, as the public saw taxing the Child Benefit as very different from targeting new tax benefits.

Nonrefundability served the third purpose of convincingly classifying the credit as revenues not collected rather than as spending. It had nothing to do with excluding nontaxpayers from the benefit. Unlike what I will describe in the US case, no allusions were made to the undeservingness of those who worked but were still too poor to pay taxes. Instead, nonrefundability was part of the Treasury Department's response to the then recent conflict with the ONS over the classification of the WFTC. The only way to ensure that the ONS would classify the Children's Tax Credit as revenues not collected was to make it nonrefundable. The ONS subsequently did so in budget statistics, helping the government make their case that they were constraining both taxes and spending.

It is possible that the Children's Tax Credit, despite being shaped by classification issues, could have served to further entrench distinctions between the unemployed and the working poor. The same policy papers that announced the Children's Tax Credit make it clear that this was not the case. At the same time that they were outlining plans for the introduction of the Children's Tax Credit , Treasury officials were also outlining longer-term plans for what was then called an Integrated Child Credit (HM Treasury 1999a: 3). Rather than being seen as a form of symbolic pollution (by combining parts of tax credits and welfare), this integrated child credit was seen as advantageous in that it would create a "seamless payment across the welfare to work divide" (39). Policymakers liked it precisely because it made no distinction between working and nonworking families, between taxpayers and nontaxpayers.

The proposal became part of the Labour government's election platform promise to remove another 1 million children from poverty. The issue of child poverty received renewed attention after the 2001 reelection of the Labour government when it was revealed that the child poverty rate was decreasing much more slowly than Blair had promised in his initial 1999 pledge. Poverty advocates, including the Child Poverty Action Group, looked to the government to step up their actions (Waugh 2002). The complexity of the existing system was still seen as part of the problem. Although the expansion of the WFTC eliminated the worst employment traps, low-income families still faced a maze of different programs to navigate as they moved from welfare to work.

Splitting Supplements: The Child Tax Credit and the Working Tax Credit

Several scholars, including Bertram (2015) and Steensland (2008), have argued that in-work benefits serve to further entrench cultural categories based on work distinctions. In the US, the introduction of the EITC in 1974 eschewed children and made workers the relevant category, according to this view. It is possible that children only became the relevant category in Canada, which did not introduce its first in-work benefit until the 2000s, because work-conditioned benefits had not yet institutionalized the work distinction until after the introduction of the refundable CTC. Had the chronology been reversed, the results might have been very different.

At first glance, there seems to be some evidence of this in the UK with the conversion of the Family Credit into the WFTC. Did the introduction of the FIS in 1970 serve to further entrench distinctions based on work, as was the case with the EITC in 1974? The answer, as I demonstrate here, is no. Although the functional structure of the WFTC makes this distinction, it was actually child poverty that motivated policymakers to introduce the WFTC in 1999. By 2002, the WFTC was split into two separate tax credits—the WTC and the CTC. Despite tracing its technical origin to the WFTC, policymakers were able to draw on the cultural legacy of family allowances as a source of legitimacy for this new benefit, transferring direct cash benefits to children regardless of their parents' work status.

Policymakers in the UK faced the same problem as Canadian policymakers in 1992. Complexity made it hard for families to recognize which benefits they would be eligible for as they moved from income support into work. The solution was to rationalize the system by simplifying it. The Treasury Department did this by separating "support for adults in a family from support for the children, so as to provide a clearer focus (UK Inland Revenue 2001: 10). The result was a proposal to replace the child and work components of Income Support, the WFTC, and the Children's Tax Credit with two separate tax credits—the refundable WTC and the CTC. Although each tax credit embodied a distinct goal, they were both governed by an overarching logic of income supplementation. The WTC was a modified version of the WFTC, stripped of its child-related components, so that it went to low-income workers with and without children. By removing children from the equation, policymakers shifted to an emphasis on "making work pay" (HM Treasury 2002b) for all low-income workers as a way to reduce poverty.

The new CTC was fully refundable, going to families regardless of the parents' employment status. It still excluded high-income families, with 80% of all families receiving the full or partial credit (Waldfogel 2010: 7). The exclusive goal of the CTC was to "tackle child poverty" (HM Treasury 2002b). By redirecting child-related funds from social assistance and the WFTC to the CTC, policymakers hoped to achieve a "reduction in stigma" (9), as was the case with the Canadian strategy of "taking children off welfare." It was simply seen as an income-tested supplement for low- and middle-income families, on top of the Child Benefit, which would still go to all families with children. Although a tax credit in name and administered by the UK's revenue collection agency, it fell squarely under the category of income supplements for children in the eyes of the public. This allowed it to transgress boundaries based on taxpaying and work distinctions that hindered similar proposals in the US. The WTC and the CTC passed as part of the Tax Credits Act of 2002 and were implemented in 2003. This represented the completion of the fiscalization process, which had begun several years earlier, as well as the triumph of the logic of income supplementation over the logic of tax relief.

Discussion

The process of fiscalization came to the UK starting much later than in the other two countries examined here. The UK case is interesting because several factors, including the path dependency of early programs and the close ties between American and British policymakers, might lead some scholar to expect it to parallel the US case. Yet on close inspection, we find it is really most similar to the Canadian case.

As early as the 1960s, with the founding of the Child Poverty Action Group, children clearly took center stage in British social policy. This is reflected in policymakers' response to the stagflation crisis of the 1970s. As was the case in Canada, policymakers in the UK traced growing economic pressures on families to the erosion of family allowances rather than the erosion of tax expenditures, as was the case in the US. Rather than pursuing a fiscalization strategy, though, British policymakers pursued income-testing at the top with the introduction of the FIS. In many ways, the FIS is structurally similar to the US EITC at the time, but this is where the similarities end. Unlike the EITC, the British FIS was clearly not seen as tax relief or aimed at taxpayers, nor was it aimed at excluding the "undeserving" nonworking poor. Instead, it was seen as the most efficient strategy for supplementing the incomes of poor families with children in the face of a new austere environment. A broader tax base, including less salient VATs, enabled successive governments to avoid deficits by increasing broad-based consumption taxes while continuing to enrich the Child Benefit and the FIS and its successor programs.

The UK reached the limits of this strategy in the 1990s after almost two decades of popular Conservative government resistance to higher taxes. The Labour government was elected in 1997 with the expectation that it would continue to balance the budget while reining in both taxes and spending. Like other countries, it first took aim at social assistance programs, leading to similar welfare reforms, as I have shown, in the US and Canada. In addition, the Treasury Department, under the leadership of Gordon Brown, quickly turned to fiscalization as their primary strategy. By converting the Family Credit into the WFTC, the government was able to expand the program while obfuscating its true effect on the budget. This was neither a workfare measure nor one that followed the logic of tax relief. Like subsequent reforms, it stemmed from Blair's pledge to end child poverty in the UK. As was the case in Canada, British reforms were dominated by the logic of income supplementation. The eventual splitting of the WFTC into the WTC and the CTC demonstrates the advantages of fiscalization, as well as this logic.

In summary, the changes we find during this period were rooted in the cultural legacies of the family allowance, introduced during the 1940s. The UK, like Canada, followed a logic of income supplementation that can be traced to family allowances as a springboard for the changes I have described during the 1990s and early 2000s. In the next chapter, I will show how this scenario stands in stark contrast to that in the US, where the lack of family allowances led to the shaping of the structure of tax credits by the dominant logic of tax relief.

6

The United States

TAX RELIEF FOR FAMILIES

THE 1990S WAS the most momentous period in the US for the expansion of policies aimed at reducing child poverty, though they were often overshadowed by welfare reform and the failure of comprehensive healthcare reform proposals.[1] The most striking aspect of the 1990s is how little the US differed from the UK and Canada during this period in many respects, following the same general trajectory I described in chapters 4 and 5. Growing concern with child poverty, beginning in the late 1980s, ultimately led to the creation of the bipartisan National Commission on Children (NCC), which published their findings in 1991. The commission's recommendations for tackling child poverty included an expansion of the EITC and the conversion of the dependent exemption into a fully refundable CTC, for all the same reasons these policies were popular in other countries. From the vantage point of 1991, one might have expected US social policy to converge completely with that of the UK and Canada by the end of the decade.

The policy episodes that followed quickly dispelled any such notion that American exceptionalism was coming to an end. Policymakers did indeed expand the EITC and introduce a new CTC, but they continued to see some children—particularly those in the poorest families—as "undeserving" of these tax credits. According to the US literature on this topic, the EITC and the CTC were structured this way (with limited refundability or nonrefundability) because of popular and elite demands that they be antiwelfare and prowork (Bertram 2015; Howard 1997; Steensland 2008; Ventry 2000). This view neglects the fact that concepts such as "antiwelfare" and "prowork" do not necessarily require exclusion of the welfare poor. As the cases of Canada and the UK demonstrate, these policy goals are completely compatible (in theory) with the extension of tax credits to families on welfare and working families too poor to pay taxes through provisions for full refundability. Tax credits in all three countries *were* perceived as antipoverty, antiwelfare, and prowork.

As this chapter reveals, the chief obstacle in the US was the continued dominance in policy debates of the logic of tax relief over tax credits for families. The idea that economic pressure on families stemmed from rising taxes due to a combination of payroll tax increases and the erosion of tax exemptions, which emerged in the 1970s, continued to serve as the frame of reference for policymakers across the political spectrum in the 1990s. Without a legacy of family allowances, the alternative logic of income supplementation remained unavailable to the US policymakers and antipoverty advocates who were pushing for more inclusive refundable tax credits. As such, opponents of refundability found it easy to label the provision of tax relief to families who bore no tax liability as inappropriate.

This chapter begins with liberal congressional Democrats' attempts to make good on the NCC recommendations to introduce a fully refundable CTC. These Democratic proposals quickly ran into opposition from conservative Republicans as well as more moderate Democrats. Without the appropriate policy legacy, justifications for a refundable CTC using the logic of income supplementation fell on deaf ears. Instead, because these early proposals provided benefits to nontaxpayers, opponents strongly criticized them as equivalent to "welfare," robbing them of their legitimacy and leaving Democrats without an effective counter-argument. Unified Democratic control of Congress and the White House was not enough to save any of these proposals. Within two years, the concept of a refundable CTC was dead in the water.

The Clinton administration, sensing where the political winds were blowing, pivoted toward a set of antipoverty policy reforms that accounted for the constraints set by the logic of tax relief. The first was the expansion of the EITC as part of the Deficit Reduction Act of 1993. Like policymakers in Canada and the UK, Clinton saw this expansion as part of a larger antipoverty program aimed at "making work pay" for low-income families caught in welfare or poverty traps. The key difference is that Clinton successfully tapped into the rhetorical dimension of tax credits to explicitly frame them as a tax offset against federal income, payroll, and excise taxes.

The importance of the logic of tax relief in shaping the structure of the EITC was driven home when Republicans took over Congress in 1995.

Worried that the EITC had drifted from its original intent as a form of pure tax relief, several prominent Republicans argued that it had become a fraud-prone welfare program that needed to be cut back down to size. These accusations were premised explicitly on the fact that maximum EITC benefits now exceeded the total income and payroll tax liability for many families. Remarkably, whereas Republicans defeated refundable CTC proposals using this kind of rhetoric, it was unsuccessful against the EITC, because Democrats were able to effectively counter-frame their criticisms, using the logic of tax relief, by portraying Republicans as raising taxes on poor families.

The new Republican Congress also resurrected a modified CTC proposal. Unlike the previous Democratic proposals, newer versions were in accord with the logic of tax relief by limiting refundability to total income and payroll tax liability. Even this was too much for some tax relief purists in the GOP, who pushed instead for a totally nonrefundable CTC. Controversy ensued over the issue of "stacking"—whether families would be able to claim the partially refundable EITC before or after the nonrefundable CTC. Having learned their lesson after the defeat of the fully refundable CTC, Democrats strategically adopted the logic of tax relief in order to extend benefits to more working-class families. It proved highly effective, giving Democrats a victory with the introduction of the CTC as part of the Taxpayer Relief Act of 1997 in an otherwise unfavorable environment.

While the decade started off with what seemed to be a promising focus on tackling child poverty though the introduction and expansion of tax credits, the US ultimately diverged from Canada and the UK because of policy legacies that privileged the logic of tax relief rather than the logic of income supplementation. The counterintuitive consequence was that taxpayers trumped children in the fight against child poverty.

One in Five Children

The nascent concern over child poverty that began in the mid-1980s (Congressional Budget Office 1985; Primus 1989) became a major political issue by the end of the decade. After rising significantly early in the decade, child poverty gave no sign of declining again as the economy picked up. American antipoverty advocates emphasized that a staggering one in five children now lived in poverty. The issue spurred Congress into action in 1987. Representatives George Miller (D-CA) and Martin Russo

(D-IL) and Senator Lloyd Bentsen (D-TX) sponsored a bill to create the bipartisan NCC, which would be tasked with examining the causes of child poverty and coming up with recommendations (133 Cong Rec E 3747, vol. 133, no. 151, p. E 3747 1987). Having made a "children's agenda" an important part of the 1988 Republican platform, President Reagan readily signed it into law.

It took several years for the commission to draft their final report. In that time, several important actors who went on to play major roles in the expansion of the EITC and the introduction of the CTC served on the commission. Bentsen, the bill's sponsor in the Senate, became treasury secretary under future president Clinton, who also served on the commission. Dan Coats (R-IN) went on to sponsor and spearhead the Republican's CTC proposal. The NCC released its first interim report in 1990, highlighting in particular, among a number of family issues, the problem the problem of child poverty (National Commission on Children 1990; *New York Times* 1990b). This piqued public interest in preparation for the release of their final report in June the following year.

The final report, *Beyond Rhetoric: A New American Agenda for Children and Families*, is significant for the way it portrayed the problems of child poverty and families in general. The NCC framed the issue as one affecting both low- and middle-income families, tracing the problem to the growing economic pressures on families that had begun with the stagflation crisis of the 1970s (National Commission on Children 1991: 48). The NCC also highlighted the problem of poverty or welfare traps, in which families rapidly lost benefits as they moved from social assistance into work. This was in line with the diagnosis of the sources of the problem of child poverty in other countries. The US report was notably unique in one important respect: it pinpointed rising taxes on families as the primary source. Echoing the well-known Steuerle (1983) Report on the taxation of families (discussed in chapter 3), the NCC report argued that rising taxes had "harmed most American families with children, especially low-income working families," and that the "erosion of the value of the [dependent] exemption" since its peak in 1948 "has been one factor contributing to the declining economic well-being of American families with children" (National Commission on Children 1991: 124, 126).

One of the most remarkable observations we can make of this period is of the extent to which proponents of tax credits, whether liberal or conservative, cited, either directly or indirectly, Steuerle's work on the erosion of the dependent exemption and the rising burden of payroll taxes. The logic of tax relief dominated policymakers' thinking on child poverty from the very beginning. Keeping in line with worries about family tax burdens, the report argued: "U.S. tax policy should bolster families and . . . government should not tax away that portion of a family's income which is needed to support children" (National Commission on Children 1991: 94).

The report went on to recommend tax credits as the best way to tackle child poverty. This included a proposal for a fully refundable $1,000 CTC and support for current efforts already under way to expand the EITC and adjust it for family size. In the commission's discussion of the rationale behind the proposed CTC, they echoed many of the same arguments that, as I have shown, led to the successful introduction of refundable tax credits in Canada and the UK—they were nonstigmatizing, antiwelfare, prowork, profamily, and pro–middle class as well:

> Because it would assist all families with children, the refundable child tax credit would not be a relief payment, nor would it catego-rize children according to their "welfare" or "nonwelfare" status. In addition, because it would not be lost when parents enter the work force, as welfare benefits are, the refundable child tax credit could provide a bridge for families striving to enter the economic mainstream. It would substantially benefit hard-pressed single and married parents raising children. It could also help middle-income, employed parents struggling to afford high-quality child care. Moreover, because it is neutral toward family structure and mothers' employment, it would not discourage the formation of two-parent families or of single-earner families in which one parent chooses to stay at home and care for the children. (National Commission on Children 1991: 95)

Theoretically, a refundable CTC had something for everyone. These arguments had been enough to sustain a powerful coalition of profamily conservatives and antipoverty liberals in Canada, leading to the introduc-tion of the refundable CTB there. An analogous coalition of profamily conservatives, including the Family Research Council, the Christian Coalition, and the Heritage Foundation, and antipoverty liberals, including the Center on Budget and Policy Priorities, was active in the debate of tax credits in the US but differed fundamentally, in that the US groups tapped into the logic of tax relief rather than the logic of income supplementa-tion to make their case. As such, the arguments that helped establish a refundable CTC as the most appropriate policy response to child poverty in Canada were not effective on US audiences. Without the proper policy legacy to anchor understanding of them, tax credit proposals premised on the logic of income supplementation had trouble garnering support and quickly ran into formidable opposition from important actors.

The Rise and Fall of the Refundable Child Tax Credit

Given that Eugene Steuerle's earlier report had acted as a major benchmark event in reinforcing the logic of tax relief in the US, it is ironic that he proposed the first serious plan for a fully refundable CTC. In April 1991, Steuerle, now at the Urban Institute, coauthored a report with Jason Juffras advocating for a $1,000 RCTC. As Steuerle and Juffras worked with Jay Rockefeller (D-WV), the chair of the NCC, the proposal eventually found its way into the report *Beyond Rhetoric*. Focusing on child poverty in particular, Steuerle and Juffras (1991) identified two problems afflicting families under the current tax and welfare system. First, the "tax problem" stemmed from the familiar fact that "over the past few decades, the tax system has forced households with children to bear a larger share of the total tax burden." Second, the "welfare problem" consisted of the "perverse incentives on mobility, work, and marriage" (Steuerle and Juffras 1991: 5–7) of Aid to Families with Dependent Children.

From a technical standpoint, a refundable CTC made perfect sense. Steuerle, an economist, went to great lengths to explain how replacing the dependent exemption and a portion of benefits with his proposed CTC would solve both the tax and welfare problems while reducing child poverty by restoring benefits for families and smoothing out labor market transitions. This technical standpoint was uncontroversial in other countries where the logic of income supplementation dominated. In the absence of this logic, though, Steuerle's indifference to the boundaries of tax relief and social assistance destined the proposal for trouble.

The difficulty came swiftly when Steuerle testified before Congress at the hearing "Reclaiming the Tax Code for American Families" that same month (US House 1991c). The hearing was arranged by Representative Patricia Schroeder (D-CO) in order to highlight the growing tax burden on families and act as a platform for advocacy of her proposal to increase the personal exemption. As witnesses began to testify, the topic of discussion quickly changed from the personal exemption to proposals for

CTCs. Steuerle and another economist, Timothy Smeeding, argued on behalf of a refundable CTC for all of the economic reasons discussed above. Steuerle emphasized the benefits of it for what he called "those of lower-middle income, or if you wish, upper-lower income say between $6,000 and $15,000, or $20,000 of income" (105), as well as the desirability of lowering the penalties for moving off of welfare through work or marriage (24). Smeeding argued that "if we work toward a refundable tax credit . . . we help remove children from poverty and we do it on an equitable basis, across all children and across all mothers" (62).

Both also explicitly pointed to other countries' family allowance model, which Smeeding again tied to child poverty: "as you well know, we have about 19 to 20% of our children who are poor. The next nearest country is Britain with 12%. The Canadians only have 9% of their kids poor. Why? Because they have this refundable child allowance, this child grant, that is relatively modest, but it underlies the rest of the system" (US House 1991c: 62). Representative Wolf (R-VA) inquired further into the difference between a family allowance and a refundable CTC and their political viability, to which Steuerle responded: "I've been talking to people on all ends of the political spectrum about the notion of a credit and I'm actually surprised by the extent of its acceptability. In some ways, there's a game that's played, in calling a 'tax credit' what is little different than a 'family allowance.' In fact, the difference is just a question of who administers the system" (105). Steuerle was mistaken, though. Several individuals present pushed back against this characterization. Gary Bauer, president of the conservative Family Research Council, took issue with the economists' indifference toward whether families received cash through the tax system or some other means. Bauer went on to unveil a proposal, in coordination with the Heritage Foundation, that would introduce a partially refundable CTC as part of their Tax Freedom for Families Plan. The proposal would "offer a per-child tax credit worth $1,800 for preschool children and $1,200 for children ages 6 and up. This credit, which would be refundable up to the combined employer-employee level of the payroll tax, is superior to an across-the-board cut in the payroll tax because it targets assistance to the taxpayers that need help most— families with children" (59; emphasis added). In his written statement submitted to the committee, Bauer emphasized that his proposed tax credit should only go to those who are actually paying taxes. "Refundable," in his view, only meant that it should be offset against a family's total federal income and payroll tax liability. Under the Family Research Council/Heritage proposal, families would never receive more than they paid in total income and payroll taxes. However, he quickly tagged fully refundable tax credits as inappropriate, emphasizing the need for a policy that "separates tax relief mechanisms from wage supplement mechanisms" (60). Similarly, Dennis Hastert (R-IL) emphasized the "fine line between family tax policy and welfare reform" and argued: "we need to be careful not to get the two mixed up" (112). The competing logic of tax relief drew a sharp line between taxpayers under economic pressure, who deserved a CTC because of an unfair tax burden, and other families, who had no inherent claim to government benefits except perhaps as welfare recipients drawing on the logic of income support. The hearing marked the first skirmish in a larger conflict between competing logics of appropriateness.

The release of the NCC's *Beyond Rhetoric* the next month ensured that discussion of CTCs would continue in Congress. Several weeks later, the Senate Committee on Labor and Human Resources held a hearing on "economic pressures on working families" that revisited the question of a CTC. While the initial topic of the hearing was the eroding dependent exemption, Juffras's testimony returned the emphasis to a CTC. Juffras, like Steuerle and Smeeding, alluded to tax relief in his statements about the increasing tax burden on families. But he also emphasized income supplementation as an appropriate type of benefit for families with children: "a child credit, something like that of $1,000, would provide a floor of income for all families. It would be something that would be available whether you were on welfare or not on welfare, if you are in a single-parent family or not in a single-parent family" (US Senate 1991b: 56).

Yet once again, the pushback from critics using the logic of tax relief was almost immediate. The Family Research Council's William Mattox drew a line around "taxpayers" as the appropriate target population and disparaged the NCC's proposed refundable CTC as "welfare-style cash transfers" (US Senate 1991b: 71). While the poorest children might at times need income support, what was called for in this case was "a pure tax relief mechanism" (70). Additional hearings in the House saw similar pushback, with Martin Kosters of the American Enterprise Institute arguing that refundable CTC proposals were "much more akin to increasing means-tested transfer payments than they are to giving tax relief" (US House 1991a; 1991b: 12).

At the same time they were chipping away at arguments for a fully refundable CTC, conservatives concerned with making sure that the tax and welfare system was "profamily" were lining up behind what they saw as more appropriate CTC proposals. Earlier that year, the conservative journal *Policy Review* had asked thirteen conservative and libertarian experts if they thought there should be tax cuts in the face of budget deficits, and if so, which kind of cuts they would like to see. Only two mentioned a CTC. Both were from profamily advocacy groups. Whereas similar groups supported a fully refundable CTC in Canada, their American counterparts opposed it. Among Republican policymakers, the so-called House Wednesday Group, made up of moderate Republican members of the House, endorsed a partially refundable CTC as well (Wednesday Group 1991).

Later that summer, a Heritage Foundation report by Robert Rector, one of the architects of the 1996 welfare reforms, and Stuart Butler came out in favor a partially refundable CTC that would eliminate both income and payroll tax liabilities (Rector and Butler 1991). The report rests part of its argument on the idea that "mushrooming federal taxation has played a key role in the financial and personal strains that afflict many families" (Rector and Butler 1991: 9). At this point, "refundable" was still synonymous with the elimination of payroll tax burdens among conservatives. Rector and Butler explicitly endorsed the CTC over an increase in the personal exemption, based on the rationale that most low-income families pay substantially more in payroll taxes, while the personal exemption only eliminates income taxes. The report emphasized the distinction between refunding payroll taxes and a fully refundable credit, which would provide "cash welfare benefits to non-working families" (12).

During the 102nd congressional session, fourteen different CTC proposals floated around Congress (see Table 6.1). Of the ten sponsored by Democrats, seven were fully refundable. None of the four Republican-sponsored bills included fully refundable credits. Senator John "Jay" Rockefeller's proposal for a fully refundable $1,000 CTC was the first to be introduced in Congress, but both the Democrat-controlled Congress and the Republican administration of Bush deemed it too expensive. As the CTC idea gained steam, more hearings on it were held in late 1991. In Canada and elsewhere, such conversations had been opportunities for conservatives to demonstrate their profamily, antiwelfare positions by positioning refundable CTCs as a means of "taking children off welfare." But in the US, the logic of tax relief, with its concomitant view of full refundability as equivalent to welfare, rather than an alternative to it, remained dominant among moderates and conservatives. This shaped which bill Democrats favored.

Among liberal Democrats, a proposal by Representative Thomas Downey (D-NY) and Senator Al Gore (D-NY) was the favorite. The

Table 6.1 Bills introduced in the US Congress containing child tax credit provisions, 1991–1998

Congressional session	Republican sponsor		Democratic sponsor		Total
	Fully refundable	*Partially or not refundable*	*Fully refundable*	*Partially or not refundable*	
102 (1991–1992)	0	4	7	3	14
103 (1993–1994)	0	5	1	1	7
104 (1995–1996)	0	5	0	0	5
105 (1997–1998)	0	5	0	0	5
Total	0	19	8	4	31

Source: Author's analysis of bills containing "child tax credit" between 1991 and 1998.

Gore-Downey proposal provided a minimum $400 refundable CTC to families with no income that would increase to $800 for working- and middle-class families. Increasingly, however, a proposal by Senators Lloyd Bentsen, William Roth (R-DE), and Barbara Mikulski (D-MD) gained ground. This much smaller $300 nonrefundable CTC was governed, like conservatives' proposals, by the logic of tax relief. The problem, as the latter senators explained it, was that "families with children saw their taxes increase while their income dropped" since the 1970s (US Senate 1991a: 2). These legislators defined the problem in the terms determined by the dominant policy legacy of dependent exemptions—as families struggling with the burden of taxes, a logic entirely different from that used by profamily conservatives in Canada and elsewhere. It was because of this congruity with the logic of tax relief that the centrist Bentsen proposal was able to gain the favor of groups like the conservative Family Research Council. In their statement supporting Bentsen-Roth-Mikulski, the Council noted: "curiously, several prominent proposals promising 'middle-income tax relief' (including the Rockefeller and Gore-Downey plans) make little or no distinction between welfare recipients and taxpayers with children. They offer refundable tax credits to all families, including low-income, child-present households where the household head is not married, gainfully employed, or receiving child support. . . . Even if one believes greater cash assistance to welfare recipients is warranted, it is disingenuous to use the banner of 'middle-income tax relief' to secure this result" (326).[2] Assertions that the fully refundable proposals were not true tax relief almost always went unanswered by their proponents because they had no policy legacy based on the logic of income supplementation from which to draw. The vast majority of US policymakers viewed the issue of refundability through the dichotomous distinction of tax relief versus welfare.

Liberal Democrats argued that making the credit nonrefundable would mean one-quarter of American children would receive no benefit whatsoever while another third, from working families, would receive less than the full amount (US Senate 1991a: 44). However, it was the Bentsen nonrefundable tax credit that found its way into a doomed tax bill that was passed by Congress and vetoed by President Bush in March 1992 (Clymer 1992). The election of President Clinton, a member of the NCC and initially a supporter of a refundable CTC, the following year was not enough to keep the refundable CTC on the agenda. Realizing that refundable CTC proposals had been effectively stigmatized as "welfare," the Clinton administration and congressional Democrats quietly dropped them from consideration (Evans and Novak 1993). No bills proposing fully refundable CTCs appeared after 1993—well before the Republican takeover in the next year's midterm elections.

Expanding the Earned Income Tax Credit as Tax Relief

The defeat of proposals for a fully refundable CTC stands in stark contrast to the success of the partially refundable EITC during this period. The difference stems from two factors. First, the birth of the EITC almost two decades earlier had institutionalized a logic of tax relief that continued to advantage it well into the 1990s. Second, policymakers could tap into the rhetoric dimension of the tax credit to portray it as an offset against other taxes beyond income taxes. This was important because new budget rules made the EITC's refundability problematic in terms of the technical dimension of tax credits.

The 1990 budget enacted new "PAYGO" restrictions that would tie the hands of future policymakers. As a result of growing concerns over increasing budget deficits, Congress passed the Budget Enforcement Act of 1990. The new rules required that any tax or expenditure changes not increase the deficit. This meant that any tax cuts had to be paid for with revenue increases elsewhere or expenditure reductions. Conversely, expenditure increases required revenue increases. Unlike previous tax cuts (i.e., Reagan's in 1981), any losses in revenue in the 1990s would have to be made up with cuts in spending or tax hikes elsewhere. The cost of the EITC were only scored as "revenues not collected," where they reduced income tax liabilities. While this portion of the credit was rhetorically portrayed as offsetting payroll taxes as well, it was technically scored as traditional spending. If advocates wished to expand the EITC, they had to do so without this advantage. Conservative critics of the EITC, as I will show later, used the technical dimension as a weapon against the tax credit.

Building on the momentum of the discussion of child poverty and tax relief sparked by the NCC report, nearly elected President Clinton turned to the EITC as part of a larger strategy to "make work pay" for poor families as an alternative to welfare. The impetus for the EITC came from the fact that it helped lower implicit marginal tax rates on the transition from welfare to work. There was a consensus that part of the problem with Aid for Families with Dependent Children was that it created a "poverty trap" or "welfare wall" where beneficiaries could find themselves with less income overall or still in poverty if they chose to work full-time (Ellwood 1988; Murray 1984). As an antipoverty, prowork measure, the EITC made economic sense, but more important, it made sense according to the logic of tax relief. The Clinton administration and congressional Democrats could and did frame the EITC as a form of tax relief for low-income families in the face of deficit reduction measures.

Congressional Democrats first used this strategy to justify the EITC expansion already under way when the NCC released its interim report in 1990. The 1990 expansion, which increased the value of the credit and adjusted it for family size for the first time, was labeled a "progressivity offset" against a payroll tax bump and several excise tax increases that would disproportionately affect low-income families (Steuerle 1991: 179). Senator Gore testified that it was necessary "in order to provide tax relief for the working poor" (US House 1989: 11). The *New York Times* (1990a) argued: "deficit reduction measures, especially the excise taxes on gasoline, alcohol and cigarettes, will hit the working poor hard. Increasing the tax credit would offset those losses." By arguing that the EITC could be used as an offset against taxes beyond income and payroll taxes, congressional Democrats were breaking new ground.

The Clinton administration had the success of the 1990s expansion, based on the logic of tax relief, in mind when they proposed to substantially further expand the EITC in 1993.

Robert Greenstein of the liberal Center on Budget and Policy Priorities was well aware of the EITC's political advantages. Greenstein, sometimes called the "godfather of the plan to expand the tax credit" worked closely with the administration to push for it (Noah and McGinley 1993). His role directly parallels that of his Canadian counterpart, Ken Battle of the Caledon Institute, who worked with the Liberal government to expand the CTB there. It was Greenstein who first suggested that the administration sell the EITC as an offset against increasing energy taxes for low-income families in the same budget (National Security Council, Speechwriting Office, and Robert Boorstin, "Deficit Budget Options," Clinton Digital Library). The administration and Congressional Democrats took Greenstein's advice, not only emphasizing the EITC's antipoverty and prowork features but also justifying it as an instrument of working-class tax relief (Cloud 1993a).

According to Howard (1997: 157) there was little debate in Congress on the merits of the EITC. He sees this as an "indication of general support for expansion" rather than of the fact that it was simply hidden in a larger tax bill. When the EITC was discussed in the Congressional Record, it was as a tax cut or tax offset for low-income taxpayers (see also US House 1993; Ventry 2000). According to a *New York Times* (1993) editorial, "the credit insulates the poor from Social Security payroll taxes and, looking ahead, higher energy taxes. It thus acts to untax the poor who work."

The final Clinton budget proposed a $28 billion increase in the EITC. The expansion consisted of phasing in higher rates for families and adding a new, much smaller credit for low-income taxpayers with no children. The same proposal included a hike in corporate taxes and the top personal income marginal tax rate, as well as a new BTU (energy) tax worth $70 billion. The goal was to increase taxes on high-income earners, decrease them on low-income families, and reduce the deficit. Advocates framed the EITC as a tax cut to offset the regressive BTU tax included in the proposal (Center on Budget and Policy Priorities 1993a, 1993b). The administration originally hoped that the expansion would be large enough to pull any family working full-time out of poverty, but budget constraints caused them to scale back their proposal (Cloud 1993a). The House version that came out of the Ways and Means Committee was very close to Clinton's proposal, except the corporate tax hikes were smaller (Howard 1997: 157). The biggest issue was the inclusion of the BTU tax, which made many Democrats from energy-producing states reluctant to vote for the bill. Still, the House bill squeaked by in late May by two votes.

The bill faced trouble as it headed to the Senate, where opposition to the BTU tax was stronger among conservative Democrats from energy-producing states. The Senate Finance Committee version of the bill dropped the BTU tax and shrank the EITC expansion by $10 billion by limiting it to taxpayers with children (Cloud and Hager 1993). Congressional Democrats' narrow majority in both chambers gave substantial power to any group of holdouts on any aspect of the bill. While this empowered senators opposed to the BTU tax, it also empowered the Congressional Black Caucus. In early June, the Caucus sent a letter to Clinton in response to the Senate cuts demanding the restoration of the reduced EITC as "nonnegotiable" (Cloud 1993b). The Clinton administration reacted by putting forth a modified proposal that replaced the BTU tax with a smaller gasoline tax increase and slightly scaled-back EITC expansion (Howard 1997: 157–158). The Center on Budget and Policy Priorities followed up with a public relations campaign highlighting the regressive effects of combining new gasoline taxes with the Senate's EITC cuts (Center on Budget and Policy Priorities 1993c). In reconciliation, negotiators were able to work out an EITC expansion totaling $21 billion—less than Clinton's original proposal and more than the original Senate version.

The changes were enough to satisfy the Congressional Black Caucus and senators from energy-producing states. The vote was still extremely close, though, because of the complete absence of Republican support due to the bill's provisions raising personal and corporate income taxes. In order to shore up support in Congress, Clinton held a press conference reminding the public what his EITC meant to taxpayers: "thanks to the Earned Income Tax Credit in our tax code, which reduces the tax burden on low-income workers, they are supporting their children instead of going on welfare. . . . This plan has a revolutionary expansion of the earned-income tax credit so that for the first time ever, we can say to American workers: If you work full time and you have children in your home, you will not live in poverty. The tax system will lift you out of poverty, not drive you into it" (Clinton 1993). Clinton's framing of the EITC as both tax relief and an alternative to welfare made it hard for many congressional Democrats to vote against the bill. It was a winning combination. In the House, the attention brought to the BTU tax led some members to change their votes for fear of upsetting constituents. The reconciliation bill again squeaked by the House. In the Senate, the vote was so close that a tie had to be broken by Vice President Al Gore. In early August the Senate passed the reconciliation bill 51–50 and sent it to the president for signing. When fully phased in over the next few years, the EITC expansion substantially increased benefits for families and childless workers.

The expansion also pushed the boundaries set by the logic of tax relief. The original rationale for the EITC was to provide income and payroll tax relief in the 1970s. Democrats had stretched the EITC to include excise taxes. This would have major ramifications for their ability to tap into the logic of tax relief when Republicans took over Congress after the 1994 midterm elections.

The Triumph of Tax Relief

The defeat of the refundable CTC in Congress and the veto of the first nonrefundable CTC by President Bush in 1992 did not spell the end for CTC proposals. Despite little interest from the Bush administration, the Heritage Foundation continued its call for the introduction of a partially refundable CTC throughout the 1992 presidential campaign. Citing heavy taxation as one cause of welfare dependency, Robert Rector made a CTC part of his larger welfare reform strategy: "the federal government currently imposes heavy taxes on low-income working families with children. A family of four making $20,000 a year currently pays $3,780 in federal taxes. This heavy taxation promotes welfare dependence by reducing the rewards of work and marriage relative to welfare" (Rector 1992:46).

In January 1993, the National Commission on America's Urban Families, established by President Bush in 1992 and chaired by social conservative John Ashcroft, released their report *Family First*, which recommended, among other things, replacing the dependent exemption with a CTC (National Commission on America's Urban Families 1993). The report was picked up by a number of conservative family groups who cited it approvingly. The turning point came in the summer of 1993, when Christian Coalition leader Ralph Reed wrote an article in *Policy Review* calling for major changes in the electoral strategy of the so-called Christian Right. Arguing that charismatic leaders and calls for a return to traditional values weren't enough to gain evangelical and orthodox Catholic voters, Reed called on conservative profamily activists to focus on concrete policies that affected voters. "Their primary interest is not to legislate against the sins of others, but to protect the health, welfare, and financial security of their own families. . . . One promising step," Reed continued, "is a bill offered by Representatives Rod Grams and Tim Hutchinson that would provide a $500 tax credit for each child and pay for it with a cap on discretionary domestic spending" (Reed 1993:32).

The Grams-Coats bill, as it was called, would provide a $500 credit for each child under eighteen. As a modified version of the Heritage proposal, families could claim the credit against their total income and payroll tax burden, making it partially refundable. The proposal soon caught on among conservatives, but Republicans still lacked a majority in Congress. As part of their electoral strategy, Republicans made it the "crowning jewel" of Newt Gingrich's famed Contract with America (Gingrich 1995). Republican victories in both the House and Senate in the 1994 elections allowed Republicans to follow through on their campaign promise. One congressional observer remarked that the time was right for a "tax bidding war." She was correct, as the Clinton administration soon launched a new proposal for a *nonrefundable* $500 CTC for families making less than $75,000 (Rubin 1994).

The new Republican majority in the House wasted little time bringing their plans to fruition. On January 6, 1995, they introduced a modified version of the Grams-Coats bill, the American Dream Restoration Act, which provided a partially refundable (against income and payroll taxes) $500 CTC. Two weeks later, the House Committee on Ways and Means held a hearing on the family tax provisions in the Contract with America. As usual, the growing tax burden on families was a central concern of members of both parties and across the ideological spectrum. Senator Rod Grams (R-MN), in reference to his previous testimony before the same Democratic-controlled committee a year before, remarked: "our arguments then were simple. Taxes were too high. The burden of tax increases fell disproportionately on the middle class and big government was forcing more workers out of the working class and into the welfare class" (US House 1995b: 11). Early support for the Grams-Coats bill ran into trouble when some Republicans detected a potential issue with its partial refundability in the wake of the 1990 and 1993 EITC expansions.

Most Republicans had never been comfortable with Democratic arguments that increasing the EITC was justified in response to rising excise taxes. Representative Bill Archer (R-TX), who went on to chair the powerful House Ways and Means Committee, had supported Reagan's EITC expansion as part of the 1986 tax reforms because the total value of the credit could not exceed a family's combined income and payroll tax liability. Despite his antiwelfare and prowork attitudes, he vehemently opposed both the 1990 and 1993 expansions, which he saw as violating the logic of tax relief (Archer 1991; Bertram 2015: 184). These expansions enabled families to receive tax credit benefits far above their total income and payroll tax liabilities. In his mind, this turned the EITC into just another welfare program.

Even those who took a less harsh view of the expansion as "welfare," such as many profamily groups, still took issue with the continued characterization of the EITC as tax relief. During the same 1991 hearing in which he testified in favor of a (nonrefundable) CTC, the Family Research Council's Gary Bauer submitted written testimony in which he proposed replacing the EITC with something he called a Family Wage Supplement. Functionally, Bauer's proposed wage supplement was identical to the EITC. Why, then, would such a change be necessary? According to Bauer, "this is a significant advantage over the existing EITC, which blurs the critical distinction between taxpaying families receiving tax benefits and non-taxpaying income-earners receiving wage-based cash assistance. Certainly, both groups are deserving of assistance, but both should not be treated the same. For example, limitations on family size (both the EITC and the proposed Family Wage Supplement currently cut off benefits after two children) are justifiable for cash transfer recipients who are not yet self-sufficient, but are inappropriate for low-income taxpaying families" (US House 1991c: 60). Bauer saw the EITC as another form of "welfare," albeit one that he thought had merit. To call it a tax credit transgressed the boundary between the logic of tax relief and income support. Even in this case, where working families are still "deserving" of assistance, the logic behind that deservingness makes a difference. It is inappropriate to provide tax relief to working families who pay no income or payroll taxes.

The issue received little attention at the time because the difference between families' EITC and total income/payroll tax burden was small and Democrats controlled Congress. The 1993 expansion and subsequent takeover of Congress by Republicans gave conservatives a chance to contest this perceived violation of the logic of tax relief. For conservatives, the transformation of the EITC from a tax offset to a wage subsidy sparked many of the same fears they had about welfare (Schiffren 1995; Ventry 2000: 1005). One in particular was fraud. This began after the 1990 expansion when studies came out in the early 1990s showing high error rates, which Republicans perceived as fraud.

Between 1993 and 1997, Congress held a number of hearings to investigate the EITC's noncompliance and fraud issues (Ventry 2000: 1006). The new Republican orthodoxy that refundability beyond a certain threshold turned tax credits into welfare programs shaped their approach to the EITC and the CTC, in two ways. First, they conducted a full-scale assault on the 1993 EITC expansion. Second, they turned against their own initial promise to make the CTC partially refundable.

Republicans Turn Against Partial Refundability

The Republican tax package that emerged in 1995 would eliminate the EITC for childless workers and freeze the rate at 36% (which was scheduled to rise to 40% as part of the 1993 legislation) for families with two or more children. Under these circumstances, Republicans sympathetic to the EITC, like Representative Shaw (R-FL), lost out to tax relief purists including Archer, Roth, and Don Nickles (R-OK) in the Senate (Haskins 2006: 235–236). Democrats reacted as they had in the past by framing any EITC cut as a tax hike on the poor. Majority leader Richard Gephardt (D-MO) told reporters that the Republican bill "raised taxes on working families to give a tax cut to the people that already have it made" (Rosenbaum 1995).

Both the House and Senate held hearings on the EITC in June, focusing both on the issue of noncompliance in order to bolster Republican proposals to scale it back. In the eyes of EITC critics, there was no doubt that these issues stemmed from the program's growth. Representative Nancy Johnson (R-CT) concisely laid out the logic behind GOP arguments about fraud: "as long as the payroll tax and the EITC subsidy are roughly equal, taxpayers have no incentive to overstate income from self-employment to increase their EITC. Doing so would result in a larger credit, but would also obligate the taxpayer to pay higher Social Security taxes on their self-employed income. As a result of recent expansions of the EITC, there are now strong incentives for taxpayers to manipulate the level of their income from self-employment" (US House 1995a:4). Drawing on the EITC's legacy as a tax relief measure, Representative Tim Hutchinson (R-AR) lamented: "unfortunately, in many ways the EITC has strayed far from its original mission. It was designed as a small supplement to help compensate working families who pay payroll taxes. It has evolved into an alternative to traditional forms of welfare assistance" (15). Others suggested it would be proper to transfer administration of the credit to a welfare bureaucracy where there was more experience with fighting fraud (97).

The discussion before the Senate Finance Committee was much more contentious, even though, unlike the House, they had already passed a resolution proposing substantial EITC cuts. Those present made repeated references to the EITC's legacy as relief from payroll taxes and their perception that it had strayed far from this original mission. "We were trying to find some way to relieve lower income working people—it was not intended as a welfare program—from the burden of the Social Security tax," said Senator Bob Packwood (R-OR) (US Senate 1995: 1). In one terse exchange, the Treasury's assistant secretary for tax policy, Leslie Samuels, testifying on behalf of the Clinton administration, continued the long-standing strategy of rhetorically framing the EITC as a broad offset against federal taxes, including excise taxes: "under current law, over 78 percent of the EITC offsets Federal payroll and incomes taxes. I would note, this does not include excise and other tax burdens borne by low-income workers. Under the Senate budget resolution, the EITC would be reduced and tax burdens increased for over 14 million working families. Working families with two or more children would be hit the hardest, with an average tax increase of $305 per year" (2). While Packwood laughed at the accusation that Senator William Roth (R-DE), an ardent tax cut proponent who had helped craft the 1981 tax cuts, would raise taxes on anyone, Roth himself was not amused and fired back: "well, Mr. Chairman, just let me point out that EITC is basically an income redistribution, it is not a tax matter. What we are really talking about is welfare. . . . It is the only program where you get a tax credit without having to pay any taxes" (9). Senator Nickles, using a narrower definition encompassing only income taxes, claimed that more than 80% of the EITC was disbursed as a welfare check rather than a tax refund, bluntly telling the committee: "it is a welfare program, it is an income redistribution program, and it is fraudulent" (19). In response, Democrats on the committee continued to emphasize that the EITC acted as a tax offset against regressive excise taxes as well. Democratic protestations notwithstanding, the Republican-controlled Congress went on to include provisions to cut the EITC in the 1995 budget.

Relatedly, the logic of tax relief and worries over refundability also led congressional Republicans to abandon their initial plan for a partially refundable CTC in the same budget (Rubin 1995). The change to a nonrefundable credit was the work of Representative Archer. By itself, the Grams-Coats proposal for a partially refundable CTC was unproblematic because a family's total refund could not exceed their income and payroll tax liability. In combination with the EITC, though (even a much smaller one), a family's combined EITC/CTC benefit could potentially greatly exceed their total tax liability and thus turn the Republicans' "crown jewel" into another welfare program. In the eyes of many conservatives, "refundable" had increasingly become synonymous with the EITC—and, by extension, welfare (Staff Memo to Rod Grams, 3 May 1995. Rod Grams Senitorial Files, Box 51, File 15, Minnesota Historical Society). Conservative profamily groups, including the Heritage Foundation and the Christian Coalition, were initially upset by this decision but eventually accepted it when they realized that a nonrefundable CTC was the only way to ensure that tax relief was limited to families who actually paid income and payroll taxes (House Republicans Break Their Contract with Low-Income Families, 23 March 1995. Rod Grams Senitorial Files, Box 51, File 16, Minnesota Historical Society; US House 1995a).

After weeks of intense negotiations, the House and Senate finally agreed to $245 billion in tax cuts, under the assumption that they would later agree on enough expenditure cuts to avoid any more deficits. Several more weeks of intense negotiations led to a scaled-back nonrefundable CTC for families with children under eighteen making less than $110,000 per year and to the retention of the provisions to eliminate the EITC for childless workers and to scale back its value for families with children. With the final bill was hashed out in reconciliation, both the House and the Senate passed it in October 1995.

Congressional Democrats were powerless to stop Republicans from pushing through EITC cuts. In an attempt to get Congress to drop the cuts during the reconciliation process, President Clinton tapped into the logic of tax relief, telling reporters and the public that "no one should be taxed into poverty" and imploring Congress not to "raise taxes on working people while we're lowering taxes on everybody else in the country" (Purdum 1995). Elsewhere, Clinton claimed: "17 million working families who seek to share in the American dream will have to pay $42 billion in income taxes through reductions in the Earned Income Tax Credits for working families" (Wines 1995). Several members of Congress subsequently sparred in the *New York Times* over whether the Republican proposal was a legitimate welfare cut (Shaw 1995) or a tax increase on the working poor (Sabo 1995).

Much to Republicans' chagrin, the charges of fraud and the characterization of EITC beneficiaries as welfare recipients generally fell on deaf ears. The public was in agreement with the Democrats (Bartels 2006). The final bill cut taxes for most families making more than $30,000 but raised them slightly for many making less than $30,000. A study released by the Joint Committee on Taxation (1995) showed that the EITC cuts would adversely affect 6.8 million low-income taxpayers. This study, along with a Treasury study that came to similar conclusions, gave President Clinton the political cover to veto the bill. On vetoing the bill over the EITC cuts, he remarked: "while cutting taxes for the well-off, this bill would cut the EITC for almost 13 million working families. . . . Even after accounting for other tax cuts in this bill, about eight million families would face a net tax increase" (Gitterman 2010: 93).

Despite cutting taxes for middle- and upper-income families, the bill did not become law, because it was perceived as raising taxes on poor families. The logic of tax relief, which had been used to undermine refundable CTC proposals, was used to protect the EITC against critics. Congressional Republicans, realizing that they were losing the public relations battle, dropped the proposed cuts from future tax and welfare reform packages. Whereas Republicans found that they could split off welfare reforms and pass them as a stand-alone package, according to Myles and Pierson (1997: 464), "there was never any suggestion that a similar open assault on the EITC would be politically feasible." Notably, Clinton's veto demonstrates that it was the logic of tax relief—not a logic of income supplementation or support for the working poor—that allowed him to veto a budget full of otherwise popular measures and claim victory over a hostile Republican-controlled Congress.

Co-opting the Logic of Tax Relief

The Democrats had successfully co-opted the logic of tax relief by counter-framing Republican attempts to cut the EITC as raising taxes on working-class families. With the EITC now safe from possible retrenchment, Democrats turned their attention to strategizing how to expand the benefits of the still popular proposal for a nonrefundable CTC. Most notably, arguments based on the logic of income supplementation were completely absent by this point. The logic of tax relief prevailed. After the 1996 election, which left Clinton in the White House and Republican majorities in both chambers of Congress, there was a sense that some form of CTC would now be hammered out (Rubin 1996). The approach taken by liberal Democrats, who wanted a CTC that reached more low-income families, was particularly noteworthy. Any attempts to make the CTC refundable would be tainted by the stigma of welfare. Democrats' only chance was to strategically work within constraints set by the logic of tax relief.

Their opportunity arose in the summer of 1997, when three distinct nonrefundable proposals emerged from the House, the Senate, and the

Clinton administration (President Clinton's Tax Cut Proposal Summary Documents, 30 June 1997. Elena Kagan Domestic Policy Council Files, Box 2, File 18. William J. Clinton Digital Library). The difference between each involved the procedure for claiming tax credits referred to as "stacking." In this case, the question was whether low-income families should be able to claim the proposed nonrefundable CTC before the refundable EITC. The order would determine whether working families making less than $30,000 annually would receive any benefits from the CTC (see Figure 6.1).

The Clinton administration wanted to stack the CTC before the EITC, but the proposal approved by the House Ways and Means Committee made families apply their EITC before claiming the CTC. The proposal approved by the Senate Finance Committee split the difference, requiring families to apply half of their EITC before they could claim the CTC. Because the EITC wiped out some or all income tax liability for most families making less than $30,000 a year, they would receive little or nothing from the House CTC proposal, which could only be claimed against income taxes. The Clinton proposal on the other hand allowed families to apply the nonrefundable CTC to their income tax liability before claiming the refundable EITC. The decision to focus on stacking rather than refundability

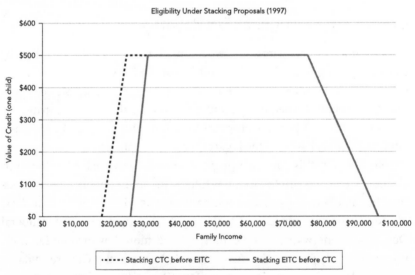

FIGURE 6.1 Eligibility under stacking proposals (1997).

Source: Joint Committee on Taxation (1995). Present Law and Analysis Relating to the Earned Income Credit and the Child Tax Credit as Contained in the H.R. 2491 Conference Agreement. Washington DC: Government Printing Office.

was a conscious one made by administration officials in order to co-opt the logic of tax relief:

> all of us agreed that we did not want to allow the Republicans to be able to frame the message as Democrats for welfare payments at the expense of Republicans for tax credits for teens in middle class families. We reached consensus around a proposal that would give the tax credit to teenagers, and have partial refundability—but only to the degree that people paid payroll and income taxes beyond what they get in their EITC. In this way, we take away the Republican message on teenagers, keep some element of refundability, but keep our message that this is a tax cut only for people who owe federal payroll and income taxes. (President Clinton's Tax Cut Proposal Summary Documents, 30 June 1997. Elena Kagan Domestic Policy Council Files, Box 2, File 18. William J. Clinton Digital Library)

Republicans pushed back, though, arguing that stacking a partially refundable CTC before the refundable EITC would allow some families to receive more in combined CTCs and EITCs than they paid in federal income and payroll taxes. House Ways and Means Committee chair Bill Archer set off a firestorm when he declared that allowing families to claim the CTC before the EITC was tantamount to "welfare." He wrote to the *New York Times*: "giving taxpayer money to people who pay no taxes allows for a backdoor increase in welfare spending. My plan protects taxpayers by reserving relief only for those who pay taxes. It is not fair if lower- and middle-income workers get less tax relief so that Americans who pay no taxes at all can receive a larger check" (Archer 1997).

Weeks later, he told reporters: "this is a bill for people who pay income taxes. It will be very hard for the American people to accept the president's proposal to increase welfare spending by providing tax relief to people who pay no taxes" (Rubin and Hosansky 1997). Gingrich also weighed in on the matter, announcing: "we don't think a tax-cut bill designed to help people who pay taxes should be turned into a welfare bill" (Bennet 1997). The implication, of course, was that those receiving both the CTC and the EITC were no longer taxpayers. They were just like any other welfare recipient.

Democrats responded aggressively, wielding the same logic of tax relief that had been used to defeat refundable CTC proposals. Now, they exclusively emphasized that Republicans were trying to deny the CTC to worthy taxpaying families. The Center on Budget and Policy Priorities released reports on both the House and Senate proposals contesting the notion that these families were not paying any federal taxes. Using the hypothetical example of a family of four making $24,000 a year, the report showed that the family paid a considerable amount in taxes. It concluded: "most of the children who would be denied the credit or have their credit reduced live in families that owe federal taxes. Their tax burdens often amount to several thousand dollars even after the effects of the Earned Income Tax Credit are accounted for. Claims these families owe no federal tax are not correct" (Shapiro and Greenstein 1997:1).

Columnists and editorial boards at newspapers ranging from the *New York Times* and the *Washington Post* to the *Wall Street Journal* took Archer, Gingrich, and the Republicans to task for characterizing low-income working families as welfare recipients. The writers often included stories of hypothetical or real-life families who would be denied the CTC under the GOP proposals. Significantly, writers framed this as a denial of tax relief. Writing in the *Wall Street Journal*, Albert Hunt (1997) told the story of a hypothetical family in Georgia:

> A starting police officer in Gwinnett County, GA: coincidentally part of Speaker Gingrich's district—is paid $23,078 a year. If his family has two kids, it gets a $1,668 earned income tax credit, which offsets its $675 in federal taxes and yields a check for $993. But that family pays $1,760 in payroll taxes (most economists would also add the employer's share of payroll taxes too) and another $354 in federal excise taxes. Thus, even after the EITC, this police officer's family's out-of-pocket federal taxes would be at least $1,121 and in reality more like $2,881. . . . Mr. Gingrich and company apparently believe giving that young police officer and his family the child credit is welfare.

Writing in the *New York Times*, Bob Herbert (1997) told the real-life story of the McCumber family in West Virginia.

> When politicians talk about tax cuts to help working families with children, you would think they had families like the McCumberses in mind. You would certainly think they were talking about children like Beckie and John McCumbers if they came up with a plan to provide tax credits worth $500 per child. . . . But if you thought that, you would be wrong. The McCumberses are among several million working and tax-paying families that will get nothing from

the ballyhooed child tax credit passed by the House and Senate last week. They are ineligible for the child credit because their incomes are not high enough.... If anyone needs tax relief, those families do.

The editorial board of the *Washington Post* (1997) specifically took issue with the characterization of the families being denied the credit as welfare recipients:

the sponsors say it's only fair to do as they propose, since the purpose of this bill is to give relief to taxpayers, not add to welfare. Of all the distortions they have used to grease and sell this awful bill, none matches this. The implication is that the people who would lose from this provision are freeloading. The absolute opposite is true. These are working people, typically with children and with incomes in the range of, say, $17,000 to $27,000 a year—precisely the kind of struggling, taxpaying, not-on-welfare Americans for whom the Republicans profess to bleed. The EITC may wipe out the income tax liability of many of them; it doesn't wipe out their total liability, counting the payroll tax. They remain net taxpayers.

The Clinton administration took note of the newspaper coverage (President Clinton's Tax Cut Proposal Summary Documents, 30 June 1997. Elena Kagan Domestic Policy Council Files, Box 2, File 18. William J. Clinton Digital Library). The administration and Congressional Democrats explicitly pursued a strategy in which they trotted out police officers, nurses, and schoolteachers as the face of taxpayers being denied the CTC under GOP proposals (President Clinton's Child Tax Credit, 10 July 1997. Domestic Policy Council, Bruce Reed, and Subject Files, Clinton Digital Library). The *Congressional Record* is filled with stories of taxpaying families much like the ones discussed in the newspapers. Republicans simply doubled down on their assertion that these families were not taxpayers and that this amounted to welfare (143 Cong Rec H 4668, vol. 143, no. 92, p. H 4668; 143 Cong Rec S 6401, vol. 143, no. 92, p. S 6401; 143 Cong Rec S 8453, vol. 143, no. 111, p. S 8453 1997).

By mid-July, as the House and Senate were entering conference talks to reconcile the bills that had passed in both chambers, it was clear that Democrats were winning this public relations battle. Polls showed that the public strongly supported Clinton on the issue. Congressional aides to Republicans in both chambers were admitting that the tax package would "include more taxpayers in lower-income brackets" going forward (Taylor and Carey 1997). Republican rhetoric about the CTC as welfare ceased. Gingrich told the *Wall Street Journal* that the House would move toward Clinton's position on the CTC (Rubin 1997). The change was a direct result of Democrat efforts to categorize low-income families receiving the CTC as taxpayers (Taylor 1997).

The logic of tax relief and the conflict over the taxpayer/welfare recipient distinction was not simply a matter of public relations and superficial framing by policymakers. Behind-the-door negotiations over the CTC/EITC issue reveal that the policymakers involved saw the distinction as a deep moral issue. Conference negotiators were now working with a modified proposal from the Clinton administration. The CTC was now stacked before the EITC but would only be refundable against any payroll taxes left over after the EITC was applied for families with three or more children. Democratic negotiators assured Republicans that this would prevent families who were receiving both the EITC and the CTC from receiving more than they paid in total federal taxes.

John Hilley, who represented the administration in the negotiations, recalls that this seemed to satisfy hostile Republicans who had previously opposed the change because it was referred to as refundable. According to Hilley (2008: 197), Gingrich was content, saying: "we wouldn't be sending people a check." The same logic that appeared in public also appeared in private: "after Gingrich spoke, Armey chimed in. He did not like the EITC one bit, but he would support this provision. Giving people a check—welfare—was one thing. But letting them pay less taxes was another" (197).

The deal fell apart a few days later when it was revealed that a small number of families would actually get back more in combined CTC/EITC than they paid in income and payroll taxes. For these families, the CTC would wipe out their entire income tax liability, and their EITC was worth more than their payroll tax liability. The cost difference was small, but, according to Hilley, it was not about money at that point. On informing Gingrich of the issue, Hilley (2008: 211) recalls him responding: "I cannot carry this in my caucus. If it means the loss of the bill, then so be it. My caucus will never agree to an expansion of welfare. I cannot and will not carry it!"

The administration, having just waged a long public relations battle on the same issue, realized that the "particular line in the sand was drawn across the word welfare" and set out to find a solution that would satisfy Republican critics. They did this by adding EITC compliance measures aimed at cutting down on "waste, fraud, and abuse" in the program, which was estimated to result in $2.5 billion worth of savings. Specifically, the administration came up with the idea of denying the EITC to welfare recipients taking part in "workfare" programs. This was done so that there would be no net change in EITC outlays broadly, but it also helped reinforce the distinction between tax relief and welfare. Congressional Republicans were happy that the legislative changes would result in no net increase in EITC spending and would deny the CTC to families whom almost everyone agreed were welfare recipients, even if a small number of families got more than they paid in federal income and payroll taxes (Hilley 2008: 214; Tax Cuts for Middle Class Working Families, 22 July 1997. Rod Grams Senitorial Files, Box 52, File 7, Minnesota Historical Society). The compromise was passed by both the House and Senate and sent to President Clinton, who signed it into law in August. The US finally introduced a *nonrefundable* CTC as part of the Taxpayer Relief Act of 1997.

Discussion

Over the course of the 1990s, child poverty became a major issue across liberal welfare regimes. As I showed in chapters 4 and 5, such conversations had been opportunities for conservatives and "third way" liberals in Canada and the UK to demonstrate their profamily, antiwelfare positions by positioning RCTCs as a means of "taking children off welfare" and refundable in-work tax credits as "making work pay." Buoyed by the cultural legacy of family allowances, Canadian and British policymakers tapped into a logic of income supplementation so as to structure these tax credits in ways that most efficiently and effectively reduced child poverty in the face of continued pressures for austerity.

US policymakers had the same goal of reducing child poverty and faced the same pressures for austerity, but the dominant logic of tax relief limited their ability to structure the CTC and the EITC in ways that best reduced child poverty. Measured in both absolutely and relative terms, child poverty did decline by the end of the decade but still remained much higher in the US than in the UK and Canada (Smeeding 2006). This stemmed from the marked shift in benefits away from the poorest families to poor and working-class families further up the income distribution scale (Moffitt 2015).

The absence of family allowances is critical in explaining this divergence. Unable to tap into the logic of income supplementation that was institutionalized in that policy legacy, even liberal policymakers had no alternative but to accept the logic of tax relief. Democrats demonstrated ingenious political adeptness in strategically adopting the logic of tax relief, as it gave them major victories in otherwise unfavorable circumstances, but even these victories pale in comparison to the ease with which liberals and conservatives expanded similar refundable tax credits in the UK and Canada. Only when viewed from the perch of comparative politics do the successes and limits of fiscalization in the US make sense.

But how do we know that it is logics of appropriateness, rather than antiwelfare attitudes, mobilization of conservative forces, shifts toward workfare, or racial antagonisms, that explain continued American exceptionalism in this case? The next chapter steps back and summarizes the support for my theories of fiscalization, presents an extensive discussion of alternative arguments, and explains why these other theories are wrong or cannot explain as well as my theories do the timing or the shape that fiscalization took in the US, the UK, and Canada.

7

Conclusion

THE YEARS 2000–2010 became the decade of the "temporary" tax package. In 2001, in an effort to offset the regressive distributional effect of his tax plan, President George W. Bush proposed doubling the CTC to $1,000 per child and making it partially refundable for families making at least $10,000 per year. The expanded CTC eventually became policy as part of the administration's 2001 temporary tax package. Several years later, the Obama administration again enacted temporary legislation to lower the eligibility threshold to $8,500 and then $3,000, as part of a large stimulus package in the wake of the 2008 financial crisis. As the tax packages were set to expire, making the CTC once again nonrefundable, a familiar battle played out between a Republican-controlled Congress and the Obama administration. This time, the Obama administration claimed victory, as the CTC remained refundable at the low threshold of $3,000.

Does this victory indicate that the US has finally broken free of the logic of tax relief and embraced the logic of income supplementation? There's good reason to believe that the permanence of the policy change conceals the tenuous foundation on which CTC refundability rests. Concurrent events suggest that even moderate Republicans still do not accept the idea of the CTC as anything other than a mechanism for family tax relief. From its inception, policymakers built symbolic boundaries between the original nonrefundable CTC and its more recent refundable portion, which is technically a separate credit called the Additional Child Tax Credit. What at first glance seems like a minor technicality has actually been a major political issue for most Republicans.

In November 2015, the Republican-controlled House Ways and Means Committee held a hearing on "welfare programs" at which Representative Charles Boustany (R-LA) unveiled a chart highlighting the maze of welfare programs he believed were in need of reform. The chart listed four cash aid programs in particular. Temporary Assistance to Needy Families and Supplemental Security Income are both widely perceived as traditional social assistance programs for the unemployed and disabled. More interestingly, the chart also listed the refundable portions of the EITC and the Additional Child Tax Credit—but not the nonrefundable portions. In the eyes of Republicans, refundability is still synonymous with welfare.

This does not mean that Republicans have been opposed to any and all expansions of the EITC or the CTC. On the contrary, they have proposed a number of expansions in line with the logic of tax relief. Speaker of the House Paul Ryan (R-WI), who has led efforts to make poverty a major policy issue among Republicans, recently proposed expanding the EITC for childless workers as part of a comprehensive antipoverty agenda (Ryan 2014). Much like the 1974 Senate report that originally outlined the rationale for the EITC as an offset against payroll taxes, Ryan has proposed doubling the value of the EITC for childless workers to 15.3%—an amount equal to the combined employee-employer payroll tax burden.

Also in 2014, Senators Mike Lee (R-UT) and Marco Rubio (R-FL) unveiled a new "pro-family, pro-growth" tax reform that included a proposal for another $2,500 CTC in addition to the existing one. Building off of the work of former Treasury official Robert Stein (2010), the proposed CTC was explicitly governed according to the logic of tax relief. Keeping in line with Ryan's emphasis on emphasizing the plight of working-class families, Lee and Rubio emphasized that it was "applicable against income taxes and payroll taxes—i.e., the taxes that most burden lower- and middle-income families" (Lee and Rubio 2014). Even limited refundability against payroll taxes was too much to handle for some Republicans, though. In a subsequent presidential primary debate in which Rubio framed his CTC proposal as a form of family tax relief, his rival Senator Rand Paul (R-KY) attacked it as a "welfare transfer payment" rather than true tax relief. Despite limited forays into refundability, the logic of tax relief still acts as a powerful force structuring the extent to which policymakers may deviate from using tax credits as mechanisms for what is considered pure tax relief.

In examining the history of how the US got to this point today, while policymakers in Canada and the UK. pay little attention to whether tax credits conform to the logic of tax relief, I have made two arguments about (1) the convergence toward the fiscalization of social policy via child and in-work tax credits, and (2) the divergence in the cultural legacies of public policies that institutionalized distinct logics of appropriateness in the US versus other liberal welfare regimes. Before turning to this book's theoretical and policy implications, it is necessary to summarize my findings, discuss possible alternative explanations, and note the argument's limitations.

Explaining Convergence: Fiscalization

My theory of fiscalization accounts for both its timing and extent across liberal welfare regimes. The proliferation of child and in-work tax credits is an adaptation to austerity. As for traditional social security benefits, policymakers can claim credit for their expansion. Where they differ is that tax credits possess advantages due to their classification as "revenues not collected" in government budgets, which has enabled policymakers to obfuscate the effect of expansion, in two important ways. First, the conversion of social security programs into tax credits has allowed policymakers to signal austerity to financial watchdogs such as the IMF and credit markets. Second, introduction or expansion of tax credits has given policymakers a rhetorical weapon to wield against budget critics by taking advantage of seemingly objective budget scoring techniques to shape the distribution of benefits. This explanation departs from the traditional view of tax expenditures in the literature about American political development.

Beginning with Christopher Howard's groundbreaking work, scholars of American political development have extensively studied the US's "hidden," "divided," or "submerged" welfare state (Faricy 2015; Hacker 2002; Howard 1997; Mettler 2011). Despite the wide array of policy issues examined, there is a broad consensus in this literature on factors contributing to the fiscalization of social policy in the US: the unique structure of Congress empowers conservative legislators who are ideologically hostile to traditional social spending but friendlier to disbursing benefits in the form of tax expenditures.

In this view, the fragmentation of the American state is the biggest obstacle to more robust social spending. The problem for advocates of traditional welfare state expansion is that the committee structure in Congress disproportionately empowers conservative southern Democrats who, like Republican members of Congress, are opposed to the expansion of social welfare benefits, for reasons ranging from petty racial hostility to principled ideological opposition to "big government." At the same time, conservative policymakers prefer tax expenditures for a number of reasons, ranging from antitax, antispending ideology to distributing benefits to their upper-class supporters. Conservative intransigence on spending makes it harder for moderate and liberal Democrats to deliver benefits for their own constituencies during the periods of divided government that mark much of US history. As a result, moderate and liberal Democrats are forced to compete in the arena of tax policy, where there are fewer obstacles to obtaining benefits via tax expenditures for their constituencies. Party competition for the provision of tax expenditures reinforces tax credits' political popularity vis-à-vis traditional social spending.

Although the broad consensus among scholars of American political development suggests that these factors are important, the centrality of a constellation of distinctively American institutions (Congress) and actors (southern conservatives) suggests that this explanation may be less useful in explaining the international trends in fiscalization of social policy since the 1970s. By adding Canada and the UK as case studies, I have shown the shortcomings of this previous consensus. Two factors in particular are advantageous. First, Canada and the UK have parliamentary systems with strong parties. The fragmentation that is so central to US-based theories is completely absent in both countries. Second, even in the absence of this fragmentation and conservative veto players, left-leaning governments in Canada and the UK both introduced and expanded these tax credits. Further comparative analysis reveals that alternative explanations for fiscalization based on ideas, cost savings, and the salience of tax credits do not stand up to cross-national scrutiny.

Ideational explanations posit that the child and in-work tax credits are the result of resurgent conservative movement emphasis on being antitax, prowork, or both (Block 2009; Howard 1997; Moffitt 2015). While antitax sentiments did indeed contribute to the introduction of these tax credits in the US, I have shown that Canadian and British policymakers understood tax credits as income supplements delivered through the tax system rather than tax relief. The rationale behind them elsewhere was simply not antitax in nature. Relatedly, while policymakers everywhere perceived child and in-work tax credits as being prowork, this was related to their structure, not their classification as tax credits. This becomes clear in the UK case, where the traditional Child Benefit and the FIS had long been considered prowork before their conversion into tax credits.

Cost-saving explanations see tax credits as the "progeny of austerity," in that they allow policymakers to increase benefits for lower-income families by redistributing benefits from high-income families (Levy 1999; Myles and Pierson 1997). In many cases, the introduction of tax credits has gone hand in hand with income-testing that excludes middle- or upper-income families. Like the prowork explanation, this one confuses structure with classification. Any cost Savings come from income-testing, not conversion into tax credits. There is little evidence that administrative costs for tax credits are lower than those for traditional benefits. If anything, the reluctance of the UK Inland Revenue to take over administration and congressional criticisms of EITC administration and recommendations that it be moved to other agencies suggest that costs may be somewhat higher. In addition, this explanation makes little sense where tax credits were introduced wholesale rather than converted from already existing programs, as was the case with the American CTC and the Canadian WITB—both of which increased budget pressures in the absence of other changes.

Finally, a number of scholars suggest that the advantage of tax credits lay in the fact that they are less salient or "hidden" relative to traditional benefits (Howard 1997; Mettler 2011; Myles and Pierson 1997). This might be true for some—mostly corporate—tax expenditures, but it is not the case for the tax credits examined here. The American CTC, for example, was the "crown jewel" of the Republican Party's famous Contract with America, and both Canadian and British policymakers made tax credits the center of high-profile campaigns to tackle child poverty. Policymakers counted on voters taking notice of these policy changes and rewarding them for it. None of this is to say that the perception of tax expenditures is unimportant. On the contrary, previous explanations have been right to focus on how tax credits have been perceived in the new era of permanent austerity. We must simply shift the focus and ask what we mean by austerity and from whom tax credits are hidden.

My comparative case design is useful for pinpointing the specific mechanisms that advantage tax credits over traditional social benefits, but unfortunately, the use of three liberal welfare regimes limits the generalizability of the findings. While I have been able to eliminate the alternative factors that American political development scholars think explain the proliferation of tax credits in the US, it is uncertain whether additional factors have played a role in policymakers' decisions to use tax credits. For example, the pressure to resort to using tax credits may be (and is likely) lower or absent in countries that have broader tax bases on which they can fund traditional welfare states (Kato 2003; Prasad and

Deng 2009). It is also unclear whether corporatist structures have any effect on this decision (Huber and Stephens 2001). One issue is that we lack comprehensive cross-national databases comparable to those typically used in large-N welfare state studies. Future research should focus on developing such a database (i.e., Ferrarini, Nelson, and Höög 2012) in order to expand the countries we can study and the methods with which we can study them.

Explaining Divergence: Distribution

In the beginning of this book, I noted a paradox. One of the primary motivations for the growth of these tax credits across all three countries was that they were part of conscious strategies for tackling child poverty. Despite this common goal, the poorest families were made ineligible for the benefits of these tax credits in the US but not in Canada or the UK. I then traced this divergence back to the 1940s, when Canada and British policymakers introduced family allowances but contingent events in the US prevented American policymakers from ever considering them. The result was the institutionalization of a logic of income supplementation elsewhere but not in the US, where the logic of tax relief, institutionalized in tax exemptions for children, remained dominant.

Fast-forward to the 1970s, when the onset of stagflation across the developed world led to new and intense economic pressures on families. Policymakers faced uncertainty about how to deal with inflation-induced erosion of tax and social benefits for families. In countries with family allowances, like Canada and the UK, policymakers and the public traced these pressures to the erosion of family allowances. Because the US had no family allowance, policymakers and the public instead traced these pressures to the erosion of dependent exemptions in the tax system. In doing so, they reinforced the dominant logic of appropriateness behind policy responses in each country. The decisions made during this period paved the way for full transformation in the 1990s.

During this decade, child poverty became a major political issue, leading to complete fiscalization in liberal welfare regimes. Despite sharing the common goal of reducing child poverty, policymakers' responses were powerfully shaped by the distinct logics of appropriateness that were institutionalized in the available policy legacies. Canadian and British policymakers saw tax credits as providing more inclusive income supplements. American policymakers saw tax credits as a form of tax relief for a narrower population of taxpayers. Whereas children dominated in the UK and Canada, taxpayers trumped children in the fight against child poverty in the US. Once again, my explanation departs from the traditional view of American exceptionalism in the political sociology literature. Explanations based on power resource, state-centered, cultural, and race-based approaches do not stand up to scrutiny in these cases.

Power resource approaches focus on the support or opposition of influential actors, such as business and labor groups, political parties, and advocacy groups, in explaining the structure of public policies (Brady, Blome, and Kleider 2016; Gitterman 2010). These interest-based explanations might predict that left-leaning parties, labor groups, and antipoverty advocates would favor the expansion of tax credits while right-leaning parties, business groups, and conservative movements would oppose it. While power resource theory has traditionally had good predictive power, the study of tax credits poses a special problem.

The vast majority of this research, especially those utilizing quantitative methods, operationalizes the welfare state as public social spending, usually measured as a percentage of GDP or on a per capita basis (Castles and Obinger 2007: 207). Reliance on such aggregates masks many the changes that need to be uncovered here, because tax credits often do not show up in the measures of spending used by welfare state scholars to test power resource theories. This may be part of the reason Huber and Stephens (2001) find that the exploratory power of power resource theory is relatively muted by the 1990s. Reliable historical and cross-national statistics are still hard to find and infrequently used (Faricy 2015). Instead, this study has looked at the moments when policies were introduced or blocked to see who supported or opposed them and finds a much more complicated picture.

Evidence for the influence of business groups is inconsistent across countries. British business groups did indeed come out against the WFTC when proposed, but this stemmed from their reluctance to be tasked with its administration more than anything else. Despite this opposition, the Labour government went ahead and introduced the tax credits anyway. Consistent with Howard's (1997) observation about other tax credits, we find little concern among US business groups with the distributive structure of tax credits. American business groups were concerned with their overall cost, in that it crowded out business tax cuts (US House 1991b), but offered little opinion on whether they should be refundable or not. Canadian business groups took surprisingly little interest in these tax credits as well. Labor groups took no strong positions either, offering tepid support for whichever policies were proposed by left parties but mounting no serious campaigns for or against proposed policy changes.

The evidence on partisanship is equally problematic. In the UK, the WFTC was introduced and subsequently split into the WTC and CTC under a Labour government, but we must also keep in mind that they were building on the previous Conservative government's expansion of the predecessor of the WFTC, the Family Credit. In Canada, the RCTC was first introduced under a Liberal government in 1978, expanded under successive Progressive Conservative governments through the 1980s and 1990s, and then expanded again under another Liberal government in the late 1990s. The WITB has a similar story, in that it was initially proposed (but never introduced) under a Liberal government in 2005 before a Conservative government introduced it in 2007.

In the US, the EITC and the CTC were introduced under divided government. Gitterman (2010: 105) argues that the CTC's introduction as nonrefundable, which resulted in fewer benefits for low-income families, was a consequence of Republican control of Congress, but Congress passed bills with nonrefundable credits three times between 1992 and 1997—once under Democratic control (1992) and twice under Republican control (1995 and 1997). Democrats did not pass refundable credits even when they controlled Congress. Moreover, we find that Republicans did support expansion of the EITC throughout the 1970s and 1980s, with opposition arising only in the 1990s. While this observation is inconsistent with power resource theory, it makes perfect sense in light of dominant logics of appropriateness. Republication support of EITC expansion in the 1970s and 1980s and opposition to it in the 1990s were both governed by the logic of tax relief.

A comparison of US and Canadian support for CTCs in the 1990s is must telling here because, as I have shown, the *same exact constellation of policy actors* was involved. Political parties, profamily conservatives, and antipoverty advocates all took positions on the structure of CTCs. In both Canada and the US, right-leaning parties introduced the credits with the support of both conservative profamily groups and liberal antipoverty advocates. On other social policy issues, Canadian and US groups took similar positions. For example, in both countries conservative groups supported welfare reform, and antipoverty groups opposed it. But US and Canadian interest groups diverged on the issue of CTC refundability. In Canada, the Progressive Conservative Party, with the support of the Family

Caucus and the Caledon Institute, introduced a refundable CTC. In the US, congressional Republicans, with the support of the Family Research Council and the Center on Budget and Policy Priorities, introduced a nonrefundable CTC. The different outcomes were due not to the relative strength of left and right interest groups in the two countries but to whether those groups perceived tax credits through the logic of tax relief or the logic of income supplementation. This is consistent with institutional criticism of power resource theories on the basis that political actors are relatively constrained in their actions (Brady, Blome, and Kleider 2016: 124).

State-centered approaches to social policy emphasize that successful programs require cross-class support (Korpe and Palme 1998; Prasad 2006; Skocpol 1991). This suggests that universal programs will be more resilient relative to targeted programs. The inclusion of both in-work (targeted) and child (universal) tax credits enables us to see how this approach stands up in the cases presented here. The evidence suggests that program structure had relatively little impact on the expansion of tax credits.

Robert Greenstein of the Center on Budget and Policy Priorities has offered the strongest challenge to this view, both theoretically and practically. In 1991, Greenstein first challenged Skocpol's contention that programs for poor people make poor programs, noting that she makes an inappropriate comparison between a contributory program for the retired elderly and a noncontributory program for the working-age poor (Greenstein 1991; Skocpol 1991). The point was that other factors might matter as much or even more. He used the example of the EITC as a case in point. As the architect of the 1993 EITC expansion and the chief defender of Republican efforts to cut it in 1995, Greenstein then offered a real-world demonstration of the weakness of arguments about targeted programs. The expansion of in-work tax credits targeted exclusively at the working class in Canada and the UK provides further evidence that the lack of cross-class coalitions was not an obstacle in these cases.

In regard to universal programs, this approach also has trouble explaining the variance I have shown in cross-class coalitions across national contexts. If anything, this explanation would lead us to expect initial proposals for a refundable CTC to succeed in the US as elsewhere, since refundability would bring low-income families into the supporting coalition (Pierson 1994; Prasad 2006). Thus while the outcome in Canada and the UK is compatible with a state-centered approach, such an approach has no obvious explanation for American exceptionalism. Whether coalitions formed was not based on economic interests, as these theories would predict, but rather on cultural factors—whether potential coalition members were seen as appropriate beneficiaries of a given benefit. Whether the logic was more inclusive (income supplementation) or exclusive (tax relief) determined whether successful cross-class coalitions formed.

Political culture explanations focus on the legacy of the English Poor Laws in institutionalizing distinctions between the "deserving" working poor and the "undeserving" welfare poor in social policy (Bertram 2015; Moffitt 2015; Steensland 2008). These explanations suggest that this legacy has resulted in a trend toward "workfare" in the US in recent decades. Such explanations would suggest that tax credits would be favored if they were seen as encouraging work and disfavored if they were seen as expanding welfare. While this theory is one of the most enduring ones in the sociology of US welfare policy, it suffers from complete lack of comparative analysis. The problem is that all three of the countries examined here have Poor Law legacies that make distinctions between the deserving and the undeserving poor. Moreover, these legacies played central roles in shaping welfare reform in all three countries in the 1990s (Bashevkin 2002). The US is simply not unique in this respect.

This approach treats the Poor Law legacy, or what I have been calling the logic of income support, as governing all of US social policy, but the fact is that this logic largely applies to only a small set of social assistance programs. It neglects other logics/legacies that may govern other social policies. I have highlighted two in particular—tax exemptions institutionalizing a logic of tax relief and family allowances institutionalizing a logic of income supplementation—that offer alternative springboards on which political actors may move social policy in other directions. What seems like a pervasive distinction based on work in the US does not stem from the Poor Law legacy of the 1830s. Rather, it stems from the absence of a legacy of income supplementation more recently in the 1940s.

Whereas the introduction of a nonrefundable CTC in the US is mistakenly attributed to the country's Poor Law legacy, both Canada and the UK introduced refundable CTCs without issue—at the same time they were undertaking punitive welfare reforms. Importantly, policymakers in all three countries saw their preferred version of the CTC as promoting work over welfare. The key difference is that Americans saw refundability above and beyond total tax liability as equivalent to welfare, while Canadians and the British saw it as a distinct alternative that helped "take children off welfare." The legacy of family allowances (or lack thereof), not Poor Laws, best explains this divergence.

Furthermore, the Poor Law legacy explanation even has trouble explaining conflicts within the US alone during the 1990s. Battles of the expansion or retrenchment of the EITC and over CTC stacking had little to do with distinctions between the welfare poor and the working poor. In each case, it was a question of who, among the working poor alone, should be eligible for these tax credits. The fault line was drawn according to the logic of tax relief. Not all of the working poor were deserving of tax relief. While the existence of the "undeserving working poor" makes little sense according to previous cultural explanations, it fits perfectly with my theory, which sees the absence of family allowances leading to the domi-nance of the logic of tax relief in the US but not in otherwise similar liberal welfare regimes.

Finally, a number of scholars have argued that racial animosity has had a key role in shaping the development of the US welfare state both historically (Quadagno 1994; Lieberman 1995) and contemporarily (Tesler 2016). Social policy has been extensively racialized in the US—programs perceived as assisting black families receive less support than programs perceived as assisting white families (Gilens 1999; DeSante 2013; Kinder and Kam 2009; Winters 2006). Given that the scope of racialization extends beyond negative assessments of social assistance to include pos-itive assessments of contribution-based pensions, it is possible that tax credits for families are similarly racialized and that this may affect support in terms of their structure. I discussed the problems with this approach in explaining the development of New Deal social programs and planning for postwar reconstruction in the US in chapter 2 (see also Davies and Derthick 1997; DeWitt 2010; Rodems and Shaefer 2016), but it is neces-sary to explore the possible effects of the racialization of social assistance in the postwar period.

Most prominently, Gilens (1999) argues that stereotypes about the work ethics of black parents are mediating factors in Americans' attitudes toward social assistance. He demonstrates that the media increasing portrayed poverty in highly racialized terms beginning in the 1960s, leading many Americans to see Aid to Families with Dependent Children as a program for poor black parents with questionable work ethics. This portrayal exacerbated very specific and already existing worries about the work ethics of welfare recipients in general. As a result, racial animosity lowers support for social assistance even lower than it would be otherwise. More recent research continues to find that racial animosity helps to explain why Americans hate welfare. Extrapolating from this, it is not unreasonable to suggest that Americans' aversion to making tax credits fully refundable is a spillover effect from racial animosity toward welfare recipients (i.e., Tesler 2016) rather than from the logic of tax relief as I argue here.

If this is the case, then we should expect it to apply in any country where social assistance has been stigmatized and racialized. Until recently, though, research on this issue focused entirely on the role of race in the US. Fortunately, new research has emerged looking at the possibility of racialization in other countries. In a series of articles, Allison Harell and colleagues have found evidence that, like their American counterparts, racial animosity reduces both British and Canadian support for social assistance (Harell et al. 2014; Harell et al. 2016). Despite this, both the UK and Canada introduced refundable tax credits without issue. This leads to a new question: Why were British and Canadian tax credits protected from racial spillover effects while American tax credits seemed so susceptible to it? This is where the explanatory power of my logics of appropriateness approach is at its greatest. The particular logic of appropriateness governing policymakers as they consider a social policy determines whether and how it becomes racialized.

Both Gilens (1999) and Harell and colleagues (2014), in the US and Canada, respectively, find little support for spending on "welfare." At the same time, they find widespread support for spending on "the poor." This is because the logic behind policies often delineates the social construction of the target population. The logic of income support makes welfare beneficiaries more susceptible to being portrayed as racial and stigmatized "others," but this does not necessarily spill over into the poor more generally. The literature finds an absence of racialization (i.e., spending on public education) or even a "positive" racialization related to whiteness (i.e., Social Security pensions) for most other social programs (Kinder and Kam 2009; Winter 2006). The direction and extent of racialization depends on how people perceive the logic behind the policy in question.

In fact, the issue of racialized welfare took center stage in Canada in October 1993, when Liberal opposition leader Lynn McLeod accused a Somali refugee organization of "importing refugees to systematically pillage our vulnerable and exposed social welfare systems" at a cost of tens of millions of dollars to Ontario taxpayers (Little 1998: 159). Canada found its very own welfare scapegoat as Toronto tabloids ran stories about Somali single mothers who were accused of "asylum shopping" in order to get the highest welfare benefits (Pratt and Valverde 2002: 153). Such rhetoric continued as the Progressive Conservative Party of Ontario, under the leadership of Premier Mike Harris, began a similar series of welfare reforms there. Harris's rhetoric became more punitive and moralistic as the New Democratic Party government and the Liberal opposition zeroed in on fraud and abuse as a major issue. Whereas the previous government had constrained social assistance benefit rates in 1994 as a deficit-fighting measure, Harris called for "removing from the rolls those who are ripping us off, those who are staying home and doing nothing because they want to do nothing," actively calling for workfare measures for the first time (Walker 1994). Just as conservative policymakers were doing in the US at the time, Harris began to continually juxtapose the deserving status of taxpayers with the undeserving status of welfare beneficiaries and the latent conflict between the two: "anyone in Ontario with the courage to say the words 'welfare reform' in public has the attention of most taxpayers" (Harris 1995). Harris had spent many years positioning himself as defender of the taxpayer, and it was finally paying off. In anticipation of the 1995 provincial election, Harris and the Progressive Conservatives released an election pamphlet under the banner of the "Common Sense Revolution." Much like the Republicans' Contract with America, the pamphlet was geared toward taxpayers rather than social assistance beneficiaries. Harris promised to slash income taxes by 30%, cut "Cadillac" welfare benefits by 20%, and eliminate fraud and abuse within the system (Progressive Conservative Party of Ontario 1995). The racialization and stigmatization of welfare did not stop at the 49th parallel.

This is key because, as I have shown, tax credits have been governed historically either by the logic of tax relief or the logic of income supplementation. It is only within the context of the logic of tax relief that refundability has become synonymous with "welfare" for those without any income or payroll tax liability. To the extent that tax credits have become racialized in the US, it is a spillover effect from their partial refundability and the boundaries of tax relief. The logic of income supplementation, which has governed tax credits in the UK and Canada, is not susceptible to the same accusation of being "welfare" and thus has been protected from racialized spillover effects. This was most clear in the Canadian case when policymakers simultaneously reduced welfare benefits (racialized logic of income support) while increasing CTCs (nonracialized logic of income supplementation) for the *exact same families* without any problem. It is fair to conclude that if American policymakers had access to the same institutionalized logic of income supplementation as their British and Canadian counterparts, then the idea of tax credits as welfare, and thus their racialization, would never have been an issue in the first place.

Accordingly, although racialized welfare politics are not the main focus of this book, I hope my approach brings some insightful nuance to the literature on race in American politics by bringing a comparative perspective back in. Too often, we become mired in arguments about whether race matters in American politics. That much is clear. The real question, as scholars like Evan Lieberman (2003) have showed, is not whether race matters but under what circumstances and to what extent race shapes politics and to what extent political institutions make race salient in politics. This opens up the possibility that there have been paths the US might have taken in which race was less salient in social policy and the hope that we may yet find new paths to minimize racialization's effects on the fight against poverty.

American Exceptionalism Revisited

Dating perhaps as far back as Alexis de Tocqueville's *Democracy in America*, theories of American exceptionalism have been one of the most enduring research programs in comparative politics and political sociology (Amenta et al. 2001; Lipset 1990; Prasad 2016). This book challenges the traditional conception of American exceptionalism in two ways.[1]

First, this book undermines previous arguments—often made implicitly, in that scholars emphasize the unique structure of Congress—that the US is exceptional when it comes to the use of tax credits for social policy purposes. Whereas scholars of American political development implicitly assume this is a uniquely American phenomenon (Faricy 2015: 10; Hacker 2002: 46–48; Howard 1997: 17; Mettler 2011), we find that other countries have converged on the same set of child and in-work tax credits. Despite this global trend, sociological research on tax policy and welfare states has yet to account for this new development in our theories. This book begins the process of catching up theory with the world around us, extending the literature on tax expenditures beyond the US case, and proposing a novel theory to explain their relatively recent international proliferation.

Fiscalization has flourished in these countries because policymakers have seen tax credits as a way to get around budget constraints in an environment that has emphasized spending cuts as the primary route to austerity. Tax credits have flourished because of their budget classification as revenues not collected rather than spending. This has obfuscated their effect on the budget for financial watchdogs, concerned principally with aggregate spending rather than the individual programs that have constituted it. By examining one strategy often associated with retrenchment—obfuscation—and showing how the same strategy has successfully been used to expand the welfare state, we can begin to reinvigorate the "new politics of the welfare state" with new and interesting questions.

Although not explicitly examined credit and loan guarantee programs here, this study also suggests that the same characteristics that make tax expenditures so attractive to policymakers may also make those programs attractive for similar reasons. A number of recent studies on "financialization" argue that policymakers in the US turn to credit programs when faced with tight fiscal restraints (Krippner 2011; Prasad 2012a; Quinn n.d.). Much like tax expenditures, credit programs often do not show up as spending in government budgets. As the welfare state evolves into new forms, including fiscalization and financialization, our theoretical analyses must evolve with it.

Second, the enduring differences between US tax credits and those in other liberal welfare regimes suggest that we need to modify existing theories of American exceptionalism to account for differences in historical trajectories. The book identifies one specific mechanism through which historical policy decisions can have ongoing political effects. Other scholars have shown how policies institutionalize target populations or cultural categories (Katz 1996; Schneider and Ingram 2005; Steensland 2008). Building on March and Olsen's (2008) concept of "logics of appropriateness," this study has shown how past policies can institutionalize matches between particular categories of beneficiaries and types of benefits. The presence or absence of such legacies constrains policymakers seeking to provide new kinds of benefits, even to populations (like children) otherwise seen as deserving. Though the subsequent history of the EITC and the CTC suggests that ongoing efforts can partially counter such legacies, it is clearly a long, upward struggle. In other countries, by comparison, the bright line between refundability and nonrefundability, which has been so meaningful in the US, has been simply irrelevant.

The focus on logics of appropriateness also leads us to rethink the historiography of the American welfare state. Two periods in particular, the 1930s and the 1970s, are called into question. First, the majority of the scholarship focuses on the interwar and the Depression period—when President Roosevelt first introduced the series of New Deal programs that grew into what we know today as the foundation of the American welfare state—as the most important critical juncture (Amenta 1998; Katznelson 2014; Prasad 2012a). These accounts portray failed efforts at postwar construction, such as the failure of the Wagner-Murray-Dingell bill, as foregone conclusions that came after the window of opportunity closed. Rather than reflecting this closure, chapter 2 shows that the Roosevelt administration's decision to forgo the chance to craft a new "American Beveridge plan" that included family allowances was the source of this closure.

The literature indicates that this divergence had major effects on the development of the US welfare state. The failure to adopt family allowances left the US with no universal, noncontributory benefits program. Brown (1999) suggests that much of the racialization of the US welfare state stems from its reliance on means-tested welfare programs stereotyped as handouts to poor black families and contributory programs premised on regular employment from which black workers were excluded. Family allowances had the potential to create cross-racial coalitions otherwise unheard of in the US. In addition, the advantage of universal programs for creating cross-class (Prasad 2006) and symbolic (Steensland 2008) coalitions in favor of expansion and as a vanguard against retrenchment is clear. In light of the experiences of other countries, it is doubtful that continued antipathy toward the welfare state among American conservatives would be so severe if the US had adopted family allowances. In doing so, this book follows an emerging literature that lays some of the blame for America's underdeveloped welfare state on the choices made by liberal state builders in the 1940s (Michelmore 2012; Prasad 2012a) rather than conservatives or business groups.

Second, my findings challenge accounts of why Americans have become so antitax since the 1970s. Rather than attributing this phenomenon to racial animosity, the power of antitax movements, or the structure of taxation (Block 2009; Martin 2008; Harvey 2005; Phillips-Fein 2009; Prasad 2006), this book finds that Americans are intensely antitax because they have been left with no other choice. As chapter 3 suggests, the unusually strong antitax movements in the US would not have arisen if policymakers had been able to assist families with children through family allowance programs rather than the expansion of child-related tax exemptions and credits. Tax relief only became a salient issue because policymakers in the US, unlike policymakers in the UK and Canada, have not had and still do not have alternative programs to expand as economic pressures have mounted since the 1970s. Whereas the antitax goals of Thatcherism have largely been abandoned in the UK, Reagan's antitax legacy remains strong in the US.

This is because antitax policies, rather than being a conservative way to undermine antipoverty policies, are themselves broadly popular economic security policies with a role equivalent to the role family allowances played in other countries until they were converted into refundable tax credits. Antitax activists are successful not because Americans are reflexively antitax but because protax activists have no universal, noncontributory program to which they can point as a legitimate reason to raise taxes. Even the most "neoliberal" leaders, such as Thatcher in the UK and Mulroney in Canada, raised taxes to pay for popular social benefits. On the other hand, while Reagan was able to raise earmarked payroll taxes to pay for Social Security benefits, he faced no popular pressures to raise taxes in order to bolster noncontributory programs.

Rather than asking why American voters and policymakers are so antitax, fiscal sociologists should be asking why people might be protax in the first place. This gets at the heart of one of the great debates among fiscal sociologists: whether lack of fiscal capacity has undermined support for the welfare state or whether support for the welfare state has led to tolerance of higher taxes (Kato 2003; Lindert 2004; Prasad 2012a; Prasad and Deng 2009). My view, based on the evidence presented here, is that at least one relatively universal, noncontributory program is necessary to stem the tide of antitax sentiment in the US.

Child Poverty: Crafting Viable Policies

In chapter 1, I noted that there is a consensus among poverty scholars that broad and generous cash benefits are the most effective policy for reducing child poverty.[2] Despite budget constraints, the combination of refundable child and in-work tax credits enabled Canada and the UK to lower their child poverty rates over time and relative to the US. As such, the ultimate goal for American policymakers should be to move toward full policy convergence with other successful liberal welfare regimes. This includes making the CTC completely refundable and separating the child- and work-related components of tax benefits so the EITC becomes a pure in-work tax benefit unrelated to family size. The history of other countries suggests that US policymakers need to proceed with the former before they attempt the latter, which is why I will conclude with a discussion of CTC reform while leaving EITC reform for another day.

In recent years, a number of antipoverty advocates on the left, looking at the success of Canada and the UK, have made policy recommendations to substantially expand the CTC and make it fully refundable so that all families with children are eligible for it (Children's Defense Fund 2015; Garfinkel et al. 2010; Garfinkel et al. 2016; Waldfogel 2010; West et al. 2015). From a poverty reduction standpoint, this would make for an excellent reform, substantially lowering the poverty rate among children. From a political viability standpoint, these proposals all suffer from the exact same problems as the refundable CTC first recommended by the NCC over twenty-five years ago. Unfortunately, if left in their current forms, they are likely to follow its fate. This leaves us with quite the conundrum. Conservative proposals (like the Rubio-Lee proposal) would successfully resonate with logic of tax relief but would be ineffective at reducing child poverty. Liberal proposals would effectively reduce child poverty *if enacted*, but there is little chance that they will survive the policymaking process.

Institutions, such as those imbued with logics of appropriateness discussed in this book, are durable constraints on even the most determined reformers, but the obstacles to institutional change, however great, are not insurmountable. While sociologists spend most of their time explaining institutional continuity, there is also an important literature on the circumstances under which institutional change becomes possible. In this case, child-related tax benefits in the US are ripe for what Streeck and Thelen (2005: 31) call "conversion" or the "redeployment of old institutions to new purposes." Conversion is possible because of growing gaps in the unique coalition that brought tax relief for families to the fore of American politics in the first place. Much of the success of the GOP's tax-cutting agenda has been premised on cooperation between the profamily and antitax factions in the Republican Party coalition.

Since the 1970s, these two rivals have coexisted peacefully, based on a compromise in which Republicans put forth a strategy of providing profamily tax relief in the form of policies like the expansion of the dependent exemption, the EITC, the CTC, and the elimination of marriage penalties in the tax code. As I showed in earlier chapters, this strategy has been wildly successful in fostering a coalition for policies that have gained wider support among the voting public. More important, these compromises have enabled both factions to retain their ideological purity. Taxpayers and families each receive recognition that they are worthy and important players in American life.

Recent events suggest that we have reached the limits of this strategy, testing the strength of the coalition in the process. Ironically, it is a victim of its own success. There is simply very little tax relief to offer working-class families with children anymore. The combination of broad-based tax cuts and the growth of child-related tax benefits has relieved families of much or all of their federal tax burdens. Mitt Romney's infamous comment about the 47% of Americans who pay no federal income taxes is a case in point. Of those who pay no income tax, almost one-third of them are families who are made nontaxable by these various child-related credits and exemptions. The refundable EITC, which was introduced in 1975 with the explicit goal of offsetting rising Social Security taxes for working-class families, wipes out much of these families' payroll tax liabilities as well. In 2014, a family of four earning one-half of the median income (about $38,000) had an effective tax rate of 0% for their income and for the employee portion of their Social Security and Medicare taxes. For the same family earning the median income (about $76,000), their effective tax rate has dropped from a high of 18.4% in 1981 to about 13% today.

On the one hand profamily and antitax activists should celebrate this achievement. The rising tax burden on families that Americans worried so much about in the 1970s has not only been halted but substantially beaten back or eliminated altogether. On the other hand this achievement poses a major problem for the aforementioned coalition, exemplified by Rubio's CTC proposal.

Rubio has gone to great lengths to frame his CTC as a decidedly profamily measure in order to garner support from social conservatives concerned with making sure public policy supports stable families. At the same time, Rubio has been pushed to clarify that only families with a positive income and payroll tax liability are eligible for his CTC in order to appease antitax conservatives who will not support it unless it is a pure tax relief measure. Because most working-class families already pay little or no federal income and payroll taxes, they will receive little or no benefit from Rubio's proposed CTC. A middle-class family of four earning the median income would receive the full $5,000 value of the credits for their two children. The same working-class family earning half the median income would only receive about half this amount for the same two children. The disparities only grow for larger families.

The most strident antitax conservatives are fine with this, concerned primarily with limiting tax relief to taxpayers, but it has given pause to some profamily and so-called reform conservatives have pause. How "profamily" can a policy really be if it excludes some poor and working-class families altogether? We've reached the point where one can no longer be antitax and profamily. One must either be antitax or profamily when it comes to child benefits. The gap leaves profamily and reform conservatives open to the possibility of supporting a fully refundable CTC—if, and only if, it aligns with their other priorities, though. For profamily conservatives, supporting marriage and family stability are major priorities. Among reform conservatives, fiscal responsibility and streamlining government are major priorities. The best chance for making the CTC fully refundable is to "convert" it from an antitax policy to a profamily, fiscally responsibly reform policy.

Steven Teles (2013) has written about the problem of complexity—what he calls America's kludgeocracy—as overlapping programs, often working at cross purposes, are introduced haphazardly over the years. It has become increasingly hard for parents to navigate the plethora of government policies and programs aimed at strengthening families. One important step that advocates of a refundable CTC can take is to push for rationalization of this system as it manifests itself in child-related tax/transfer benefits. Representative Paul Ryan recognized this issue in his proposal to consolidate a number of means-tested programs into a single block grant to states to spend as they see fit. While consolidation is a good goal, there is no promise that the vertical consolidation Ryan proposes will result in a simpler, more effective system for families or savings for taxpayers. Simply put, there is no reason to believe that state governments are any less dysfunctional than the federal government. Instead, antipoverty advocates should work with reform conservatives to craft a fiscally responsible profamily horizontal consolidation of current tax-transfer programs aimed at children. Shifting the conversation to revenue/spending neutral simplification would lower the stakes and push rhetoric in a more technocratic, less morally charged direction.

Depending on their income, family structure, and childcare situation, parents may be eligible for the head of household filer status, the dependent exemption, the CTC, the EITC, the child and dependent care tax credit, or the Supplemental Nutritional Assistance Program. This alphabet soup is enough to confuse any parent (including the author of this book, who still needed help filling out a W-4 form after the birth of his daughter). Elaine Maag (2013) of the Urban-Brookings Tax Policy Center recently estimated that these child-related tax benefits amounted to $171 billion in 2013. If we exclude the EITC but include Supplemental Nutritional Assistance Program benefits for children, then the total drops to just about $139 billion in child-related benefits across five different programs. This is a lot of money, but it is being distributed ineffectively. Complexity, not cost, is the problem. This system is inefficient, ineffective, and unfair to families. It penalizes work and marriage while doing little to tackle child poverty.

The Canadian experience of the 1990s offers an attractive model for reform. As I showed in chapter 4, their goal was to consolidate portions of means-tested programs together with various child-related tax and transfer policies into a single refundable CTC. In 1992, the Progressive Conservatives introduced the refundable Child Tax Benefit—rationalizing a fragmented system, reducing penalties on work and marriage, and cutting child poverty at the same time. Left-leaning antipoverty groups fought the reforms tooth and nail because they would not increase benefits for those on social assistance. If they had gotten their way, the reform would have fallen apart. In retrospect, it was clearly a good thing that the critics lost the battle. The Progressive Conservative reforms provided the foundation for subsequent types of expansions of the CTB that would not have occurred otherwise.

Antipoverty advocates need to work with profamily and reform conservatives to craft a bipartisan policy that similarly consolidates various child-related benefits into one refundable CTC. Importantly, this reform should *not* be aimed at raising total benefits for the poorest families. Doing so would raise red flags among conservatives that the reform is really just a Trojan horse for the kind of redistribution to welfare families they currently oppose. Simplifying child-related benefits for all families is a worthy goal in and of itself.

If policymakers took the $139 billion spent on the current maze of child-related programs and scrapped them in favor of a single refundable CTC worth $2,500 per child, they could strengthen families by reducing complexity (Campbell 2015; Levine 2013), increasing income stability (Charles and Stephens 2004; Conger et al. 1990; Eliason 2012; Western et al. 2016), and eliminating marriage penalties (Carusso and Steuerle 2005). This benefit would also eliminate work disincentives (Steuerle 2012) as well as the stigma and underreporting associated with the Supplemental Nutritional Assistance Program (Teihan et al. 2016). Best of all, it would do all this while ensuring that poor, working, and middle-class families were as well or better off than under the current system, without increasing the deficit one penny. This combination of benefits from consolidation enables what Teles and Dagan (2016: 118) call "trans-partisanship," or "agreement on policy goals driven by divergent, deeply held ideological beliefs."[3] In this case, profamily conservatives and reform conservatives would divorce supply-side tax cutters in order to build an ad hoc coalition with traditionally liberal antipoverty advocates.

Americans are increasingly politically polarized on a number of issues, but tackling child poverty should not and need not be one. A transpartisan coalition in favor of reforms leading to a refundable CTC could be the solution to gridlock and obstructionism. It is up to policymakers to make it happen, because American families deserve it.

Notes

1. Tax credits can either be refundable or nonrefundable. Nonrefundable credits allow the beneficiary to receive the value of the credit insofar as it offsets the beneficiary's income tax liability. Because the progressive nature of some income tax systems may leave many low-income families without any tax liability, they may only be able to claim part of a nonrefundable tax credit or none at all. In contrast, beneficiaries meeting the eligibility requirements of refundable tax credits may claim their full value regardless of income tax liability.
2. North America is unique in using absolute measures of poverty rather than the relative measures used by most other rich democracies. Following the norm in comparative research, I have chosen to use the most commonly used relative measure (those falling under 50% of the median income) over absolute measures, such as the American supplemental poverty measure or the Canadian low-income cutoff.

CHAPTER 2

1. This includes Australia (1941), Canada (1944), the UK (1945), and New Zealand (1946).
2. Sociologist Joya Misra (2003) has done the most comprehensive comparative analysis on the introduction of family allowances during the interwar and World War II periods. Using a Qualitative Comparative Analysis for eighteen industrialized democracies, she examines a number of explanations for their adoption. Unfortunately, she finds no common path to the adoption of family allowances (or nonadoption in the US case) among liberal welfare regimes.
3. In South Africa, a constitution outlining a racially exclusive unitary state led wealthy white South Africans to see poor whites as belonging to the same

community, encouraging tax compliance to help them. In Brazil, a constitution outlining a racially inclusive federal state led wealthy white Brazilians to see only those in their immediate region as belonging to the same community, encouraging tax evasion, on the belief that tax revenues paid are otherwise extracted by those outside the community.

4. Indeed, the failure of family allowances in the 1960s stems, in part, from the fact that they came on the political agenda after the racialization of social assistance and increasing dominance of economists in policymaking (Steensland 2008).

5. Pearson identifies several mechanisms as they affect the public at large. The focus here is on how the sequence of events affects elites within the government.

6. That is, the welfare state consisting of the big five programs of workers' compensation, old-age pensions, health insurance, unemployment insurance, and family allowances.

7. One wonders whether gender played some role as well. Burns likely had a great disadvantage in getting her voice heard relative to Marsh, especially when it came to senior bureaucrats and cabinet members.

CHAPTER 4

1. The Department of Human Resource Development was the heir to the DNHW, which was created under the previous government. It combined jurisdiction over four areas previously under the control of other departments, including job training, unemployment insurance, labor standards, social assistance, education, old-age pensions, and CTBs.

CHAPTER 5

1. The other three papers focused on increasing the savings rate among families and were thus excluded.

2. It is worth noting that the few mentions of taxpayers and tax relief we find in the series The Modernisation of Britain's Tax and Benefit System are almost always in reference to reducing National Insurance Contributions—not tax credits.

CHAPTER 6

1. In addition to the EITC and CTC, the decade also saw the largest expansion of health insurance for children, the State Children's Health Insurance Program, since the introduction of Medicaid in 1965.

2. See also US House (1991b) for similar examples of this logic at work.

CHAPTER 7

1. It is worth noting that I have not offered a grand unified theory of American exceptionalism here. Nor do I believe it is possible to construct one. Given the importance of contingency and policy legacies, it has become clear to me that an explanation of American exceptionalism looking at family allowances and refundable tax credits will likely look different from one looking at social assistance, healthcare, federalism, immigration, or any other set of policies in which the US is exceptional in some way. Scholars may one day discover a sui generis factor broadly explaining American exceptionalism, but I remain skeptical.

2. Work and marriage are the other two important factors, though they may be less amenable to policy solutions.

3. Transpartisanship differs from bipartisanship, where compromise is based on agreeing to the lowest-common-denominator policies between liberals and conservatives. As the recent American Enterprise Institute/Brookings Working Group on Poverty and Opportunity (2015) report reveals, this has led to more of the same old policies that have failed to reduce child poverty in the past.

Bibliography

Aaron, Henry (ed.). (1976). *Inflation and the Income Tax.* Washington, DC: Brookings Institution.

Advisory Commission on Intergovernmental Relations. (1976). *Inflation and Federal and State Income Taxes.* Washington, DC: Government Printing Office.

Advisory Commission on Intergovernmental Relations. (1980). *The Inflation Tax: The Case for Indexing Federal and State Income Taxes.* Washington, DC: Government Printing Office.

Alesina, Alberto and Edward Glaeser. (2005). *Fighting Poverty in the US and Europe: A World of Difference.* Oxford: Oxford University Press.

Amenta, Edwin. (1998). *Bold Relief: Institutional Politics and the Origins of Modern American Social Policy.* Princeton: Princeton University Press.

Amenta, Edwin, Chris Bonastia, and Neal Caren. (2001). "US Social Policy in Comparative and Historical Perspective: Concepts, Images, Arguments, and Research Stratregies," *Annual Review of Sociology* 27: 213–43.

American Enterprise Institute. (1974). *Essays on Inflation and Indexation.* Washington, DC: American Enterprise Institute.

American Enterprise Institute/Brookings Working Group on Poverty and Opportunity. (2015). *Opportunity, Responsibility, and Security: A Consensus Plan for Reducing Poverty and Restoring the American Dream.* Washington, DC: American Enterprise Institute and Brookings Institution.

Archer, Bill. (1991). "Who's the Fairest of Them All?" *Policy Review* 57: 67–73.

Archer, Bill. (1997). "Tax Plan Gives Most Relief to the Middle Class." *New York Times.* 16 June: A14.

Auditor General of Canada. (1999). *Observations of the Auditor General on the Financial Statements of the Government of Canada.* Ottawa: Queen's Printer.

Auditor General of Canada. (2000). *Report of the Auditor General of Canada (October).* Ottawa: Queen's Printer.

Bakija, Jon, and Eugene Steuerle. (1991). "Individual Income Taxation since 1948." *National Tax Journal* 44(4): 451–475.

Banks, James, Richard Disney, Alan Duncan, and John Van Reenen. (2005). "The Internationalisation of Public Welfare Policy." *Economic Journal* 115: C62–C81.

Barnett, Joel. (1982). *Inside the Treasury*. London: Deutsch.

Bartels, Larry M. (2006). "A Tale of Two Tax Cuts, a Wage Squeeze, and a Tax Credit." *National Tax Journal* 59(3): 403–423.

Bartels, Larry M. (2010). *Unequal Democracy: The Political Economy of the New Gilded Age*. Princeton: Princeton University Press.

Bashevkin, Sylvia. (2002). *Welfare Hot Buttons: Women, Work, and Social Policy Reform*. Toronto: University of Toronto Press.

Battle, Ken. (1990). "Social Policy by Stealth." *Policy Options* 11(2): 17–29.

Battle, Ken. (1999). "Child Benefit Reform: A Case Study in Tax-Transfer Integration." *Canadian Tax Journal* 47(5): 1219–1257.

Battle, Ken. (2003). "The Role of a Think-Tank in Public Policy Development: Caledon and the National Child Benefit." *Horizons* 6(1): 11–15.

Battle, Ken, and Sherri Torjman. (1993). *The Welfare Wall: Reforming the Welfare and Tax Systems*. Ottawa: Caledon Institute of Social Policy.

Battle, Ken, and Sherri Torjman. (1995). *How Finance Re-Formed Social Policy*. Ottawa: Caledon Institute of Social Policy.

Benford, Robert D., and David A. Snow. (2000). "Framing Processes and Social Movements: An Overview and Assessment." *Annual Review of Sociology* 26: 611–639.

Bennet, James. (1997). "Gore and Gephardt, Potential Rivals in 2000, Join in Criticizing of G.O.P. on Taxes." *New York Times*. 11 July: A16.

Bertram, Eva C. (2007). "The Institutional Origins of 'Workfarist' Social Policy." *Studies in American Political Development* 21(2): 203–229.

Bertram, Eva C. (2015). *The Workfare State: Public Assistance Politics from the New Deal to the New Democrats*. Philadelphia: University of Pennsylvania Press.

Best, Rachel K. (2012). "Disease Politics and Medical Research Funding: Three Ways Advocacy Shapes Policy." *American Sociological Review* 77(5): 780–803.

Beveridge, William. (1942). *Social Insurance and Allied Services*. London: HMSO.

Beveridge, William H. (1943). "Social Security: Some Trans-Atlantic Comparisons." *Journal of the Royal Statistical Society* 106(4): 305–332.

Blair, Tony. (1999). "Beveridge Revisited: A Welfare State for the 21st Century." In *Ending Child Poverty*, edited by Robert Walker. Bristol: Policy Press: 7–18.

Blake, Raymond B. (2009). *From Rights to Needs: A History of Family Allowances in Canada, 1929–92*. Vancouver: UBC Press.

Block, Fred. (2009). "Read Their Lips: Taxation and the Right-Wing Agenda." In *The New Fiscal Sociology: Taxation in Comparative and Historical Perspective*, edited by Isaac W. Martin, Ajay K. Mehrotra, and Monica Prasad. Cambridge: Cambridge University Press: 68–85.

Blyth, Mark. (2002). *Great Transformations: Economic Ideas and Institutional Change in the Twentieth Century*. Cambridge: Cambridge University Press.

Blyth, Mark. (2013). *Austerity: The History of a Dangerous Idea*. Oxford: Oxford University Press.

Bochel, Hugh, and Andrew Defty. (2007). *Welfare Policy under New Labour: Views from Inside Westminster*. Bristol: Policy Press.

Bower, Tom. (2005). *Gordon Brown*. London: Harper Perennial.

Bowker, Geoffrey, and Susan Star. (1999). *Sorting Things Out: Classification and Its Consequences*. Cambridge, MA: MIT Press.

Brady, David. (2009). *Rich Democracies, Poor People: How Politics Explains Poverty*. Oxford: Oxford University Press.

Brady, David, Agnes Blome, and Hanna Kleider. (2016). "How Politics and Institutions Shape Poverty and Inequality." In *The Oxford Handbook of the Social Science of Poverty*, edited by David Brady and Linda M. Burton. Oxford: Oxford University Press: 117–140.

Brady, David, and Rebekah Burroway. (2012). "Targeting, Universalism, and Single-Mother Poverty: A Multilevel Analysis across 18 Affluent Democracies." *Demography* 49: 719–746.

Breul, Frank R. (1953). "The Genesis of Family Allowances in Canada." *Social Service Review* 27(3): 269–280.

Brewer, Mike, Tom Clark, and Matthew Wakefield. (2002). "Social Security in the UK under New Labour: What Did the Third Way Mean for Welfare Reform?" *Fiscal Studies* 23(4): 505–537.

Brodie, Janine. (2010). "Globalization, Canadian Family Policy and the Omissions of Neoliberalism." *North Carolina Law Review* 88(5): 1559–1592.

Brown, Colin. (1999). "Budget 1999: Family Tax Reform—Middle Class Loses Out as Children Gain." *Independent*. 10 March: 2.

Brown, Gordon. (1998). Budget Speech. *Hansard*. 17 March. Col. 1104–1105.

Brown, Hana E. (2013). "Race, Legality, and the Social Policy Consequences of Anti-immigration Mobilization." *American Sociological Review* 78(2): 290–314.

Brown, Michael K. (1999). *Race, Money, and the American Welfare State*. Ithaca: Cornell University Press.

Brownlee, W. Elliot (ed.). (1996). *Funding the Modern American State, 1941–1995: The Rise and Fall of the Era of Easy Finance*. Cambridge: Cambridge University Press.

Brownlee, W. Elliot. (2004). *Federal Taxation in America: A Short History*. Cambridge: Cambridge University Press.

Brownlee, W. Elliot, and C. Eugene Steuerle. (2004). "Taxation." In *The Reagan Presidency: Pragmatic Conservatism and Its Legacies*, edited by W. Elliot Brownlee and Hugh Davis Graham. Lawrence: University of Kansas Press: 155–181.

Bruce Reed Papers and Elena Kagan Papers. William J. Clinton Presidential Library and Museum. Little Rock, Arkansas.

Bryce, R. B. (1985). "The Canadian Economy in the 1930s: Unemployment Relief under Bennett and Mackenzie King." In *Explorations in Canadian Economic History: Essays in Honor of Irene M. Spry*, edited by Duncan Cameron. Ottawa: University of Ottawa Press: 7–26.

Burk, Kathleen, and Alec Cairncross. (1992). *Goodbye, Great Britain: The 1976 IMF Crisis*. New Haven: Yale University Press.

Burns, Eveline M. (1925). "The Economics of Family Endowment." *Economica* 14: 155–164.

Burns, Eveline M. (1943). "The Beveridge Report." *American Economic Review* 33(3): 512–533.

Burns, Eveline. (1944). "Social Insurance in Evolution." *American Economic Review* 34(1): 199–211.

Campbell, Andrea L. (2015). *Trapped in America's Safety Net: One Family's Struggle*. Chicago: University of Chicago Press.

Campbell, Andrea L., and Kimberly J. Morgan. (2005). "Financing the Welfare State: Elite Politics and the Decline of the Social Insurance Model in America." *Studies in American Political Development* 19(2): 173–195.

Canada. Department of Finance. (1978). *Report on the Integration of Social Security Program Payments into the Income Tax System*. Ottawa: Queen's Printer.

Canada. Department of Finance. (1984). *A New Direction for Canada: An Agenda for Economic Renewal*. Ottawa: Queen's Printer.

Canada. Department of Finance. (1993). *The Budget 1993*. Ottawa: Queen's Printer.

Canada. Department of Finance. (1994). *A New Framework for Economic Policy*. Ottawa: Queen's Printer.

Canada. Department of Finance. (2000). *Better Finances, Better Lives*. Ottawa: Queen's Printer.

Canada. Department of Finance. (2005). *A Plan for Growth and Prosperity*. Ottawa: Queen's Printer.

Canada. Department of Finance. (2006). *Focusing on Priorities*. Ottawa: Queen's Printer.

Canada. Department of Finance. (2007). *Aspire to a Stronger, Safer, Better Canada*. Ottawa: Queen's Printer.

Canada. Department of Finance. (2013). *Tax Expenditures and Evaluations*. Ottawa: Queen's Printer.

Canada. Department of Human Resources Development. (1994). *Improving Social Security in Canada: A Discussion Paper*. Ottawa: Queen's Printer.

Canada. Department of National Health and Welfare. (1992). *The Child Benefit: A White Paper on Canada's New Integrated Child Tax Benefit*. Ottawa: Queen's Printer.

Canada. Federal-Provincial Social Security Review. (1975). *Working Paper on Income Support and Supplementation*. Ottawa: Federal-Provincial Conference of Ministers of Welfare.

Canada. House of Commons. (1929). *Report, Proceedings and Evidence of the Select Standing Committee on Industrial and International Relations upon the Question of Granting Family Allowances*. Ottawa: Queen's Printer.

Canada. House of Commons. (1942). *Minutes of Proceedings and Evidence of the Special Committee on Reconstruction and Re-establishment*. Ottawa: Queen's Printer.

Canada. House of Commons. (1943). *Minutes of Proceedings and Evidence of the Special Committee on Reconstruction and Re-establishment.* Ottawa: Queen's Printer.

Canada. House of Commons. (1991). *Canada's Children: Investing in Our Future.* Ottawa: Queen's Printer.

Canada. House of Commons. (1992). *Minutes of Proceedings and Evidence of the Legislative Committee on Bill C-80.* Ottawa: Queen's Printer.

Canada. Senate. (1989). *Child Poverty and Adult Social Problems.* Ottawa: Queen's Printer.

Canada. Senate. (1991). *Child Poverty: Toward a Better Future.* Ottawa: Queen's Printer.

Capoccia, Giovanni. (2015). "Critical Junctures and Institutional Change." In *Advances in Comparative-Historical Analysis,* edited by James Mahoney and Kathleen Thelen. Cambridge: Cambridge University Press: 147–179.

Carluccio, Teresa. (1993). "Tax Expenditures for Social Policy: A Study of the Federal Child Tax Benefit System." ML thesis, University of Toronto.

Carruthers, Bruce G. (2010). "Knowledge and Liquidity: Institutional and Cognitive Foundations of the Subprime Crisis." *Research in the Sociology of Organizations* 30A: 155–180.

Carruthers, Bruce G., and Wendy N. Espeland. (1991). "Accounting for Rationality: Double-Entry Bookkeeping and the Rhetoric of Economic Rationality." *American Journal of Sociology* 97(1): 31–69.

Carusso, Adam, and C. Eugene Steuerle. (2005). "The Hefty Penalty on Marriage Facing Many Households with Children." *Future of Children* 15(2): 157–175.

Cassidy, Harry M. (1943). "Review of *Report on Social Security for Canada*." *American Economic Review* 33(3): 709–712.

Castles, Francis G., and Hebert Obinger. (2007). "Social Expenditure and the Politics of Redistribution." *Journal of European Social Policy* 17(3): 206–222.

Center on Budget and Policy Priorities. (1993a). *The Administration's Earned Income Credit Proposals.* Washington, DC: Center on Budget and Policy Priorities.

Center on Budget and Policy Priorities. (1993b). *The Clinton EITC Proposal: How It Would Work and Why It Is Needed.* Washington, DC: Center on Budget and Policy Priorities.

Center on Budget and Policy Priorities. (1993c). *The Senate Finance Committee's Actions in Removing $10 Billion from the Clinton EITC Expansion.* Washington, DC: Center on Budget and Policy Priorities.

Charles, Kerwin K., and Melvin Stephens. (2004). "Job Displacement, Disability, and Divorce." *Journal of Labor Economics* 22(2): 680–701.

Chetty, Raj, John N. Friedman, and Jonah Rockoff. (2011). *New Evidence on the Long-Term Impact of Tax Credits.* IRS Statistics of Income White Paper.

Children's Defense Fund. (2015). *Ending Child Poverty Now.* Washington, DC: Children's Defense Fund.

Christie, Nancy. (2000). *Engendering the State: Family, Work, and Welfare in Canada.* Toronto: University of Toronto Press.

Clawson, Marion. (1981). *New Deal Planning: The National Resources Planning Board.* Baltimore: Johns Hopkins University Press.

Clinton, William J. (1993). "Remarks on the Economic Program." *Weekly Compilation of Presidential Documents* 29(31): 1521–1523.

Clift, Ben and Jim Tomlinson. (2008). "Negotiating Credibility: Britain and the International Monetary Fund, 1956–1976," *Contemporary European History* 17(4): 545–566.

Cloud, David S. (1993a). "Clinton Looking to Tax Credit to Rescue Working Poor." *CQ Weekly*. 13 March: 583–587.

Cloud, David S. (1993b). "It's Democrats vs. Democrats as Conference Nears." *CQ Weekly*. 10 July: 1799–1801.

Cloud, David S., and George Hager. (1993). "Deal on Deficit Sets Stage for Senate Floor Fight." *CQ Weekly*. 19 June: 1542–1545.

Clymer, Adam. (1992). "Effort to Gut Tax Bill Fails in the Senate." *New York Times*. 13 March: D1.

Conger, Rand D., Glen H. Elder, Jr., Frederick O. Lorenz, Katherine J. Conger, Ronald L. Simons, Les B. Whitbeck, Shirley Huck, and Janet N. Melby. (1990). "Linking Economic Hardship to Marital Quality and Instability." *Journal of Marriage and Family* 52(3): 643–656.

Congressional Budget Office. (1980). *Indexing the Individual Income Tax for Inflation*. Washington, DC: U.S. Government Printing Office.

Congressional Budget Office. (1985). *Reducing Poverty among Children*. Washington, DC: U.S. Government Printing Office.

Connell, Andrew. (2011). *Welfare Policy under New Labour: The Politics of Social Security Reform*. London: I. B. Tauris.

Cook, Fay L., and Edith Barrett. (1992). *Support for the American Welfare State: The Views of Congress and the Public*. New York: Columbia University Press.

Coyle, Diane. (1998). "Tax Credit 'Unworkable.'" *Independent*. 3 December: 8.

Coyle, Diane. (2000). "Brown Hits Back at Budget Criticism." *Independent*. 14 April: 20.

Cropper, P. J. (1978). "United Kingdom Indexation of Personal Income Tax Allowances." *Intertax* 6(4): 134–138.

Cross, Simon, and Peter Golding. (1999). "A Poor Press? Media Reception of the Beveridge Lecture." In *Ending Child Poverty*, edited by Robert Walker. Bristol: Policy Press: 121–138.

Daunton, Martin. (2002). *Just Taxes: The Politics of Taxation in Britain 1914–1979*. Cambridge: Cambridge University Press.

Davies, Gareth, and Martha Derthick. (1997). "Race and Social Welfare Policy: The Social Security Act of 1935." *Political Science Quarterly* 112(2): 217–235.

Deacon, Alan, and Jonathan Bradshaw. (1983). *Reserved for the Poor: The Means Test in British Social Policy*. Oxford: Blackwell.

DeSante, Christopher D. (2013). "Working Twice as Hard to Get Half as Far: Race, Work Ethic, and America's Deserving Poor." *American Journal of Political Science* 57(2): 342–356.

DeWitt, Larry. (2010). "The Decision to Exclude Agricultural and Domestic Workers from the 1935 Social Security Act." *Social Security Bulletin* 70(4): 49–68.

Douglas, Paul. (1925). *Wages and the Family*. Chicago: University of Chicago Press.

Duncan, Alan, and David Greenaway. (2004). "Tax Credits and Welfare for Working Families: A Case Study of Policy Transfer." In *The Political Economy of Policy Reform*, edited by Douglas Nelson. Bingley: Emerald Group: 195–217.

Economist. (1977). "Taxation without Misrepresentation." 30 July: 70.

Economist. (1998). "Dreams of Field." 26 March: 35–40.

Eidlin, Barry. (2015). "Class vs. Special Interest: Labor, Power, and Politics in the United States and Canada in the Twentieth Century." *Politics and Society* 43(2): 181–211.

Eliason, Marcus. (2012). "Lost Jobs, Broken Marriages." *Journal of Population Economics* 25(4): 1365–1397.

Ellwood, David T. (1988). *Poor Support: Poverty in the American Family*. New York: Basic Books.

Emigh, Rebecca J. (1997). "The Power of Negative Thinking: The Use of Negative Case Methodology in the Development of Sociological Theory," *Theory and Society* 26(5): 649–684.

Epstein, Abraham. (1938). *Insecurity: A Challenge to America*. New York: Harrison Smith and Robert Haas.

Erwin, Lorna. (1993). "Neoconservatism and the Canadian Pro-family Movement." *Canadian Review of Sociology and Anthropology* 30(3): 401–420.

Evans, Patricia M. (1992). "Targeting Single Mothers for Employment: Comparisons from the United States, Britain, and Canada." *Social Service Review* 66(3): 378–398.

Evans, Rowland, and Robert Novak. (1993). "Reviving the Family Feud." *Washington Post*. 19 March: A31.

Faricy, Christopher. (2015). *Welfare for the Wealthy: Parties, Social Spending, and Inequality in the United States*. Cambridge: Cambridge University Press.

Ferrarini, Tommy, Kenneth Nelson, and Helena Höög. (2012). *The Fiscalization of Child Benefits in OECD Countries*. Gini Discussion Paper 49. Amsterdam: Amsterdam Institute for Advanced Labour Studies.

Ferree, Myra M. (2003). "Resonance and Radicalism: Feminist Framing in the Abortion Debates of the United States and Germany." *American Journal of Sociology* 109(2): 304–344.

Freeman, Lucy. (1948). "Family Life Held Strong amid Flux." *New York Times*. 19 November: 36.

Gaillard, Norbert. (2012). *A Century of Sovereign Ratings*. New York: Spring.

Gallup, Alec. (1999). *The Gallup Poll Cumulative Index: Public Opinion, 1935–1997*. Wilmington: Scholarly Resources.

Garfinkel, Irwin, David Harris, Jane Waldfogel, and Christopher Wimer. (2016). *Doing More for Our Children: Modeling a Universal Child Allowance or More Generous Child Tax Credit*. Washington, DC: Century Foundation.

Garfinkel, Irwin, Lee Rainwater, and Timothy Smeeding. (2010). *Wealth and Welfare States: Is America a Laggard or Leader?* Oxford: Oxford University Press.

Gilens, Martin. (1999). *Why Americans Hate Welfare: Race, Media, and the Politics of Antipoverty Policy*. Chicago: University of Chicago Press.

Gill, David J. (2015). "Rating the UK: The British Government's Sovereign Credit Ratings, 1976–8." *Economic History Review* 68(3): 1016–1037.

Gillespie, Irwin. (1991). *Tax, Borrow and Spend: Financing Federal Spending in Canada, 1867–1990*. Ottawa: Carleton University Press.

Gingrich, Newt. (1995). "The Contract's Crown Jewel." *Wall Street Journal*. 21 March: A20.

Gitterman, Daniel P. (2010). *Boosting Paychecks: The Politics of Supporting America's Working Poor*. Washington, DC: Brookings Institution Press.

Glennerester, Howard. (2007). *British Social Policy: 1945 to the Present*. Oxford: Blackwell.

Good, David A. (2013). "The New Bureaucratic Politics of Redistribution." In *Inequality and the Fading of Redistributive Politics*, edited by Keith Banting and John Myles. Vancouver: UBC Press: 210–233.

Gormley, William T. (2012). *Voices for Children: Rhetoric and Public Policy*. Washington, DC: Brookings Institution Press.

Granatstein, Jack L. (1975). *Canada's War: The Politics of the Mackenzie King Government, 1939–1945*. Oxford: Oxford University Press.

Greener, Kim, and Richard Cracknell. (1998). *Child Benefit*. House of Commons Research Paper 98/79. London: House of Commons Library.

Greenspon, Edward. (1996). "Ottawa Pressed for Initiative on Child Care." *Globe and Mail*. 23 November: A8.

Greenspon, Edward. (1997a). "New Child Tax benefit Planned." *Globe and Mail*. 28 January: A1.

Greenspon, Edward. (1997b). "Ottawa Advised to Stress Welfare of Children." *Globe and Mail*. 10 November: A1.

Greenspon, Edward. (1997c). "Poverty Issue Requires Kid Gloves." *Globe and Mail*. 17 February: A4.

Greenspon, Edward, and Anthony Wilson-Smith. (1996). *Double Vision: The Inside Story of the Liberals in Power*. Toronto: Doubleday Canada.

Greenstein, Robert. (1991). "Universal and Targeted Approaches to Relieving Poverty: An Alternative View." In *The Urban Underclass*, edited by Christopher Jencks and Paul E. Peterson. Washington, DC: Brookings Institution.

Grice, Andrew. (1999). "Budget 1999: Red Gordon and the Iron Chancellor Sit Happily Together." *Independent*. 10 March: 14.

Grice, Andrew. (2000). "Brown Planning Tax Cuts for Families in Bid to Blunt Tory Election Pledge." *Independent*. 2 November: 2.

Grice, Andrew, and Diane Coyle. (1999). "Official Figures Reveal Rise in Tax under Labour." *Independent*. 19 November: 2.

Guest, Dennis. (1999). *The Emergence of Social Security in Canada.* Vancouver: UBC Press.

Guetzkow, Joshua. (2010). "Beyond Deservingness: Congressional Discourse on Poverty, 1964–1996." *Annals of the American Academy of Political and Social Science* 629: 173–197.

Hacker, Jacob S. (2002). *The Divided Welfare State: The Battle over Public and Private Social Benefits in the United States.* Cambridge, MA: Harvard University Press.

Hacker, Jacob S., and Paul Pierson. (2010). "Winner-Take-All Politics: Public Policy, Political Organization, and the Precipitous Rise of Top Incomes in the United States." *Politics and Society* 38(2): 152–204.

Haddow, Rodney S. (1993). *Poverty Reform in Canada 1958–1978: State and Class Influence on Policymaking.* Montreal: McGill-Queen's University Press.

Hale, Geoffrey E. (2002). *The Politics of Taxation in Canada.* Peterborough: Broadview Press.

Hancock, Ange-Marie. (2004). *The Politics of Disgust: The Public Identity of the Welfare Queen.* New York: New York University Press.

Handler, Joel F., and Yeheskel Hasenfeld. (2007). *Blame Welfare, Ignore Poverty and Inequality.* Cambridge: Cambridge University Press.

Harell, Allison, Stuart Soroka, and Shanto Iyengar. (2016). "Race, Prejudice and Attitudes toward Redistribution: A Comparative Experimental Approach." *European Journal of Political Research* 55: 723–744.

Harell, Allison, Stuart Soroka, and Kiera Ladner. (2014). "Public Opinion, Prejudice and the Racialization of Welfare in Canada." *Ethnic and Racial Studies* 37(14): 2580–2597.

Harris, José. (1997). *William Beveridge: A Biography.* Oxford: Oxford University Press.

Harris, Michael. (1995). "Welfare Should Offer a Hand Up, Not a Hand-Out." *Policy Options* 16(4): 33–36.

Harvey, David. (2005). *A Brief History of Neoliberalism.* Oxford: Oxford University Press.

Haskins, Ron. (2006). *Work over Welfare: The Inside Story of the 1996 Welfare Reform Law.* Washington, DC: Brookings Institution Press.

Herbert, Bob. (1997). "Topsy-Turvy Tax-Cut." *New York Times.* 30 June: A11.

Higgs, Robert. (1987). *Crisis and Leviathan: Critical Episodes in the Growth of American Government.* Oxford: Oxford University Press.

Hilley, John L. (2008). *The Challenge of Legislation: Bipartisanship in a Partisan World.* Washington, DC: Brookings Institution Press.

Hills, John. (2002). "Following or Leading Public Opinion? Social Security Policy and Public Attitudes since 1997." *Fiscal Studies* 23(4): 539–558.

HM Revenues and Customs. (2014). *Child and Working Tax Credits Statistics.* London: HM Revenues and Customs.

HM Treasury. (1997–2005). *The Modernisation of Britain's Tax and Benefit System.* Nos. 1–11. London: HM Treasury.

HM Treasury. (1997). *Employment Opportunity in a Changing Labour Market*. The Modernisation of Britain's Tax and Benefit System 1. London: HM Treasury.

HM Treasury. (1998a). *Work Incentives: A Report by Martin Taylor*. The Modernisation of Britain's Tax and Benefit System 2. London: HM Treasury.

HM Treasury. (1998b). *The Working Families Tax Credit and Work Incentives*. The Modernisation of Britain's Tax and Benefit System 3. London: HM Treasury.

HM Treasury. (1999a). *Supporting Children through the Tax and Benefit System*. The Modernisation of Britain's Tax and Benefit System 6. London: HM Treasury.

HM Treasury. (1999b). *Tackling Poverty and Extending Opportunity*. The Modernisation of Britain's Tax and Benefit System 5. London: HM Treasury.

HM Treasury. (2002a). *Budget 2002*. London: HM Treasury.

HM Treasury. (2002b). *The Child and Working Tax Credits*. The Modernisation of Britain's Tax and Benefit System 10. London: HM Treasury.

Holt, Steve. (2006). *The Earned Income Tax Credit at Age 30: What We Know*. Brookings Institution Research Brief. Washington DC: Brookings Institution.

Howard, Christopher. (1997). *The Hidden Welfare State: Tax Expenditures and Social Policy in the United States*. Princeton: Princeton University Press.

Howard, Christopher. (2009). "Making Taxes the Life of the Party." In *The New Fiscal Sociology: Taxation in Comparative and Historical Perspective*, edited by Isaac W. Martin, Ajay K. Mehrotra, and Monica Prasad. Cambridge: Cambridge University Press: 86–100.

Huber, Evelyne, and John D. Stephens. (2001). *Development and Crisis of the Welfare State: Parties and Policies in Global Markets*. Chicago: University of Chicago Press.

Hunt, Albert. (1997). "This Republican Tax-Cut Dog Won't Hunt." *Wall Street Journal*. 26 June: A19.

Immervoll, Herwig, Holly Sutherland, and Klaas de Vos. (2001). "Reducing Child Poverty in the European Union: The Role of Child Benefits." In *Child Well-Being, Child Poverty and Child Policy in Modern Nations*, edited by Koen Vleminckx and Timothy M. Smeeding. Bristol: Policy Press: 407–432.

Independent. (1998). "Outlook: Doubt Cast on Chancellor's Figures." 7 July: 15.

Iyengar, Shanto. (1991). *Is Anyone Responsible? How Television Frames Political Issues*. Chicago: University of Chicago Press.

Jacobs, Meg. (2005). *Pocketbook Politics: Economic Citizenship in Twentieth-Century America*. Princeton: Princeton University Press.

Jeffries, John W. (1990). "The 'New' New Deal: FDR and American Liberalism, 1937–1945." *Political Science Quarterly* 105(3): 397–418.

Joyce, Philip G. (2011). *The Congressional Budget Office: Honest Numbers, Power, and Policymaking*. Washington, DC: Georgetown University Press.

Kasper, Sherry D. (2012). "Eveline Mabel Burns: The Neglected Contributions of a Social Security Pioneer." *Journal of the History of Economic Thought* 34(3): 321–337.

Kato, Junko. (2003). *Regressive Taxation and the Welfare State: Path Dependence and Policy Diffusion*. New York: Cambridge University Press.

Katz, Michael. (1996). *In the Shadow of the Poorhouse: A Social History of Welfare In America*. 10th anniversary ed. New York: Basic Books.

Katznelson, Ira. (2005). *When Affirmative Action Was White: An Untold Story of Racial Inequality in Twentieth-Century America*. New York: Norton.

Katznelson, Ira. (2014). *Fear Itself: The New Deal and the Origins of Our Time*. New York: Norton.

Keck, Jennifer M. (1995). "Making Work: Federal Job Creation Policy in the 1970s." PhD diss., University of Toronto.

Kenworthy, Lane. (2014). *Social Democratic America*. Oxford: Oxford University Press.

Kesselman, Jonathan R. (1979). "Credits, Exemptions, and Demogrants in Canadian Tax-Transfer Policy." *Canadian Tax Journal* 27(6): 653–688.

Kinder, Donald R., and Cindy D. Kam. (2009). *Us against Them: Ethnocentric Foundations of American Opinion*. Chicago: University of Chicago Press.

Kitchen, Brigitte. (1979). "A Canadian Compromise: The Refundable Child Tax Credit." *Canadian Taxation* 1(3): 44–51.

Korpi, Walter, and Joakim Palme. (1998). "The Paradox of Redistribution and Strategies of Equality: Welfare State Institutions, Inequality, and Poverty in Western Countries." *American Sociological Review* 63(5): 661–687.

Krippner, Greta R. (2011). *Capitalizing on Crisis: The Political Origins of the Rise of Finance*. Cambridge, MA: Harvard University Press.

Lee, Mike, and Marco Rubio. (2014). "A Pro-family, Pro-growth Tax Reform." *Wall Street Journal*. 23 September: A17.

Leman, Christopher. (1980). *The Collapse of Welfare Reform: Political Institutions, Policy, and the Poor in Canada and the United States*. Cambridge, MA: MIT Press.

Lenkowsky, Leslie. (1986). *Politics, Economics, and Welfare Reform*. London: University Press of America.

Levine, Judith. (2013). *Ain't No Trust: How Bosses, Boyfriends, and Bureaucrats Fail Low-Income Mothers and Why It Matters*. Los Angeles: University of California Press.

Levy, Jonah D. (1999). "Vice into Virtue? Progressive Politics and Welfare Reform in Continental Europe." *Politics and Society* 27(2): 239–273.

Liberal Party of Canada. (1997). *Securing Our Future Together*. Ottawa: Liberal Party of Canada.

Lieberman, Evan S. (2003). *Race and Regionalism in the Politics of Taxation in Brazil and South Africa*. Cambridge: Cambridge University Press.

Lieberman, Robert C. (1995). "Race, Institutions, and the Administration of Social Policy." *Social Science History* 19: 511–542.

Lindert, Peter H. (2004). *Growing Public*. Vol. 1. Cambridge: Cambridge University Press.

Lipset, Seymour M. (1990). *Continental Divide: The Values and Institutions of the United States and Canada*. New York: Routledge.

Little, Bruce. (1997). "Deficit Shrinking Faster Than Expected Gives Ottawa Manoeuvring Room on Tax Reductions." *Globe and Mail*. 18 January: B1.

Little, Margaret J. H. (1998). *No Car, No Radio, No Liquor Permit: The Moral Regulation of Single Mothers in Ontario, 1920–1997*. Toronto: Oxford University Press.

Maag, Elaine. (2013). *Child-Related Benefits in the Federal Income Tax*. Washington, DC: Urban Institute.

Macnicol, John. (1980). *The Movement for Family Allowances 1918–1945*. London: Heinemann.

Macnicol, John. (1992). "Welfare, Wages, and the Family: Child Endowments in Comparative Perspective, 1900–50." In *In the Name of the Child*, edited by Roger Cooter. New York: Routledge: 244–271.

Maioni, Antonia. (1998). *Parting at the Crossroads: The Emergence of Health Insurance in the United States and Canada*. Princeton: Princeton University Press.

March, James, and Johan Olsen. (2008). "The Logic of Appropriateness." In *The Oxford Handbook of Public Policy*, edited by Michael Moran, Martin Rein, and Robert E. Goodin. Oxford: Oxford University Press: 479–497.

Marsh, Leonard C. (1943). *Report on Social Security for Canada*. Ottawa: King's Printer.

Marsh, Leonard C. (1975). *Report on Social Security for Canada*. Toronto: University of Toronto Press.

Martin, Isaac W. (2008). *The Permanent Tax Revolt: How the Property Tax Transformed American Politics*. Stanford: Stanford University Press.

Maryl, Damon, and Sarah Quinn. (2016). "Beyond the Hidden American State: Rethinking Government Visibility." In *The Many Hands of the State: Theorizing Political Authority and Social Control*, edited by Kimberly Morgan and Ann Shola Orloff. Cambridge: Cambridge University Press: 58–80.

McCabe, Joshua, and Aaron Major. (2014). "The Adversarial Politics of Fiscal Federalism: Tax Policy and the Conservative Ascendancy in Canada, 1988–2008." *Social Science History* 38(3/4): 333–358.

McCammon, Holly. (2013). "Discursive Opportunity Structure." In *The Wiley-Blackwell Encyclopedia of Social and Political Movements*, Edited by David A. Snow, Donatella della Porta, Bert Klandermans, and Doug McAdam. Indianapolis: Wiley-Blackwell. 1–3.

McLaughlin, Eithne, Janet Trewsdale, and Naomi McCay. (2001). "The Rise and Fall of the U.K.'s First Tax Credit: The Working Families Tax Credit 1998–2000." *Social Policy and Administration* 35(2): 163–180.

Meanwell, Emily, and Julie Swando. (2013). "Who Deserves Good Schools? Cultural Categories of Worth and School Finance Reform." *Sociological Perspectives* 56(4): 495–522.

Mettler, Suzanne. (2011). *The Submerged State: How Invisible Government Policies Undermine American Democracy*. Chicago: University of Chicago Press.

Michelmore, Molly C. (2012). *Tax and Spend: The Welfare State, Tax Politics, and the Limits of American Liberalism*. Philadelphia: University of Pennsylvania Press.

Ministerial Council on Social Policy Reform and Renewal. (1996). *Report to Premiers*. Ottawa: Ministerial Council on Social Policy Reform and Renewal.

Mirowski, Philip and Dieter Plehwe (eds.). (2009). *The Road from Mont Pelerin: The Making of the Neoliberal Thought Collective*. Cambridge, MA: Harvard University Press.

Misra, Joya. (2003). "Women as Agents in Welfare State Development: A Cross-national Analysis of Family Allowance Adoption." *Socio-Economic Review* 1(2): 185–214.

Moffitt, Robert A. (2015). "The Deserving Poor, the Family, and the U.S. Welfare System." *Demography* 52: 729–749.

Morgan, David R. (1977). *Over-taxation by Inflation*. London: Institute for Economic Affairs.

Murray, Charles. (1984). *Losing Ground: American Social Policy, 1950–1980*. New York: Basic Books.

Myles, John. (1998). "How to Design a 'Liberal' Welfare State: A Comparison of Canada and the United States." *Social Policy and Administration* 32(4): 341–364.

Myles, John, and Paul Pierson. (1997). "Friedman's Revenge: The Reform of 'Liberal' Welfare States in Canada and the United States." *Politics and Society* 25(4): 443–472.

National Commission on America's Urban Families. (1993). *Families First*. Washington, DC: Government Printing Office.

National Commission on Children. (1990). *Opening Doors for America's Children: Interim Report*. Washington, DC: National Commission on Children.

National Commission on Children. (1991). *Beyond Rhetoric: A New American Agenda for Children and Families*. Washington, DC: Government Printing Office.

National Council of Welfare. (1989). *Welfare Incomes 1989*. Ottawa: National Council of Welfare.

National Council of Welfare. (1993). *Incentives and Disincentives to Work*. Ottawa: National Council of Welfare.

National Council of Welfare. (1999). *Welfare Incomes 1999*. Ottawa: National Council of Welfare.

National Council of Welfare. (2009). *Welfare Incomes 2009*. Ottawa: National Council of Welfare.

National Resources Planning Board. (1941). *Security, Work, and Relief Policies*. Washington, DC: Government Printing Office.

New York Times. (1942). "'American Beveridge Plan' Submitted to President." 11 December: 5.

New York Times. (1990a). "These Bills Defraud the Working Poor. Editorial. 19 October: A34.

New York Times. (1990b). "U.S. Panel Warns on Child Poverty." 27 April: A22.

New York Times. (1993). "Help for the Poor Who Work." 27 April: A20.

Noah, Timothy, and Laurie McGinley. (1993). "Advocate for the Poor, Respected on All Sides, Secures a Pivotal Role in Expanding Tax Credit." *Wall Street Journal*. 26 July: A12.

O'Connor, Julia S., Ann Shola Orloff, and Sheila Shaver. (1999). *States, Markets, Families: Gender, Liberalism and Social Policy in Australia, Canada, Great Britain, and the United States*. Cambridge: Cambridge University Press.

OECD. (2010). *Tax Expenditures in OECD Countries*. Paris: OECD.

Ontario Social Assistance Review Committee. (1988). *Transitions: Report of the Social Assistance Review Committee*. Ottawa: Queen's Printer.

Owram, Doug. (1986). *The Government Generation: Canadian Intellectuals and the State, 1900–1945*. Toronto: University of Toronto Press.

Pal, Leslie. (1987). "Tools for the Job: Canada's Evolution from Public Works to Mandated Employment." In *The Canadian Welfare State: Evolution and Transition*, edited by Jacqueline S. Ismael. Edmonton: University of Alberta Press: 33–62.

Paterson, Stephanie, Karine Levasseur, and Tatyana Teplova. (2004). "I Spy with My Little Eye . . . Canada's National Child Benefit." In *How Ottawa Spends, 2004–2005*, edited by G. Bruce Doern. Montreal: McGill-Queen's University Press: 131–150.

Pear, Robert. (1983). "Substantial Rise Found in Federal Tax Burden on the Poor." *New York Times*. 24 October: A29.

Pearson, Elizabeth. (2014). "Saying Yes to Taxes: The Politics of Tax Reform Campaigns in Three Northwestern States, 1965–1973." *American Journal of Sociology* 119(5): 1279–1323.

Pedersen, Susan. (1993). *Family, Dependence, and the Origin of the Welfare State: Britain and France 1914–1945*. Cambridge: Cambridge University Press.

Pedriana, Nicholas, and Robin Stryker. (1997). "Political Culture Wars 1960s Style: Equal Opportunity Employment-Affirmative Action and the Philadelphia Plan." *American Journal of Sociology* 103(3): 633–691.

Phillips, Stephen H. (1999). "The Demise of Universality: The Politics of Federal Income Security in Canada, 1978–1993." PhD diss., University of British Columbia.

Phillips-Fein, Kim. (2009). *Invisible Hands: The Making of the Conservative Movement from the New Deal to Reagan*. New York: Norton.

Piachaud, David, and Holly Sutherland. (2001). "Child Poverty in Britain and the New Labour Government." *Journal of Social Policy* 30(1): 95–118.

Pierson, Paul. (1994). *Dismantling the Welfare State? Reagan, Thatcher, and the Politics of Retrenchment*. Cambridge: Cambridge University Press.

Pierson, Paul. (2001). *The New Politics of the Welfare State*. Oxford: Oxford University Press.

Pierson, Paul. (2004). *Politics in Time: History, Institutions, and Social Analysis*. Princeton: Princeton University Press.

Popp-Berman, Elizabeth. (2012). *Creating the Market University: How Academic Science Became an Economic Engine*. Princeton: Princeton University Press.

Prasad, Monica. (2006). *The Politics of Free Markets: The Rise of Neoliberal Economic Policies in Britain, France, Germany, and the United States*. Chicago: University of Chicago Press.

Prasad, Monica. (2011). "Tax Expenditures and Welfare States: A Critique." *Journal of Policy History* 23(2): 251–266.

Prasad, Monica. (2012a). *The Land of Too Much: American Abundance and the Paradox of Poverty*. Cambridge, MA: Harvard University Press.

Prasad, Monica. (2012b). "The Popular Origins of Neoliberalism in the Reagan Tax Cut of 1981." *Journal of Policy History* 24(3): 351–383.

Prasad, Monica. (2016). "American Exceptionalism and the Welfare State: The Revisionist Literature." *Annual Review of Political Science* 19: 11.1–11.17.

Prasad, Monica, and Yingying Deng. (2009). "Taxation and the Worlds of Welfare." *Socio-Economic Review* 7(3): 431–457.

Pratt, Anna, and Mariana Valverde. (2002). "From Deserving Victims to 'Masters of Confusion': Redefining Refugees in the 1990s." *Canadian Journal of Sociology* 27(2): 135–161.

Primus, Wendell E. (1989). "Children in Poverty: A Committee Prepares for an Informed Debate." *Journal of Policy Analysis and Management* 8(1): 23–34.

Progressive Conservative Party of Ontario. (1995). *The Common Sense Revolution*. Ottawa: Progressive Conservative Party of Ontario.

Purdum, Todd S. (1995). "Clinton Defends Income Tax Cut against G.O.P. Cut." *New York Times*. 19 September.

Quadagno, Jill. (1994). *The Color of Welfare: How Racism Undermined the War on Poverty*. Oxford: Oxford University Press.

Quinn, Sarah. (n.d.). "America's Hidden Credit State: A Sociology of Federal Credit Programs in the United States." University of Washington. Manuscript in progress.

Reagan, Patrick D. (2000). *Designing a New America: The Origins of New Deal Planning, 1890–1943*. Amherst: University of Massachusetts Press.

Rector, Robert. (1992). "Requiem for the War on Poverty." *Policy Review* 61: 40–46.

Rector, Robert, and Stuart Butler. (1991). *Reducing the Tax Burden on the Embattled American Family*. Washington, DC: Heritage Foundation.

Reed, Ralph. (1993). "Casting a Wider Net." *Policy Review* 65: 31–35.

Rein, Martin. (1973). "Recent British Experience with Negative Income Tax." *Journal of Human Resources* 8: 69–89.

Rice, James J., and Michael J. Prince. (2004). "Martin's Moment: The Social Policy Agenda of a New Prime Minister." In *How Ottawa Spends, 2004–2005*, edited by G. Bruce Doern. Montreal: McGill-Queen's University Press: 111–130.

Ries, Barry. (1992). "'Family Caucus' Fighting to Preserve Traditional Values." *Vancouver Sun*. 9 June: A8.

Rimer, Sara. (1995). "Cutting Tax Credit Means Much to Those with Little." *New York Times*. 16 October: A1.

Rodems, Richard, and H. Luke Shaefer. (2016). "Left Out: Policy Diffusion and the Exclusion of Black Workers from Unemployment Insurance." *Social Science History* 40(3): 385–404.

Rodgers, Daniel T. (1998). *Atlantic Crossings: Social Politics in a Progressive Age*. Cambridge, MA: Harvard University Press.

Rod Grams Senitorial Files. Minnesota History Society. St. Paul, Minnesota.

Rona-Tas, Akos, and Stefanie Hiss. (2010). "The Role of Ratings in the Subprime Mortgage Crisis: The Art of Corporate and the Science of Consumer Credit Rating." *Research in the Sociology of Organizations* 30A: 155–180.

Rosenbaum, David A. (1995). "Budget Balancing Gains in Congress." *New York Times.* 12 May: A1.

Rubin, Alissa J. (1994). "Republican Agenda: Political Terrain Is Right for Tax Bidding War." *CQ Weekly.* 19 November: 3337–3338.

Rubin, Alissa J. (1995). "$189 Billion in Tax Relief." *CQ Weekly.* 11 March: 739.

Rubin, Alissa J. (1996). "Tax Cut Free-for-All." *CQ Weekly.* 8 March 8: 580.

Rubin, Alissa J. (1997). "Tax Issues Divide Parties, Chambers." *CQ Weekly.* 19 July 19: 1682.

Rubin, Alissa J., and David Hosansky. (1997). "Taxes: Democrats Steamrolled in House but Find Senate GOP Obliging." *CQ Weekly.* 28 June: 1495–1497.

Ryan, Paul. (2014). *Expanding Opportunity in America: A Discussion Draft from the House Budget Committee.* Washington, DC: U.S. Government Printing Office.

Sabo, Martin O. (1995). "Tax Credit Helps Poor Families Survive." *New York Times.* 27 September: A22.

Sand, Ben, and Peter S. Taylor. (2011). *Harper's Tax Boutique.* Winnipeg: Frontier Center for Public Policy.

Savoie, Donald J. (1991). *The Politics of Public Spending in Canada.* Toronto: University of Toronto Press.

Schaefer, Sarah. (1999). "Economy: Hague Asks Blair to Tell the Truth over Higher Taxes." *Independent.* 25 November: 8.

Schäfer, Armin, and Wolfgang Streeck. (2013). *Politics in the Age of Austerity.* Cambridge: Polity Press.

Schiffren, Lisa. (1995). "America's Best-Kept Welfare Secret." *American Spectator.* April: 24–29.

Schneider, Anne L., and Helen M. Ingram. (2005). *Deserving and Entitled: Social Constructions and Public Policy.* Albany: State University of New York Press.

Schneiberg, Marc. (2007). "What's on the Path? Path Dependence, Organizational Diversity and the Problem of Institutional Change in the US Economy, 1900–1950." *Socio-Economic Review* 5: 47–80.

Schorr, Alvin. (1966). *Poor Kids.* New York: Basic Books.

Seltzer, Lawrence. (1968). *The Personal Exemptions in the Income Tax.* New York: National Bureau of Economy Research.

Sewell, William H. (1992). "A Theory of Structure: Duality, Agency, and Transformation." *American Journal of Sociology* 98(1): 1–29.

Shanahan, Eileen. (1975). "The Road to a Tax-Cut Bill Was Paved, as Usual, with Politics." *New York Times.* 6 April: 192.

Shapiro, Isaac, and Robert Greenstein. (1997). *House Ways and Means Child Tax Credit Proposal.* Washington, DC: Center on Budget and Policy Priorities.

Shaw, Clay E. (1995). "A Credit That's Fair." *New York Times.* 21 September: A23.

Skocpol, Theda. (1991). "Targeting within Universalism: Politically Viable Policies to Combat Poverty in the United States." In *The Urban Underclass*, edited by Christopher Jencks and Paul E. Peterson. Washington, DC: Brookings Institution: 411–436.

Skocpol, Theda. (1992). *Protecting Soldiers and Mothers: The Political Origins of Social Policy in the United States*. Cambridge, MA: Harvard University Press.

Skrentny, John D. (2006). "Policy-Elite Perceptions and Social Movement Success: Understanding Variations in Group Inclusion in Affirmative Action." *American Journal of Sociology* 111(6): 1762–1815.

Smeeding, Timothy. (2006). "Poor People in Rich Nations: The United States in Comparative Perspective." *Journal of Economic Perspectives* 20(1): 69–90.

Smith, Mark A. (2007). *The Right Talk: How Conservatives Transformed the Great Society into the Economic Society*. Princeton: Princeton University Press.

Smith, Miriam. (2008). *Political Institutions and Lesbian and Gay Rights in the United States and Canada*. New York: Routledge.

Smith, Roger S. (1995). "The Personal Income Tax: Average and Marginal Rates in the Post-war Period." *Canadian Tax Journal* 43(5): 1055–1076.

Starke, Peter. (2006). "The Politics of Welfare State Retrenchment: A Literature Review." *Social Policy and Administration* 40(1): 104–120.

Starr, Paul. (1992). "Social Categories and Claims in the Liberal State." *Social Research* 59(2): 263–295.

Steensland, Brian. (2008). *The Failed Welfare Revolution: America's Struggle over Guaranteed Income Policy*. Princeton: Princeton University Press.

Steensland, Brian. (2010). "Moral Classifications and Social Policy." In *Handbook of the Sociology of Morality*, edited by Steven Hitlin and Stephan Vaisey. New York: Springer.

Stein, Robert. (2010). "Taxes and the Family." *National Affairs* 2: 35–48.

Steuerle, C. Eugene. (1983). "The Tax Treatment of Households of Different Size." In *Taxing the Family*, edited by Rudolph G. Penner. Washington, DC: American Enterprise Institute, 73–97.

Steuerle, C. Eugene. (1991). *The Tax Decade: How Taxes Came to Dominate the Public Agenda*. Washington, DC: Urban Institute Press.

Steuerle, C. Eugene. (2012). *Statement on Marginal Tax Rates, Work, and the Nation's Real Tax System*. Joint Hearing of the Subcommittee on Human Resources and Subcommittee on Select Revenue Measures of the Committee on Ways and Means. Washington DC: Government Printing Office.

Steuerle, C. Eugene, and Jason Juffras. (1991). *A $1000 Tax Credit for Every Child: A Base of Reform for the Nation's Tax, Welfare and Health Systems*. Policy paper. Washington, DC: Urban Institute.

Streeck, Wolfgang, and Kathleen Thelen (eds.). (2005). *Beyond Continuity: Institutional Change in Advanced Political Economies*. Cambridge: Cambridge University Press.

Strickland, Pat. (1998). *Working Families Tax Credit and Family Credit*. House of Commons Research Paper 98/46. London: House of Commons Library.

Strikwerda, Eric. (2013). *The Wages of Relief: Cities and the Unemployed in Prairie Canada, 1929–39*. Edmonton: AU Press.

Struthers, James. (1987). "Shadows from the Thirties: The Federal Government and Unemployment Assistance, 1941–1956." In *The Canadian Welfare State: Evolution and Transition*, edited by Jacqueline S. Ismael. Edmonton: University of Alberta Press: 3–32.

Tanzi, Vito. (1980). *Inflation and Personal Income Tax: An International Perspective*. Cambridge: Cambridge University Press.

Taylor, Andrew. (1997). "The Budget: Internal Divisions, White House Frustrate GOP's Tax Agenda." *CQ Weekly*. 19 July: 1681–1684.

Taylor, Andrew, and Mary Agnes Carey. (1997). "The Budget: Hopeful Negotiation Schedule Threatened by Tax Battles." *CQ Weekly*. 12 July: 1609–1612.

Taylor-Gooby, Peter, and Rose Martin. (2008). "Trends in Sympathy for the Poor." In *British Social Attitudes: The 24th Report*, edited by Alison Park et al. London: Sage: 229–257.

Teihan, Laura, Dean Jolliffe, and Timothy M. Smeeding. (2016). "The Effect of SNAP on Poverty." In *SNAP Matters: How Food Stamps Affect Health and Well-Being*, edited by Judith Bartfeld, Craig Gundersen, Timothy M. Smeeding, and James P. Ziliak. Stanford: Stanford University Press: 49–73.

Teles, Steven M. (2013). "Kludgeocracy in America." *National Affairs* 17: 97–114.

Teles, Steven M., and David Dagan. (2016). "Conservatives and Criminal Justice." *National Affairs* 27: 118–136.

Tesler, Michael. (2016). *Post-racial or Most-racial? Race and Politics in the Obama Era*. Chicago: University of Chicago Press.

Torjman, Sherri. (1995). *Milestone or Millstone? The Legacy of the Social Security Review*. Ottawa: Caledon Institute of Social Policy.

U.K. Department of Health and Social Security. (1985a). *The Reform of Social Security*. London: HMSO.

U.K. Department of Health and Social Security. (1985b). *Reform of Social Security: Programme for Action*. London: HMSO.

U.K. Home Office. (1998). *Supporting Families: A Consultation Document*. London: Home Office.

U.K. Inland Revenue. (2001). *New Tax Credits: Supporting Families, Making Work Pay and Tackling Poverty*. London: Inland Revenue.

U.S. Congress. (1972). Joint Economic Committee. *Income Transfer Programs: How They Tax the Poor*. Washington, DC: U.S. Government Printing Office.

U.S. Congress. (1974). Joint Economic Committee. *Issues in Financing Retirement Income*. Washington, DC: U.S. Government Printing Office.

U.S. Congress. (1995a). *Hearing before the Joint Economic Committee: Family First Act: The Economic Effects of a $500 Per-child Expanded Tax Credit*. Washington, DC: U.S. Government Printing Office.

U.S. Congress. (1995b). Joint Committee on Taxation. *Present Law and Analysis Relating to the Earned Income Credit and the Child Tax Credit as Contained in the H.R. 2491 Conference Agreement.* Washington, DC: Government Printing Office.

U.S. Congress. (2014). *Estimates of Federal Tax Expenditures for Fiscal Years 2014–2018.* Washington, DC: U.S. Government Printing Office.

U.S. House. (1984). *Hearing before the Committee on Ways and Means: Federal Tax Treatment of Low Income Persons.* Washington, DC: Government Printing Office.

U.S. House. (1985a). *Hearing before the Committee on Government Operations: Work and Poverty: The Special Problems of the Working Poor.* Washington, DC: Government Printing Office.

U.S. House. (1985b). *Hearing before the Committee on Ways and Means: Comprehensive Tax Reform, Part 4.* Washington, DC: Government Printing Office.

U.S. House. (1985c). *Hearing before the Committee on Ways and Means: Tax Burdens of Low-Income Wage Earners.* Washington, DC: Government Printing Office.

U.S. House. (1985d). *Hearing before the Select Committee on Children, Youth and Families: Tax Policy: What Do Families Need?* Washington, DC: Government Printing Office.

U.S. House. (1987). *Hearing before the Select Committee on Children, Youth and Families: American Families in Tomorrow's Economy.* Washington, DC: Government Printing Office.

U.S. House. (1989). *Hearing before the Committee on Ways and Means: How to Help the Working Poor and Problems of the Working Poor.* Washington, DC: Government Printing Office.

U.S. House. (1991a). *Hearing before the Committee on the Budget: Challenging Distribution of Taxes and Income of Working People.* Washington, DC: Government Printing Office.

U.S. House. (1991b). *Hearing before the Committee on Ways and Means: U.S. Economy, and Proposals to Provide Middle-Income Tax Relief, Tax Equity and Fairness, Economic Stimulus and Growth.* Washington, DC: Government Printing Office.

U.S. House. (1991c). *Hearing before the Select Committee on Children, Youth, and Families: Reclaiming the Tax Code for American Families.* Washington, DC: Government Printing Office.

U.S. House. (1993). *Hearing before the Committee on Ways and Means: Selected Aspects of Welfare Reform.* Washington, DC: Government Printing Office.

U.S. House. (1995a). *Hearing before the Committee on Ways and Means: Earned Income Tax Credit.* Washington, DC: Government Printing Office.

U.S. House. (1995b). *Hearing before the Committee on Ways and Means: Tax Provisions in the Contract with America Designed to Strengthen the American Family.* Washington, DC: Government Printing Office.

U.S. Senate. (1972a). *Hearing before the Committee on Finance: Social Security Amendment of 1971*. Washington, DC: Government Printing Office.

U.S. Senate. (1972b). *Report of the Committee on Finance: Social Security Amendments of 1972*. Washington, DC: Government Printing Office.

U.S. Senate. (1973). *Hearing before the Committee on Labor and Public Welfare: American Families: Trends and Pressures, 1973*. Washington, DC: Government Printing Office.

U.S. Senate. (1974). *Hearing before the Committee on Finance: Proposals to Increase the Income Tax Personal Exemption*. Washington, DC: Government Printing Office.

U.S. Senate. (1975). Committee on Finance. *Tax Reduction Act of 1975*. Washington, DC: U.S. Government Printing Office.

U.S. Senate. (1985). *Hearing before the Committee on Finance: Tax Reform Proposals (People below the Poverty Line)*. Washington, DC: U.S. Government Printing Office.

U.S. Senate (1991a). *Hearing before the Committee on Finance: Middle-Income Tax Cuts*. Washington, DC: Government Printing Office.

U.S. Senate (1991b). *Hearing before the Committee on Labor and Human Resources: Caught in the Squeeze: Economic Pressures on Working Families*. Washington, DC: Government Printing Office.

U.S. Senate. (1995). *Hearing before the Committee on Finance: Middle-Income Tax Proposals*. Washington, DC: Government Printing Office.

Vadakin, James C. (1958). Family Allowances: An Analysis of Their Development and Implications. Coral Gables: University of Miami Press.

Ventry, Dennis J. (2000). "The Collision of Tax and Welfare Politics: The Political History of the Earned Income Tax Credit, 1969–1999." *National Tax Journal* 53(4): 984–1026.

Waldfogel, Jane. (2010). *Britain's War on Poverty*. New York: Russell Sage Foundation.

Walker, David. (1998). "Working Families Tax Credit: Help for Low-Paid Families Is More Than Doubled." *Independent*. 18 March: B2.

Walker, William. (1994). "Welfare Cuts May Come Swiftly." *Toronto Star*. 22 March: A8.

Warken, Philip W. (1979). *A History of the National Resources Planning Board, 1933–1943*. New York: Garland.

Washington Post. (1997). Tax Fraud. Editorial. 29 June: C6.

Waugh, Paul. (1998). "Field Returns to the Fray in Welfare Reform Row." *Independent*. 7 August: 2.

Waugh, Paul. (2002). "£2.7bn to Cut Poverty and Make Work Pay." *Independent*. 18 April: 5.

Weaver, R. Kent. (1986). "The Politics of Blame Avoidance." *Journal of Public Policy* 6(4): 371–398.

Weaver, R. Kent. (1988). *Automatic Government: The Politics of Indexation*. Washington, DC: Brookings Institution Press.

Weaver, R. Kent. (2000). *Ending Welfare as We Know It*. Washington, DC: Brookings Institution Press.

Wednesday Group. (1991). *Moving Ahead: Initiatives for Expanding Opportunity in America*. Washington, DC: House Wednesday Group.

Weir, Margaret, and Theda Skocpol. (1985). "State Structures and the Possibilities for 'Keynesian' Responses to the Great Depression in Sweden, Britain, and the United States." In *Bringing the State Back In*, edited by Peter B. Evans, Dietrich Rueschemeyer, and Theda Skocpol. Cambridge: Cambridge University Press: 107–168.

Wennemo, Irene. (1992). "The Development of Family Policy: A Comparison of Family Benefits and Tax Reductions for Families in 18 OECD Countries." *Acta Sociologica* 35(3): 201–217.

West, Rachel, Melissa Boteach, and Rebecca Vallas. (2015). *Harnessing the Child Tax Credit as a Tool to Invest in the Next Generation*. Washington, DC: Center for American Progress.

Western, Bruce, Deirdre Bloome, Benjamin Sosnaud, and Laura M. Tach. (2016). "Trends in Income Insecurity among U.S. Children, 1984–2010." *Demography* 53(2): 419–447.

White House Working Group on the Family. (1986). *The Family: Preserving America's Future*. Washington, DC: Domestic Policy Council.

Whitton, Charlotte. (1944). "The Family Allowances Controversy in Canada." *Social Service Review* 18(4): 413–432.

Wickham-Jones, Mark. (2003). "From Reformism to Resignation and Remedialism? Labour's Trajectory through British Politics." *Journal of Policy History* 15(1): 26–45.

Wiegers, Wanda. (2002). *The Framing of Poverty as "Child Poverty" and Its Implications for Women*. Ottawa: Status of Women Canada.

Wilensky, Harold L. (2002). *Rich Democracies: Political Economy, Public Policy, and Performance*. Los Angeles: University of California Press.

Wines, Michael. (1995). "Plan for Tax Cut Nears a Key Test." *New York Times*. 8 October: A1.

Winter, Nicholas J. G. (2006). "Beyond Welfare: Framing and the Racialization of White Opinion on Social Security." *American Journal of Political Science* 50(2): 400–420.

Witte, Edwin E. (1945). "1944–1945 Programs for Postwar Social Security and Medical Care." *Review of Economics and Statistics* 27(4): 171–188.

Witte, John F. (1985). *The Politics and Development of the Federal Income Tax*. Madison: University of Wisconsin Press.

York, Geoffrey. (1991a). "Coalition Stresses Plight of Poor Children." *Globe and Mail*. 22 November.

York, Geoffrey. (1991b). "Family Allowance Overhaul Urged." *Globe and Mail*. 13 December.

York, Geoffrey. (1991c). "New Deal for Low-Income Families Expected Next Week." *Globe and Mail*. 7 May.

York, Geoffrey. (1992). "Tory Politicians Form Family Compact." *Globe and Mail.* 3 June: A1.

Young, Robert A. (1981). "Reining in James: The Limits of the Task Force." *Canadian Public Administration* 24(4): 596–611.

Zelenak, Lawrence. (2003). "The Myth of Pretax Income." *Michigan Law Review* 101: 2261–2274.

Zelizer, Julian. (1998). *Taxing America: Wilbur D. Mills, Congress, and the State, 1945–1975.* Cambridge: Cambridge University Press.

Zollars, Cheryl, and Theda Skocpol. (1994). "Cultural Mythmaking as a Policy Tool: The Social Security Board and the Construction of a Social Citizenship of Self-Interest." *Research on Democracy and Society* 2: 381–408.

Index